The Hay Po~~~~~~

Martin Beales was born in 1945, was educated at St
Paul's School, London, and Edinburgh University,
where he read law. He came to Hay-on-Wye in 1977
knowing nothing about Herbert Rowse Armstrong.
Within three weeks he received a manuscript, setting out
the belief that Armstrong had been wrongly convicted.
By one of the many coincidences which are a feature of
this case, Martin Beales lives in Armstrong's house,
practises in Armstrong's old office and once lived in the
houses where the inquest and autopsy into Mrs
Armstrong's death was held. Martin Beales still lives in
Hay-on-Wye today – with his wife, Noelle, and their
three children.

The Hay Poisoner

Herbert Rowse Armstrong

MARTIN BEALES

ROBERT HALE · LONDON

© Martin Beales 1995 & 1997
First published in Great Britain as 'Dead Not Buried' 1995
This paperback edition 1997

ISBN 0 7090 6123 4

Robert Hale Limited
Clerkenwell House
Clerkenwell Green
London EC1R 0HT

2 4 6 8 10 9 7 5 3 1

Photoset in Sabon by
Derek Doyle & Associates, Mold, Flintshire.
Printed in Great Britain by
St Edmundsbury Press Ltd, Bury St Edmunds, Suffolk.
Bound by WBC Book Manufacturers Limited, Bridgend.

Contents

Illustrations

Acknowledgements

I wish to acknowledge Margaret, Armstrong's daughter, who after much soul searching allowed me to publish this book; Toby Kane, whose unpublished theories inspired and motivated me to research deeply into the facts; and Kate Clarke – a crime writer in Hay-on-Wye – whose continual interest kept me going and without whose contribution this book would not have been written.

I record my thanks to the partners in the firm T.A. Matthews & Co. Solicitors of Hereford, who allowed me to reproduce the illustrations.

I am very grateful to Stuart Orr, the Departmental Records Officer of the Crown Prosecution Service. Crown Copyright material in the Public Record Office is reproduced by permission of the Controller of Her Majesty's Stationery Office.

I wish that Chalky White and Fred Stokoe were still alive to read what I have written.

I offer thanks to the few remaining souls who have always kept an open mind: to Dorothy Ellen Jay, Amy Jay and Marina Knight; and those many others, such as Jack and Winifred Webb, who shared their memories of the events in Hay, over seventy years ago.

I offer thanks to Dr Derek Wilson of Hay, Professor Bussuttil of Edinburgh, Maxwell Cooper, Duncan Linklater and Frances Copping.

I am grateful to my colleagues at Williams Beales & Co. for putting up with me, to my former partner John G. Williams, Diane Williams, Mike Harris and Jeremy Langworthy.

To my wife Noelle and family, I offer my gratitude.

To those others not mentioned by name I apologize.

I dedicate this book to Toby Kane

Foreword

The Armstrong case is undoubtedly one of the notoriously select band of 'crimes of the century' – if indeed, after reading Martin Beales' book you still believe it was a crime.

Along with Crippen, Greenwood, Christie and now probably West, the events in Hay-on-Wye have been the most picked over and publicized deaths in the lifetime of even our oldest citizens. After numerous revisits in print, sound and vision, which all confirmed Herbert Rowse Armstrong in his traditional role of scheming killer, another solicitor from Hay, who lives in Armstrong's house and works in his office, has meticulously assembled a persuasive alternative to the authorised version.

The release of previously restricted documents, along with a thorough reappraisal of existing evidence, has allowed Martin Beales to write a book which in 1995 prompted the judges of the Crime Writers' Association to unanimously award it the Gold Dagger Award for the best book of non-fiction. I was one of those judges and after several readings of the book, I concluded that, whether he killed his wife or not, Major Armstrong certainly should never have been convicted on the evidence, and, one hopes, could not be so convicted today – or could he?

In the present climate of deep questioning of our criminal law system, the frequency of successful appeals, the doubts about the effectiveness of the jury and the role of expert witnesses, this book is very timely, as well as absorbing and important.

The author has shown up the bias, the unfairness and perhaps the dishonesty of senior law officers and experts which can still provoke uneasiness even after seventy-five years. Thankfully, the scaffold no longer frustrates late visits to the appeal court.

Professor Bernard Knight CBE

Six proposals are now before Parliament to abolish the penalty of death in cases of murder, but it may well be doubted whether the British public would be satisfied if they felt assured that by some process as yet undisclosed an atrocious poisoner had been painlessly and without degradation inducted to the Kingdom of the Just. This may, perhaps, be contrary to a complete Christian charity – though, even among the Fathers, authority to the contrary may be found – but among primitive, and also among highly-civilised peoples, there was no question on the subject.

Mr Justice Darling,
London Evening News, 27 March 1924

Prologue

It was almost seventy years after the date of Major Armstrong's execution that Margaret, his only surviving daughter, stood in the drive of Mayfield, the family home. It was the first time that she had returned to it since the age of six, when her childhood had been rudely shattered for ever.

Now a slight woman of seventy-five, so like her mother in looks, she walked towards the front door. Apprehensive and slightly alarmed, she waited for her husband to join her. Neither spoke as she rang the bell, and as she waited she looked round at the garden in which she had happily played those many years ago.

I welcomed her inside, into the warmth of a family home that had long forgotten the anguish of those events in the 1920s – events that were a double tragedy for her family.

Her memories of that far past were vague as for many years she was not told why her father had died. Her recollection was distant and clouded by disgrace. After her father was hanged she, together with her elder sister Eleanor and brother Pearson, had to bear his shame, and his sins were visited upon them for the rest of their days.

She recalled that she only learned of her father's fate when she was in her teens and read a magazine article in *Pearson's Weekly*. She found it difficult to believe, and when she returned to reread it, the article had been torn out, so careful were her carers to prevent her finding out about the past. For what was the past except dishonour and humiliation? And what was worse, no one would talk about it, because the disgrace would taint them as well.

Throughout her life she had coped with her misfortune. She could not lie about her father's death, but would brush off enquiries with lines such as, he fell off a scaffold, or, he had a fall. Her mind was blessed with an acute intelligence inherited from both her parents. Her spirit, too, flowed with compassion and tenderness. I was aware that I was in the presence of a person who had suffered a very great tragedy but was capable of an understanding that could transcend the pain and grief she had endured. She had come to terms with her misfortune and nothing I could say could make it worse. Or could it? What if I said her father was innocent of a crime that did not even take place? I knew that thought was more shocking than anything else. After all, her father's fate had been the subject of many publications, and not one had considered the possibility of innocence. His effigy had stood for its allotted span of fifty years in the Chamber of Horrors. Herbert Rowse Armstrong was an infamous poisoner ranking in the annals of crime with Crippen, and the only British solicitor to have been hanged.

Or was this the case? Could there have been a monstrous miscarriage of justice, which, but for the most unusual of circumstances, would have lain undiscovered? Margaret listened to my theories with fascination. She wanted them to be proved true, but at the same time she had lived in the certain knowledge that her father had slowly poisoned her mother and as a result had stained her life. She had no memory of either parent and had rationalized his hanging with the thought that the family's suffering would have been much greater if he had been sentenced to life imprisonment; but her feelings and subsequent justifications depended on a just and proper verdict having been reached – that he was guilty of wilful murder, for which he had paid with his own life. If he was innocent, the ground rules were changed. If he was indeed innocent, what was the truth?

THE LIFE OF
HERBERT ROWSE ARMSTRONG

1

It used to be a rule that the hangman should always sleep in the prison the night before an execution. Both John Ellis and his assistant Parrott arrived at 4 p.m. Their duty was indicated by a notice pinned on the front gate of Gloucester Prison:

CAPITAL PUNISHMENT AMENDMENT ACT 1868
The sentence of the law passed upon Herbert Rowse Armstrong, found guilty of murder, will be carried into execution at eight a.m. tomorrow.
Signed: Edwin Martin Dunne, Sheriff of Hereford.
H. Whyte, Governor, Gloucester Prison
30th May 1922

On the Tuesday, when his solicitor, T.A. Matthews, and Mr Chivers, his managing Clerk, visited Armstrong for the last time to take his wishes and final instructions regarding the disposal of his legal practice and the future of his children he showed emotion, but when he finally said goodbye he did so without tremor. 'Don't grieve over me, Mr Matthews,' he said, 'I am perfectly all right. I know it is tomorrow, but I have no fear.'

Armstrong always denied his guilt and made no confession. To his great friend Revd Jeffreys de Winton, vicar of Hay, he said: 'I feel better now than I ever did. I realize that the end has come and I am prepared for it. I have no confession to make: I am an innocent man.'

A large crowd of over a thousand onlookers congregated outside the prison before the appointed hour. Men, women and children flocked in to Barrack Square. When Armstrong was in the condemned cell he had been guarded by two warders night and day. The cell had two doors, one of which was not used when Armstrong was inside. Just before eight this second door opened and Ellis and Parrott came into the cell. Without ceremony Armstrong was pinioned and led into the adjoining room, where the scaffold had been erected ten years earlier. He had only to take five steps to the trapdoor of the pit. His head was covered and the rope placed around his neck. It took less than one minute from the time Ellis entered his cell to the time that he drew the bolt – before it was all over.

As the jurors left the prison after the inquest they could see the chaplain in his surplice reading the service over the doomed man. The grave was then quickly filled in and the final scene closed on one of the most sensational poisoning dramas in the history of crime in this country.[1]

Fred Davies also knew that when the Hay clock started to peal eight times on that fateful morning the vertebrae of the neck of Major Herbert Rowse Armstrong would be dislocated and that he would be dead.

He believed in the justice that was meted out to the condemned man. When Ellis pulled the lever he was convinced that Armstrong was a poisoner. Fred Davies was an ill-natured man. He had plied his trade as a chemist in Hay for over forty years. He had been wronged by Armstrong, or so he believed, and he considered it his duty to expose the man and let the full force of the law descend upon him. He could not allow himself to consider the damaging effect on the three orphaned children because he believed that he was right. After all, his conviction had been shared by the jury of twelve Herefordshire men who had considered all the evidence and had reached their verdict after a full exposure to all the facts. There could be no doubt. They had convicted him. He could rest assured that his suspicions had been justified in a court of law, and that three appeal judges led by the lord chief justice were satisfied by the fairness of the verdict. Fred Davies went about his business as usual on that day.

Fred's son-in-law, the solicitor Oswald Martin – whose evidence implicated Armstrong in attempting to poison him with a scone, using the immortal words 'excuse fingers' –

awoke earlier than usual that morning. He had arranged for his assistant to drive him to Hay, but he never made it as the car was stopped by a woman enquiring after the ghost of Armstrong, whose body, still warm and covered in quicklime, had been placed for eternity in the prison grave. Martin returned to his bed.

There was another person who waited for the town clock to ring its bell. Dr Tom Hincks, the town's only doctor, whose evidence effectively secured the conviction of his patient and former friend, also believed in the justness of the verdict. Hincks had attended Katharine Armstrong in her last illness and had also visited Martin during his sickness. He had signed Katharine's death certificate, deliberately omitting reference to her mental troubles and certified that she had died from natural causes. He had considered Martin's illness to be a mere gastric disturbance, but he changed his mind and declared in court that Katharine had died from small doses of arsenic and that Martin's sickness had been caused by acute arsenical poisoning.

The inhabitants of the little town of Hay were not so sure, for the verdict of guilty had rocked the little town to its core.

Hay is a little market town, situated at the junction of three counties, with the rich arable land of Herefordshire to the east; the sparsely populated county of Radnor to the north; and the county of Breconshire, incorporating the imposing range of the Black Mountains, to the south and west. The River Wye, teeming with salmon, passes within yards of its main thoroughfare and a little river called the Dulas, running through the neighbouring village of Cusop, separates the part of Hay which is in England from that which is in Wales.

It is a true border town and in real terms has changed little since the early 1900s. It is still dominated by the castle which is the centre point of a myriad of tiny streets – one of which is Broad Street in which the solicitors had their offices and where the chemist Fred Davies lived next door to Dr Tom Hincks, who resided above his surgery. It had a station whose line connected the town to Hereford. Although small in terms of size and population, Hay supported a whole range of shops and hostelries, the latter slaking the thirst of the labourers who poured in on market and fair days. It was a close-knit community where the English coexisted peacefully with the Welsh and where everyone knew their place despite the gulf that separated the tradesman from the gentry. In this respect the chemist was considered to be 'trade' and equated in the social strata with the ironmonger and the butcher, whereas the doctor was a professional man. Yet both chemist and doctor were in competition with each other, and Fred Davies wanted more than anything to be recognized in the higher pillars of society.

As it happened, the townsfolk of Hay blamed Davies for the execution. Their opinions were shared by those who had known Armstrong intimately and enjoyed his company, his jokes and manner. Many considered that the verdict was wrong. Despite the fact that Fred Davies was as well established as anyone in Hay, he left the town soon afterwards.

Martin stayed in Hay for less than two years and then left a broken man. He never recovered his composure or his health for the rest of his days, stating that his poisoning at the hand of Armstrong was his downfall. But was it? Why could he not make good in the same way that his younger partner Trevor Griffiths, who succeeded to his practice, had prospered?

Did both Davies and Martin take any secrets to the grave?

2

Before any criminal prosecution can be launched there must be an investigation. In order for an investigation to be initiated there must be some suspicion that a crime has been committed. Suspicious talk by itself does not always lead to a criminal investigation unless someone forces an inquiry and if that is the case there must be something to be examined.

On Sunday 30 October 1921 Tom Hincks was about to saddle his horse in readiness for an urgent visit to a patient in the Black Mountains, a journey that would take him seven hours. Hincks liked nothing more than a good ride over the hills, and all the better if he was going to be paid for his troubles. At ten o'clock Fred Davies called at his surgery and asked him if he was quite sure that there was no suspicion of poison having been given to his son-in-law Martin, who had been taken ill with vomiting and diarrhoea four days earlier. Hincks replied that he was certain. Davies then told him of Armstrong's extraordinary behaviour when Martin had gone to his house for tea. According to Hincks, Davies declared, 'There were two currant cakes on a dish and although Martin said he did not want a cake, Armstrong picked one up himself and put it on Martin's plate and Martin ate it.' Fred continued by saying that Armstrong was always intensely jealous of Martin who had poached a number of his clients, and that after the tea party he seemed jumpy and nervy.

The two men discussed the nature of Martin's illness and Davies told him that if he enquired more carefully he would find that Martin vomited a reddish vomit and was intensely ill with diarrhoea. Hincks replied that he had had no diarrhoea, only two or three loose motions, adding that he had also had no burning sensation in his throat with comparatively little pain, nothing like the amount he would expect from arsenical poisoning. Davies became more persuasive and told him that after Martin became ill he had said to him in his wife's presence, 'For God's sake don't take anything sent you anonymously,' and that they both laughed. Hincks recorded in his statement to the police, 'I don't know what made him mention anything as to anonymous presents to Martin.'

Davies then produced a box of chocolates and told him that at a dinner party at Martin's house on the evening of 8 October, one of his guests had eaten one of the chocolates and had been taken ill as a result.

The box was handed to Hincks, who examined its contents carefully. He noticed white powder impacted in the gooey mass of two of the sweets, the centres of which had been drilled. Gradually he was persuaded to believe that the alien substance could be arsenic, particularly when he was told that Armstrong had purchased arsenic from Davies's shop. After this conversation the suspicions of Hincks were aroused and he considered that he had a duty to make as certain of the matter as possible. He told Davies that the only way to obtain proof was to obtain a specimen of urine and directed him to get a Winchester quart bottle, thoroughly clean it, and wash the cork with a bottle of distilled water. Davies should then give it to Martin and tell him that he would be up shortly to ask him to pass water into it.

Hincks consulted his books on arsenic poisoning and then rode up on his horse and spent an hour with Martin going carefully into all his symptoms. He enquired about the reddish-brown vomit and was informed that it had the most filthy odour. He told Martin that he wanted him to pass water into the bottle which Davies would supply and that he would collect it the following morning. He then remounted his horse and continued on his journey through the village of Cusop and on to the Black Mountains.

On the Monday morning, 31 October, Hincks again visited Martin, who by that time was practically better. The doctor was given the bottle of urine and was told that it had been passed the evening before and again that morning. He took the bottle to Davies who parcelled it up with the chocolates and addressed it to a London laboratory known as the Clinical Research Association. Hincks wrote the covering letter specifically asking for an analysis of arsenic. Davies agreed to pay the fee.

The Clinical Research Association responded by return and with commercial thoughts foremost commented:

> ... before undertaking an investigation of this nature we require a guarantee, either that we will not be called upon to give evidence in Court, or in the event of being so called upon, that in addition to the usual fee for examining the specimen, our expert will be paid £5 5s. 0d. (Five Guineas) for each day or part of a day of attendance at any Court out of London, together with first class travelling expenses and total accommodation, if necessary. If at any Court in London, the fee will be £3 3s. 0d. (Three Guineas) for each day or part of a day of attendance.

This was an unexpected snag for Davies, who realized that he was getting into deep water if he agreed to underwrite these additional fees and he refused to do so. He asked Hincks to take it further and Hincks wrote to the Home Office asking for advice. Quite correctly the Home Office decided to refer the matter to the police and an officer was asked to speak directly to Hincks, who refused to co-operate until the result of the analysis was known. The police reported this fact to the Home Office, which responded by saying that the police should inform Hincks that in view of the fact that he refused to provide any further information the police were unable to take any action.

In the mean time Hincks wrote another letter to the Home Office asking if the analysis had taken place. The file was minuted:

> I rather sympathize with Dr. Hincks. If the police were to gossip about the matter, it might ruin his practice. I think Mr. Webster [the Home Office analyst] might be asked to make the analysis (it would be covered by his retaining fee of £500). Say to Dr. Hincks that if he will state the suspicious circumstances mentioned in his letter, which will be treated as confidential if no arsenic is found, S of S [Secretary of State] will probably be able to arrange for the analysis to be made.

Hincks responded to this suggestion immediately it was made to him. The specimens were passed from the Clinical Research Association to Mr Webster of St Mary's Hospital, Paddington, who reported to the Home Office on 3 December:

> I have examined the above articles and have to report as follows:
> (1) Bottle: I have found arsenic in the urine in this bottle. I have estimated the amount of arsenic and find it present in the amount of 1/33rd of a grain in 17½ ounces of urine.
> (2) Box: Two of the chocolates in this box had the appearance of being tampered with. A cylindrical hole nearly ½ inch long has apparently been bored and filled with a white powder, and an attempt made to conceal the white powder by covering with chocolate. The powder was found on analysis to be white arsenic (arsenious oxide). I have estimated the arsenic in one of the chocolates and find it present to the extent of slightly more than 2 grains (2.12). Two grains of white arsenic have been known to cause death in an adult.

Sir Ernley Blackwell, assistant under-secretary at the Home Office, acknowledged the report on 5 December and informed Webster that he was consulting with the director of public prosecutions (DPP).

In the mean time Hincks had again written to the Home Office asking for the results of the analysis. On 7 December he was asked to meet with a representative of the DPP at the office of the Chief Constable at Hereford. On 9 December he met Mr H. Sefton Cohen, of the DPP's office, who was present with the Honourable Captain E.S. Stanhope, the chief constable of Hereford. He was shown for the first time the results of the analysis. He then made a full statement setting out his suspicions concerning Armstrong, giving further details of Martin's illness. He also mentioned that either on 31 October or on 1 November, he had visited Dr Townsend of Barnwood Asylum and had gone with him into the symptoms of Mrs Armstrong's illness. He stated that both he and Townsend agreed that her symptoms and subsequent death presented a clinical picture of arsenical poisoning, but that they felt at the time that it was not their duty to take any action until they had been informed of the results of the analysis. His suspicions were of course those of Fred Davies, but he was the spokesman for them.

Hincks was an ebullient man, keen to demonstrate his opinions, and he wanted credit for them. Although he had absolutely no suspicions of any nature that Martin may have been poisoned when he was treating him for his illness, he went completely overboard as soon as the results of the analysis were made known to him, accepting Davies's views lock stock and barrel. As far as he was concerned his patient, former friend and brother Freemason was a poisoner and he made these views known to the police in no uncertain way:

> In my opinion he is of abnormal mentality, very clever and well read, he has run after women, no particular woman that I know of since she was in the asylum but I am informed has frequented village dances and pestered the girls there. He has three children eldest about 14. His late wife was rather inclined to keep a tight hand on him. He keeps a revolver by the side of the bed. Last Saturday week I was attending him and he asked me what the drug was I was using and I said there was arsenic in it. He then asked what a fatal dose was and I said about three grains and he replied that one grain is sufficient isn't it or words to that effect. I think the man is a homicidal maniac and if he gets to know that these questions are the subject of police or other investigations he may destroy himself, his children, Mr. Martin and me.

Sefton Cohen, armed with Hincks's extraordinary statement that Armstrong was a homicidal maniac, returned to London and spoke with the director of public prosecutions, Sir Archibald Bodkin. The latter did not need to be persuaded to launch a full investigation. He contacted Scotland Yard and the assistant commissioner of crime, Mr. F.T. Bigham, was brought into the case. Chief Inspector Crutchett was appointed officer in charge and he was ordered to Hay to take statements cloaked in secrecy.

He arrived in Hay on the 10 December and interviewed Fred and Laura Davies, who gave an account of their suspicions, both in connection with their son-in-law and Katharine herself. Fred was quite emphatic and is recorded as saying:

Some time after the sale of the arsenic I heard that Mr. Armstrong's wife, who had been away ill, was dead, and that her fatal illness was accompanied by vomiting. I had seen her a week or two before her death. She came into my shop and I noticed how much better she was looking. When I heard of her death and the symptoms of the illness the sale of the arsenic came into my mind. I wondered if Armstrong had administered any of the arsenic to his wife so causing her death but I said nothing to anyone.

Laura was equally forthcoming about her suspicions:

From various things I had heard in Hay concerning him, and his callous behaviour at the time of his wife's death, I felt no desire to cultivate his acquaintance. Some time after Oswald Martin's marriage to my daughter, I knew that he had business transactions with Mr. Armstrong, and that these transactions were not likely to result in the formation of a friendship between them. I had heard of the circumstances surrounding the death of Armstrong's wife, who, only a few days previously to her death, had been seen by a friend of mine, and was then greatly improved in health. I knew that prior to Mrs. Armstrong's death she had great vomiting and having read the reports of the Kidwelly case[2] and remembering what I had heard about Armstrong, it made me feel uneasy. When therefore some time later, my son-in-law Oswald Martin told me he had been frequently pressed by Armstrong to take tea with him, I felt instinctively that it would be better for him not to go, and I asked him not to go.

On the next day Crutchett interviewed Oswald Martin at the British Camp Hotel in Malvern where he was staying with his wife, Constance, the only daughter of Fred and Laura Davies. Martin set out his business difficulties with Armstrong and was emphatic that he had been handed a scone, which was cut in two and buttered. He was questioned about his illness and stated that after he returned to his office he was continually asked to tea, 'but I was then beginning to be suspicious that he had given me some poison'.

Constance was interviewed the following day and then Crutchett went to Tewkesbury to interview both Martin's brothers and their wives in connection with the sickness of Mrs Dorothy Martin after the dinner party on 8 October, when one of the chocolates had been eaten. He then returned to London and the various statements were forwarded to Bodkin.

Enquiries were then made of the manufacturers of the chocolates, and on 16 December, Horace Frogley of 45 Great Church Lane, Hammersmith, unequivocally declared that having examined the copy advices of all his agents in the consigning district the only agents who had been supplied with one-pound boxes of Fuller's chocolates were a firm in Radnor who had purchased three boxes on 6 October and a firm in Brecon who had been supplied with six boxes on 1 October and that these were the only sales of boxes of chocolates made in that part of England and Wales between 2 September and the end of October 1921. He confirmed that the actual box itself bore the identifying number 2451, which indicated that it had been packed on the 245th day (2 September) of the year 1921.

This statement was a bit of a problem for Crutchett, who reinterviewed Oswald and Constance Martin on the following day and asked them to identify a box of chocolates similar to the offending box they had received. Oswald mentioned that he was certain that the box had been delivered on 29 September, which was the day of a tennis party. Constance confirmed that the box must have been received either on the day of the tennis party or on the day before as she had joked about the box at the party itself. She confirmed that the tennis party had taken place on 20 September and not on the 29th. Whoever had sent the box, it must have been purchased between the date of its packing (2 September) and the date of its posting (before 19 September), and clearly the purchaser must have bought it a long way away from Hay.

By this time the line of inquiry had widened. Davies had told Crutchett of the purchase of arsenic by Armstrong in 1919. When Davies looked at his appointments book he found that Armstrong had made another purchase of a quarter of a pound of arsenic on 11 January 1921 that had not been recorded in his Sale of Poison book. Both Fred and Laura Davies had by now indirectly accused Armstrong of poisoning Katharine and the police enquiries were directed at finding a motive for a possible murder. Crutchett obtained her will made in July 1920 from Somerset House and noted that her entire estate had been left to Armstrong. He also interviewed the man who tended Katharine, Dr Townsend of Barnwood. He then reported his findings to his seniors at Scotland Yard.

On 22 December Trevor Bigham forwarded a copy of Townsend's statement together with a copy of Katharine's will to the Home Office, stating that the dates 'are very significant'. The outline of the investigation as revealed by his letter began to emerge:

July 8 1920	Will (what was Mrs. Armstrong's state of mind then. No evidence at present?)
August 15	Dr. Hincks called – mental delusions
August 22	Mrs. A certified – goes to asylum
October 3	treated with arsenic 5 minims 3 times a day
November 4	to discharge – no arsenic treatment
Jan 11 1921	A purchases ¼lb. of arsenic same day Dr Hincks wrote at A's request asking for Mrs. A's release
January 22	discharge of Mrs. A
February 15	Dr. Hincks called in – vomiting pain in stomach etc.
February 22	dead.

The inquiry had widened from the initial allegation that Armstrong had attempted to poison Martin to the issue of whether he had actually poisoned his wife.

Bigham advised that more information should be obtained about Armstrong's financial position and recommended that Sir William Willcox (the Home Office toxicologist) should give his expert opinion on the extent of the medical evidence obtained so far and comment on the effect of the arsenical tonic given to Katharine during her stay in the asylum and the time that it would have taken to be eliminated from her body.

On 23 December Sir William Willcox was telephoned by the director of public prosecutions himself. They arranged to meet the following day to discuss the evidence, and at this meeting they noted the similarities to a previous poisoning case, in which Willcox had appeared for the Crown. In this another solicitor, Harold Greenwood, had been accused but acquitted of a similar murder attempt on his wife. On 27 December Willcox produced his first report, which stated that in his opinion a near fatal dose of arsenic had been given to Oswald Martin at the tea party; that the illness of Dorothy Martin was entirely consistent with her having taken a possibly fatal dose in one of the chocolates that she ate; and that the symptoms from which Katharine had suffered, beginning with the bilious attacks in August 1919 and her subsequent symptoms in 1920 and 1921, were consistent with subacute poisoning by arsenic. The terminal symptoms, from 16 February 1921 until her death on 22 February, pointed to acute poisoning. He concluded by saying that absolute proof would be secured if arsenic was found in the body itself.

Willcox answered Bigham's question by stating that all of the arsenic given to Katharine at Barnwood would have been eliminated from her system during the 100-day period to death and none would have been left in the body except traces in the hair and nails. His report contained one caveat: there was no record in Dr Hincks's report of the occurrence of diarrhoea during the last few days of Katharine's illness. Given that this is one of the commonest symptoms of arsenic poisoning it would be unusual if it had not occurred and Willcox stated that it was important that accurate evidence be obtained on this point from both the doctor and the nurse. On 28 December he put this question to Dr Hincks in a letter. He asked Hincks to reply to the director of public prosecutions. Hincks responded on 29 December to 98 Fellows Road, Hampstead:

> I regret I cannot remember whether diarrhoea was present in either of the late Mrs. Armstrong's illnesses of August 1920 or February 1921 ... I never discussed the symptoms with Dr. Townsend, the question of diarrhoea or constipation did not arise in connection with either of her illnesses.

Undeterred by Hincks's inability to remember such an important symptom Bodkin wrote to Willcox on 30 December, commenting that despite the absence of diarrhoea being unusual in a case of arsenical poisoning he agreed that the determining factor would be the presence or absence of arsenic in the body. By now he was satisfied that there was enough evidence to order an exhumation of Katharine's body, which had lain quietly in Cusop churchyard since her interment ten months earlier. He was also satisfied that an order could be given for Armstrong's arrest on the charge of attempting to murder Martin by administering arsenic at the tea party and providing the box of poisoned chocolates, despite the fact that there was not the slightest evidence to associate Armstrong with the chocolates.

The suspicions first raised by Fred Davies to Dr Hincks had by now gathered such momentum that a full-scale murder inquiry was under way. The order for Katharine's exhumation was indicated to the coroner and Dr Bernard Spilsbury, the noted pathologist, was informed that he should attend another autopsy. Meanwhile Armstrong was arrested, not on the capital charge, but on the charge that he had administered poison to Martin with intent.

When Fred Davies later said in evidence that he was not responsible for the prosecution he should not be believed.

3

Herbert Armstrong knew nothing of the investigation under way and continued his practice as a solicitor. His office was situated across the road from the only other solicitor who practised in the town, namely Oswald Martin, but their appearance and background could not have been more dissimilar. Armstrong was a small man of five feet six inches tall, and his face was characterized by the brightest of blue eyes which always carried the hint of a roguish twinkle. When he smiled his whole face lit up, disarming whomever he was talking to. He spoke in a refined manner and tended to accentuate his closing syllables, pronouncing the word 'matter' as 'mattah', but otherwise his speech was unaffected and indicated his well-bred, university-educated origin. Prior to World War I he had rejoined the Territorial Army and was absent from Hay from the war's outbreak until his demobilization in May 1919. When he returned to his practice he bore the field rank of major and was fond of wearing his military brown, a coat which practically reached the ground. He had a perfectly waxed small moustache and walked with a swagger, for not only was he one of the town's senior solicitors, he was the clerk to three divisions of magistrates, that of Hay in Brecknock, Clyro in Radnorshire, and Bredwardine in Herefordshire, as well as being clerk to the local tax commissioners. He lived in a fine house, called Mayfield, located in Cusop, a small village within walking distance of Hay. He did not possess a motor car.

Oswald Martin could not have been more different, coming from trade origins in Tewkesbury where his two brothers and their wives continued to live. He had practised in Doncaster before he was enlisted in the army as a private and was invalided out in August 1918 as a result of a wound he sustained in the Battle of Bullecourt. When he arrived in Hay before Armstrong's return from the army he still showed signs of his wound and his face was partially paralysed, lending a strange expression to his bland features. He was considered to be a delicate man and something of a 'war crock'. He stood much taller than Armstrong and was fond of wearing outsized coats and floppy bow-ties. He was more like a 'city slicker' than a country solicitor and the pair presented an incongruous sight when seen together.

Martin had joined Robert Griffiths, who had remained in place throughout the war. Griffiths was a solicitor with a sound practice and according to Armstrong was 'a good lawyer, a straight man and a loyal friend'. Griffiths had a son, Trevor, whose legal studies were interrupted by the Kaiser's ambitions, and in 1918 as his health was failing, he decided that he could not afford to wait for his son to qualify and was forced to take on an assistant. The choice was Martin, who arrived in the early part of 1919 in a debilitated state to begin work as his managing clerk. In July 1919 Martin was made a partner and the name of the firm was changed to 'Griffiths and Martin'. Martin's future in the town appeared to be assured.

However, there was a blot on his horizon – Armstrong, who paraded back into town like a peacock and proceeded to take his place at the feet of the magistrates and reconstruct the practice that he had practically abandoned five years before. Armstrong had practised on his own after the death of his partner Arthur Cheese, who died of cancer shortly before the outbreak of the war. When Armstrong answered the call of king and country he had left the practice in the hands of Cheese's nephew Conway Samson and his managing clerk Arthur Phillips. During his absence, he drew out not a penny from the business, leaving it to pay its own way. When Armstrong returned he found that it was badly run down and, as he could no longer draw his army salary and needed serious money to buy out Cheese's share of the partnership, which was agreed at three years' gross profits, he had to get down to work fast.

Martin, too, wanted to make a name for himself; unfortunately he was not an able advocate and could not do so in the local court. However, he understood the plight of the many tenant farmers and decided that his bread and butter would be better served by furthering their interests against the gentry, whom he could not hope to emulate. The period from the end of the war was marked by rising prices, a situation that lasted until 1920 when deep depression followed. There was no protection of tenure for the tenant farmers and many tried to buy their farms from their landlords. There was much work for Martin to do.

Armstrong, on the other hand, was gentrified and attracted the legal work of the landlords in the community, his income being augmented by his salaried positions. He was anxious, too, to regain those landlords who had left his practice in the war years and consulted other solicitors. Of importance to him was a man called Williams Vaughan, to whom he had personally loaned large sums of money, secured by second mortgages over his already heavily mortgaged estates.

Before the end of the last century John Williams Vaughan had inherited from his parents vast tracts of land in Breconshire known as the Velinewydd Estate. He was a magistrate on one of Armstrong's benches and in 1912 had approached him and asked for his help in raising £12,500 to be secured by way of mortgage to the Yorkshire Penny Bank. Armstrong agreed and had arranged the deal personally with Sir Edward Holden. Armstrong also agreed to manage the estate, collect the rents and discharge the mortgage out of the rents themselves. As time progressed and Williams Vaughan became short of ready money, the solicitor continued to loan him sums of his own. As a result of Armstrong's absence abroad Vaughan instructed a land agent to deal with the rents and he then became hopelessly in arrears with his mortgage payments and the Bank threatened to sell his estate as mortgagee in possession. Williams Vaughan had instructed a Hereford solicitor to act for him in the sale of the mansion to the tenant, and it was only then that the bank discovered that their mortgage did not give them adequate security for all their loans as Williams Vaughan had previously made a settlement which had not been disclosed to them or to Armstrong. The bank was furious and insisted that the whole of the estate be sold. When Armstrong returned to his practice he was determined to regain his recalcitrant client and ensure the repayment to the Yorkshire Penny Bank of their loan and repayment to him of the sums he was owed.

The sale by auction was arranged to take place in the Castle Hotel, Brecon, in November 1919. Armstrong acted for Williams Vaughan and a Brecon solicitor acted for another mortgagee who was also owed sums by Williams Vaughan. Armstrong had hired a car and took the hapless Martin with him. There was a huge audience in the auction room and it was clear to everyone that there would be ugly scenes, for the tenant farmers considered that they had the prior right to buy their farms at a fair valuation and that the auction sale should not proceed.

A prominent local farmer called William Morgan addressed the assembled crowd and said that he was there to represent the Farmers' Union. No one, he said, should bid against a sitting tenant and that any such bidder should stand up and identify himself. When a farm was put up for sale a merchant of the name of Billy Lewis started to bid against the sitting tenant. As the farm was about to be knocked down to the luckless bidder and the auctioneer was about to lower his gavel for the third and final time there was an outcry in the saleroom and a farmer standing immediately in front of him turned round and said, 'It's Billy Lewis,' and then proceeded to drag him by the scruff of his collar and throw him out of the saleroom. Pandemonium broke loose and the auctioneer turned to Armstrong, saying 'It is enough to kill the man.' When order was finally restored the tenant farmer raised his last bid by £5 and the farm was knocked down to him. The crowd then began to sing 'God Save the King', first in Welsh and then in English, and as a result of their disruption very few farms and plots of land were disposed of and, worst of all for Williams Vaughan and the Yorkshire Penny Bank, the Velinewydd mansion, which had a reserve price of £12,500, went unsold.

Billy Lewis later sued for assault and Williams Vaughan, through Armstrong, sued for conspiracy and they were both awarded damages by a high court judge in London a year later. However, at the time, this judgment did not help Williams Vaughan in his continued negotiations with his mortgagees, who refused to allow partial releases of the land that had been sold and who insisted that all the money due to them should be repaid before they allowed him to complete any of the sales.

Unfortunately, even if Armstrong had wished otherwise, his social relations with the town's new solicitor were not allowed to prosper. In the summer of 1919 Martin had been invited to tea at the request of Katharine, who wished to be introduced to the newcomer. Armstrong set up the invitation and as he had been asked to find some fishing for an army acquaintance who was staying at a local hotel, he asked him and his wife to attend as well. Unfortunately, Martin did not realize that he should have shown more respect to the lady of the house who was entertaining him, for Katharine was 'particular' and considered that his informal dress of white flannels and tennis jacket did not befit the occasion. At her request he was never asked again as she was appalled at his manner. Martin was later questioned about the occasion and agreed that he might have been dressed in this way. Armstrong remembered the occasion well, and was recorded as saying, 'I do not think he knew any better and why he came to my house in tennis trousers I will never know as I had no facilities for the game.' Whatever the truth about Martin's attire and manner, Katharine never felt able to ask him to her house again.

Nevertheless Armstrong showed civility to Martin. He signed his papers to make him a commissioner for oaths and proposed him as a member of the local Law Society, later joking to him that he had let him in for a fee. He also introduced him to a number of his country clubs. Whatever his personal feelings about the man he seemed to have accepted him as a member of the legal fraternity in the district. Equally, he knew full well that there was no dearth of young solicitors who had been demobbed and were anxious to find positions in solicitors' practices. If Griffiths had not employed Martin he would have employed someone else.

November 1920 saw the death of Robert Griffiths, which was a misfortune to many of his clients who had entrusted their legal work to him for many years. He was widely respected and had a clientele which was far reaching, stretching well beyond the borders of Hay. Although Conway Samson, who was an able and diligent solicitor, had run Armstrong's practice to the best of his ability during the war, it was Griffiths who was by far the most senior man and clients wanted to consign their business to the more solid and better established man.

During the last year of Griffiths's life Armstrong was made aware that Martin had approached some of his (Armstrong's) clients with a view to obtaining their business and he mentioned this fact to Griffiths himself. Armstrong considered Martin to be a very 'pushing and energetic young man' and although he professed that he never bore any animosity towards him, he believed that the feeling was not mutual, since Martin had approached his clients. The position changed when Griffiths died, because Mr Gwilliam, who had been the right-hand man of Griffiths for many years, left the practice upon Martin's succession and took many of his clients directly to Armstrong.

There was clearly an uneasy truce between the two men at this stage. Armstrong did not quite know what to make of Martin because he was so different from the old Griffiths, whom Armstrong both respected and looked up to as the senior solicitor in the town. Now that Griffiths had gone he was faced with a realignment which presented him with certain difficulties, mostly because he could not fathom the newcomer. They were just not on the same wavelength and Armstrong could not predict how Martin would react to any given situation. Armstrong missed the bond that he had held with Griffiths, who had been so reliable in all his dealings with him. Above all he felt that he could not trust the competitive and point-scoring Martin.

Despite Martin's assured pushiness, Armstrong found that he could no longer recommend him to act for clients who required representation in the police courts. (Armstrong was debarred from this work because of his position as clerk to the justices.) As time progressed it became increasingly clear to him that the longer Martin stayed *in situ* the better off he would be, because gradually more and more of Griffiths's clients were now drifting over to his (Armstrong's) practice.

In June 1921 Martin married Constance Davies, the chemist's daughter, but Armstrong was not invited to the wedding. Armstrong had sent him a wedding present of two silver candlesticks and had offered to help in any way he could in business matters while the couple were on their honeymoon. Martin thanked him for his offer but did not take it up. He also thanked Armstrong for his wedding present – not in writing, as was customary, but by simply telephoning him at his office two days after receipt, which Armstrong considered to be in bad form.

After Martin returned from his honeymoon, he sent an 'at home' invitation to Armstrong, who went alone to his house on a Saturday afternoon. After the other guests had gone he remained with Martin and was shown round his garden and they had a cigar in the smoking room and discussed some of Martin's books. On his way home Armstrong noticed the name 'Bredon Hill' on the gate. The alteration from its previous name of 'Radnor View' had, according to Armstrong, caused a considerable amount of amusement in the neighbourhood and the change of name struck Armstrong as being ludicrous as Bredon Hill was in Worcestershire.

During the summer of 1921 Armstrong was very busy preparing for Captain Hope's sale of his Clifford Estate. The auction at Hay Drill Hall had been fixed for 11 August, but many of the properties which had been advertised for sale at the auction were disposed of to purchasers beforehand, demanding constant work and attention to detail by Armstrong, who was being instructed by Captain Hope's very efficient and formidable estate manager called Moyse.

On the day of the sale Martin surprised everybody, not least Captain Hope, by making a statement that no one should bid against the sitting tenant of Upper Castleton, one of Hope's biggest farms, and as a result the property was knocked down to the tenant Mrs Jane Hamer. Captain Hope was furious and told Armstrong that he considered he had lost two or three thousand pounds because of Martin's statement. Armstrong mentioned Hope's annoyance to Martin and asked him if he proposed to do anything, as it was possible Captain Hope might consider taking some action. Martin replied, 'You haven't got an earthly chance – I have done nothing that I shall regret.' Proceedings were seriously considered by Hope but eventually Armstrong was instructed not to take the matter further. Martin's comments at the sale were reminiscent of William Morgan's at the Velinewydd auction and Morgan had been ordered to pay damages to Williams Vaughan as a consequence. Martin's announcement bore its own dangers for a solicitor. He was the successor to Robert Griffiths, and his word would have carried weight in the auction room. It was very wrong of him to have made such an assertion and attempt to suborn prospective purchasers into silence. Those present knew full well what had happened at the Castle Hotel, Brecon, in November 1919 and no one wanted a repeat performance of that fiasco. It was clear that Martin was staking his claim to be the champion of the tenant farmers and demonstrating his dislike of the landed gentry and their advisors in the form of Armstrong and his class.

Unlike his rival, Martin was not at ease in the company of the gentry. It was also clear that Martin was anxious to secure more of the farmers' business at this time. In November 1921 Martin had prepared some account books that were designed to help farmers prepare their income tax returns. He showed the books to Armstrong who commented that he thought it was an excellent idea, but dismissed it from his mind. Later Armstrong was walking past the shop of Grant's, the local printer and newsagent, and noticed a poster in the window bearing the words: 'Martin's Farm Income Tax Book can be obtained within.' A few days later Grant was in Armstrong's office and Armstrong joked with him about the matter. Grant said that he did not think there was anything wrong in printing the books for Martin. Armstrong replied, 'Well, it isn't the usual thing for solicitors to advertise their wares like this' and suggested that he might have a poster exhibited bearing the words, 'Try our Guinea Wills.' Armstrong did not speak to Martin directly but clearly his words to Grant had struck home, because just before Christmas Armstrong noted that the wording of the advertisement had been altered and the word 'Martin's' was omitted.

This incident shows Martin's nature and his inability to grasp the fact that his was a learned profession distinct from trade. He was at this time losing more and more clients to Armstrong, as Griffiths would neither have had the time to prepare such books nor would he have considered it necessary to do so as he had already built up an extensive practice in and around Hay. Clearly Martin had more in common with the shopkeepers and tradesmen of the town, but even the tradesmen wanted to consult a solicitor who was above trade, as respect was still nurtured by position, standing and behaviour. Martin's father-in-law, the chemist Fred Davies, was very much the tradesman and he liked Martin, for they were similar men. They could communicate with each other. Fred Davies had been in Hay for years, but despite such long service no one could say they knew much about him because he kept himself to himself and did not involve himself in the community. He had been a Freemason but for some reason had left the lodge at the turn of the century. Fred Davies wanted his son-in-law to succeed and his wife, Laura, was equally ambitious for both Martin and her only daughter. The only obstacle to their progress appeared to be Armstrong, whom they regarded as aloof and one to be taken down a peg. Although they had had no real dealings with Armstrong it was Fred who later told Hincks, 'I wouldn't trust him a yard.'

4

Katharine Mary Friend, born on 8 February 1873, was four years younger than Armstrong. They had been childhood friends and their friendship survived his parents' move to Liverpool from Plymouth, where his father William had plied his trade as a colonial merchant in that great maritime port. Katharine's father had married twice and by his second marriage to Mary Ann Hollis Friend had sired her, and Ida Bessie two years later. He had two children by his first marriage: Arthur, who moved to New Zealand, and Iris, who died shortly before the war, leaving Katharine five nieces of whom she became very fond. Of the two daughters Bessie was the more attractive, but what Katharine lacked in looks, she made up for by an outstanding intellect. She was a rather tall, gawky woman with little dress sense, her frame typically being enveloped in voluminous swirling robes. She was also extremely religious and she shared her beliefs with Armstrong.

Katharine was highly strung, physically weak and susceptible to falls, accidents and ailments. After a particularly severe fall she required lengthy treatment for water on the knee and in 1902 a bicycle accident left her blind in one eye. The effect of this injury, which she kept to herself and her close family, was hardly apparent except, perhaps, to lend rather a strained expression to her formidable features. In 1903, shortly after the bicycle accident, she had an attack of rheumatism in her left arm which recurred at intervals throughout her life and in 1904 she had a severe attack of influenza which left her susceptible to draughts that brought on colds or neuralgia. She was so sensitive that the least nervous excitement brought on sickness.

She was devoted to her sister Bessie and they shared each other's troubles and burdens throughout their lives. Bessie neither married nor pursued a career, and after her father's death in 1909 preferred to live at home with her mother, and after her mother's death in 1917, she lived with her aunts.

In 1901 Armstrong, having taken an MA at Cambridge and qualified as a solicitor in Liverpool, where he met his lifelong friend Arthur Chevalier, decided to move back to Teignmouth, Devon, the home of Katharine's parents, and he became a partner in a solicitors' firm in Newton Abbott. He was with this firm for two years until the partnership was dissolved. He then took over the Newton Abbott branch where he practised on his own until June 1906.

It was when he was in Devon that he resumed his relationship with Katharine, who at the time was helping to run a girl's private school with a Miss Seymour who was twelve years her senior. Despite Katharine's obvious frailties they had much in common. Both shared a love of music and Katharine, although her frequent bouts of rheumatism hindered her, was a gifted pianist. Both loved to converse and discourse, and there was nothing Armstrong enjoyed more than a good discussion. They also shared an interest in homeopathy, to treat their various ailments.

Their relationship flourished and on 7 September 1904 they announced their engagement. This was a blow to Miss Seymour, who now had to find another partner or sell the school. She chose the latter course, but remained in close contact with her former partner for the rest of her life. Without doubt Armstrong knew of Katharine's physical frailties before their engagement as when he offered her his engagement ring she could not wear it because at that time she was suffering from aches in the joints of her hands.

In 1906 Armstrong moved to Hay and within six months was admitted as a partner by Arthur Cheese, with whom he had lodged for the first six months. As his position seemed a safe one he decided that he could at last marry Katharine and their wedding took place in Katharine's home town on 4 June 1907.

At the time of their marriage Katharine had no money of her own and no settlement, except for a policy of £1,000, which Armstrong settled on her. He chose as the trustees of the settlement Arthur Chevalier and Bessie.

Their first child, Eleanor, was born in 1908; then a son, Pearson, followed in 1912. In December of that year the family moved into Armstrong's house, Mayfield, and took on a nanny, Emily Pearce, who was faithful to them both to the end.

Their immediate neighbour, Tunnard Moore, who as a magistrate later signed Katharine's committal papers, certifying her as insane, recounted two of her peculiarities. When she first came to Hay she stated that she lived by rules and that afternoon tea was an abuse and she should never allow it. However, this rule was soon afterwards dispensed with and she not only gave tea but took it herself. He remembered, too, that one Sunday Armstrong was tele-phoned at Mayfield and the caller was told in no uncertain way not to telephone on a Sunday. However, on one or two occasions when their home telephone was out of order, she asked Moore if she could use his telephone, which, it being a Sunday, rather amused him, as he knew about her strong objection to using it on that day.

Other facets of her character are revealed by the Revd Edward Stredder of Cusop Church who knew Armstrong and his wife intimately. He stated that she was never 'normal' in the usual sense of the word, explaining that people could be described as 'abnormal' either because they had a deficiency of 'mental power' or an excess of 'mental power'; he placed Katharine in the latter category, portraying her as a remarkably intelligent woman. He said that her brain was always very active and that she was one of the best 'talkers' that he had ever come across. 'But one got tired of the ceaseless flow of words, but she always had a thorough grasp of the subject she was discussing. She was one of those people whose mental powers are far in the excess of the physical and sooner or later with these people there comes a breakdown. She was a regular bundle of nerves.'

Revd Stredder described an occasion when he motored to Hereford with one of his parishioners.

You know there are two trains for Bristol, the West one about 12.15, the other about 12.30. The 12.15 is express and the other slower. Catching the first meant a difference of three hours on the way. The railway officials arrange things so beautifully that travellers from Hay by the 11.25 generally arrive at Hereford Station to see the 12.15 just going out. Well I knew that Mrs. Armstrong and her Aunt were coming in by that train, so I was on the look out, and sure enough as the guard began blowing his whistle the Hay train came along. Fortunately Mrs. Armstrong and her Aunt were in the front. I dashed their door open and practically lugged them both out. The ticket inspector was demanding tickets and poor Mrs. Armstrong in her frantic excitement was jumping up and down the platform like a cat on hot bricks. I got hold of her and told the Aunt to follow me and ignoring the collector shoved them both into the Bristol train as it was on the move, so they got it alright but their luggage arrived next day. But if you had seen that poor woman you would understand what I mean when I say I never considered Mrs. Armstrong normal. She had so completely lost herself that she didn't know whether she was standing on her head or her heels.

Apart from Miss Pearce they had a serving girl at Mayfield. They also needed help to manage their large garden, which had over 800 square yards of path, and employed William Jay, who ran a market garden in Hay. Katharine made the necessary arrangements with him, supervised his work and paid him, although Armstrong used to see him occasionally to give him general instructions.

Jay used patent ready-mixed weedkiller on the paths and purchased a gallon of the stuff in 1912. The following year, on 23 June, he purchased three gallons more. On 2 May 1914 Armstrong himself purchased weedkiller, but this time he purchased its ingredients to make it himself and bought a quarter-pound of arsenic and one pound of caustic soda from the local chemist, Fred Davies. He decided to make the weedkiller himself rather than buy the prepared sort, because he had always been interested in chemistry and the preparation of weedkiller appealed to him. It was also much cheaper to buy it this way and he followed a recipe which he had cut out from the 'Gardening Notes' of *The Times*.

He kept the recipe in a box file in his library at Mayfield, and in this file he kept other newspaper cuttings relating to weeds and their destruction that he had taken from various newspapers from time to time, together with lists and catalogues of various weedkillers and appliances.

He told Fred Davies why he required the arsenic and was informed that by law arsenic could not be sold unless a colouring matter was added, the favourites being soot, charcoal or indigo. The object of the Act is obvious, for pure white arsenic can easily be mistaken for a variety of innocuous household substances such as salt, bicarbonate of soda or even sugar. It is a highly poisonous and dangerous substance.

He made up the weedkiller according to the recipe by mixing up the arsenic and caustic soda in a mortar in equal proportions of four ounces each and boiling the ingredients in a large saucepan on the kitchen range. He weighed the caustic soda on an old letter-weighing machine belonging to his wife and used all the arsenic that he had bought. He then poured the dry mixture into a saucepan and added the correct amount of water, which in this case was one gallon and boiled up the whole lot together. He then bottled this concentrated solution, ready for dilution and use. He did this by filling a three-gallon watering-can with water and added a teacup full of weedkiller solution for each gallon and poured the solution on to the weeds on the path. When he had used up all the solution in the bottle he refilled it from the saucepan. The one bottle that contained the concentrated solution was an old black port wine bottle that was put away in the loft above the stable and never brought into the house.

Katharine, a woman of frugal instincts, approved of this course of action and readily agreed that Armstrong should make his own solution. The idea appealed to her too and she read the recipe taken from the press cutting. They both realized that the solution was highly poisonous and the stable door was kept firmly locked to ensure that the children never got hold of it.

Much happened in 1914 and the purchase of arsenic to make weedkiller paled into insignificance in the scheme of things. Armstrong was in Switzerland when the war broke out and he was kept there until 6 September 1914. Except when he was on leave he was not to return to Hay until five years later in March 1919.

He had been offered and accepted the commission as

second-in-command bearing the rank of captain and from December 1914 to 1915 he was adjutant to the Wessex Division and in command of the 2/2nd Wessex Field Company, 58th Division, under orders overseas. He was no conscript but a volunteer holding up the flag of his country for his fellow countrymen. In June 1916 he was promoted to major and from August 1916 to August 1917 he served with 3/2nd Wessex Field Company and was stationed at Christchurch for some of this period. From August 1917 to February 1918 he was with 647 South Midland Field Company Royal Engineers, stationed first on the East coast and then at Cambridge. He was then posted to the 5th Reserve Battalion of the Royal Engineers based at Christchurch. On 23 June 1918 he was posted to France as officer in command of the 547th (Kent) Field Company Royal Engineers and saw active service. In September 1918 he was transferred to the Royal Engineers base depot in France, and it was not until October of that year that he returned to England to be stationed at Aldershot. In December 1918 he took up an appointment under the Ministry of Labour where he remained until he was demobilized on 23 May 1919.

Whatever has been written about Armstrong's military career the facts speak for themselves. He did not wait to be enlisted as did many of his fellow countrymen. He was an able and efficient administrator, well-liked in his mess and he commanded men. Not every one gained glory on the battlefield. Not every one died in the appalling waste of that war. Some like Armstrong helped matters to tick over with efficiency, attention to detail and correctness. He was not a man to be put out when his work was questioned, as he was fastidious in the minutiae and could answer any criticism. He served his country well and played his part in ensuring success against a formidable war machine. No person should belittle this record, whatever judgements are made against him for future actions. His military career spanned from 1900, when he first joined the Volunteers, until 1921 when he was officially retired from the Army, a period of over twenty years. He was entitled to a territorial decoration, which was bestowed on him in November 1919, and was allowed to keep possession of his title of major when he was officially retired in 1921. Whatever the truth about Armstrong, when unsung heroes are remembered Armstrong did his bit and for this he should be recognized.

5

Katharine remained at Mayfield for the first few months of the war but found the house much too big for her and decided to move to Teignmouth. In the spring of 1915 she removed her small family and Miss Pearce into rented accommodation to be close to her mother and sister. She let Mayfield to tenants and kept a close eye on their financial affairs. She also supervised the garden and the planting of various vegetables. She took these duties seriously.

Armstrong returned to his family whenever he could get leave and they also visited him at various places. Katharine went to him at Christmas 1914 when he was based at Christchurch and stayed in the room in which he was billeted. In March 1915 he spent three days at Teignmouth, at which time the youngest daughter Margaret was conceived. In November of that year he again stayed with her at Teignmouth for a three day period during the occasion of Margaret's christening. In July 1916 he spent seven days with her at Bovey Tracey, followed by three days with her at Teignmouth in the September. He also spent three days with her at Teignmouth in December 1916, March 1917, June 1917 and September 1917. In December 1917 she spent a fortnight with him at Cambridge and he again visited her at Teignmouth for three days in March 1918. On returning from France in October 1918 he spent several days with her at Teignmouth until ordered to report at Exeter for duty with the Ministry of Labour. The only occasion that he did not spend his leave with her was in the summer of 1915, when at her special request he visited Hay to attend to his practice.

During the war years she became greatly worried by his absence, especially during the period when he was posted overseas. She found her accommodation cramped and the three children had to share the same bedroom with Miss Pearce. She was also worried about the letting of Mayfield, which for a time was without a tenant. To top it all her mother died in August 1917. All these events accentuated her nervous condition. She made a will on 17 January 1917, but did not tell Armstrong about it until much later. The will was a secret one and appointed her sister Bessie Friend and Arthur Chevalier to be trustees. It was also a foolish will, leaving more money than she had, and it bore heavily on her mind that she had not told her husband about it. The will was kept by Bessie in safe custody.

At this time Katharine had a small income of her own from her mother's estate, which had been the subject of detailed dealings with other members of her family – particularly Bessie, with whom she had been in daily contact for the last four years. Although this estate was not complex, her mother had been left a life interest in her late husband's capital. Upon her death this fell to be divided among the four children, which necessitated complex dealings in shares, bonds and stocks. The administration was not helped by the fact that Katharine's half brother was in New Zealand and her late half sister's interest had passed to her husband Mr Sayle whom Katharine considered to be a lazy good-for-nothing. In addition her mother's sisters, both frail old ladies in their nineties who were being looked after by Bessie, had transferred further securities to Katharine on the understanding that the income would be paid over to them for the remainder of their lives. The aunts had also guaranteed a number of loans for the benefit of one of the Sayle girls and had taken further security by way of second mortgages. In short, the whole business became an incredible tangle. Katharine had been left to sort the matter out and Bessie looked to her for guidance throughout.

On 6 October 1917 Katharine wrote a letter to Conway Samson:

> Please excuse my wretched scribble, but Miss Pearce is away, & my head and hands have almost more than they can possibly accomplish. I have had Eleanor in bed three days, & both the little ones poorly, which has meant almost sleepless

nights, so I am somewhat tired now they are practically well again.

Five days later she again wrote to Conway Samson and her letter included a little note:

STRICTLY CONFIDENTIAL

Perhaps I should frankly explain to you my sentiments about paying Duty out of *my* income from my mother's estate. I do not propose at present to spend any of it on myself or my children. My sister has to take her share in the expenses here, and my mother feared my sister's income would hardly be sufficient for this, yet she can't move the two old ladies, especially as the house might not let, & Mrs. Friend and Miss Farley are mortgagees in possession of the rents. I promised my mother years ago not to take my share if it crippled my sister's resources unreasonably – though, since War has impoverished my husband, she told me I might not feel myself <u>bound</u> by the promise, I naturally feel I must do my best for a sister whose life has been devoted to us all. Major Armstrong is the first to acknowledge that my sister's claim on me is very real: she has always shared my burdens in no ordinary degree, & I shall share hers. So we don't want to decrease the Capital which provides her income. I think we shall divide the investments.

Please burn this

I shall not spend my money in case I have to help my sister, or in case I need it if anything happens to my husband. I tell you this as my friend & adviser.

Before Armstrong finally returned to Mayfield in the spring of 1919 Katharine wrote to him with the news that Miss Pearce was ill and the children had whooping cough. At this time she had no other servants at all and had to manage the house and deal with all the chores without help. She complained to him that she had had another nervous attack, which she attributed to a strain that she had received in her right arm caused by stoking up the central-heating boiler with a large poker. When he finally returned home he noticed that her nervous condition was more pronounced than it was in 1914.

Armstrong collected his family from Teignmouth and brought them home to spend Christmas at Mayfield before returning to Exeter to continue his duties with the Ministry of Labour. He finally returned to Mayfield in March 1919, having been given indefinite leave, and remained there until his final demobilization in May 1919.

The Hay to which he returned was not the same place as the Hay that he had left in October 1914. He found that Robert Griffiths had taken on Oswald Martin and, of more immediate concern, his practice was very run down. He discussed his financial position and business prospects with Katharine and she too was worried to a considerable extent, especially as she was fully aware of the problems with Williams Vaughan, to whom Armstrong had loaned most of his personal fortune.

In May 1919 she had a recurrence of pain and her husband begged her to see the local doctor, Tom Hincks, which she did. She complained to him about numbness in her fingers and pains in the right arm and particularly in the shoulder joint. She described her medical history and Hincks diagnosed her condition as brachial neuritis. He prescribed a battery, which Armstrong obtained for her in the town. While he turned the handle she would grip the two holders. Whatever the efficiency of this apparatus she began to recover, although all that summer she was unable to play the piano.

In July she went to stay with her sister in Bath and whilst there she made arrangements for her little boy, Pearson (known as 'Sonny'), to go to Monkton Combe School in Bath. She also discussed with Bessie her wish to make a new will as she felt that now Armstrong had returned safely from the war and as she had not left him enough in her present will, it should be changed.

In September of that year, five months after Katharine had first complained to Hincks about the pain in her right arm, Arthur Chevalier paid a visit to Mayfield. Chevalier had not seen Katharine for five years and was greatly shocked by the extent of her change. He knew that Katharine was highly strung and that she used to worry over trifles, but he had never seen her in such a state as she appeared to him in the autumn of 1919. She complained to him that she was suffering from rheumatism and used the word neuritis to him. She told him that she suffered in her fingers and arms. At the time he did not form any opinion about her complaints, and assumed that the word neuritis had been suggested to her by the doctor who was treating her 'rightly or wrongly for his own purposes'. He discussed the position with Armstrong and told him that she was in a nervous and excited state of mind.

One evening both Chevalier and Armstrong were in the smoking room. Katharine interrupted them and complained that she had been left alone in the drawing room. Both Armstrong and Chevalier said afterwards that this was a very unusual thing for her to do, but at her request they both went into the drawing room, where Katharine had been playing the piano. She told them that as this was the first time she had played since her attack of neuritis, she could not understand why they had not joined her in the drawing room immediately she had started to play. While Chevalier knew that his friends were a close and affectionate couple, he went back to Liverpool concerned about Katharine.

In December of that year he received a letter from Armstrong saying that 'my wife varies; she does not get so much rheumatism but a lot of troublesome indigestion with resulting trouble'.

The following spring Miss Pearce was taken ill. Armstrong used to attend to the kitchen fire but Katharine had to attend to all the nursing. Mrs Jay, the gardener's wife, was asked to come up after breakfast to do the rough housework during the day, and sometimes she was accompanied by her two small children, who used to play with Sonny and Margaret in the day nursery at Mayfield, the large rocking horse being a great delight to them all.

Armstrong believed at that time that the first signs of Katharine's menopause were manifesting themselves. Katharine by this time was forty-seven years old and had started to worry about the most inconsequential of routine domestic matters. He believed that a holiday would do her good and begged her to take one. He was not able to go himself as he was working himself to the bone, trying to reconstruct his practice after its years of neglect. Eventually, in June 1920, he persuaded her to go and stay with an old schoolfriend of hers, a Mrs Way, in Hoddesdon, Hertfordshire. She stayed away for ten days and spent part of the time visiting Miss Seymour.

Unfortunately, her stay away from Hay did not appear to have benefited her, because on her return she again started to worry unnecessarily over small details. For the first time she mentioned to Armstrong that she had made a will in 1917 and explained the contents of it to him. She mentioned that because Sonny's education was just starting she did not have enough money out of her income to pay for the schooling of all the children and that she wished to change it. However, she did not know how to draft it, in order to balance all the conflicting interests. He tried to reassure her that she really had nothing to worry about and that if she wished he could write out a short and simple will saying that he would ensure that the children would be properly educated.

According to Armstrong there was nothing wrong with the execution, or the attestation, of the will that he wrote out in his own hand and that appointed him sole executor and sole beneficiary. He said that he wrote down the will in the drawing room of Mayfield on 8 July 1920 and that after Katharine signed it Miss Pearce was asked to witness her signature. Lily Candy, who was the housemaid, was called into the room by Katharine with the words, 'There is Lily, she will do as the other witness.' The importance of this will cannot be overestimated, as the prosecution alleged that the document was vital evidence of the prime motive for Katharine's subsequent murder, alleging in the magistrates court that Katharine's signature had been forged and in the assizes (although the allegation of forgery was dropped) that it had been improperly witnessed. These matters will be gone into in more depth later, but suffice to say that there existed a will, apparently bearing Katharine's signature; and the names following her signature were those of Miss Pearce and Lily Candy.

This was not a secret will. Katharine had already talked to her sister Bessie about changing her previous one and Armstrong declared that he brought no pressure on Katharine to make it. The original was placed by Katharine in a small safe in Eleanor's bedroom, which held the remainder of her securities.

The house was clearly in turmoil during the summer of 1920. Before Katharine's holiday a favourite niece of hers, Miss Pearl Sayle, had come to stay with the view to becoming

Katharine's companion. Unfortunately, during Katharine's holiday in the summer, the niece was certified and transferred to Talgarth Asylum. There was nothing insidious about this illness and there has never been any question of foul play. Pearl was an extremely highly strung young woman who spent the rest of her life in and out of mental hospitals, suffering from cyclical manic depression, and she became a great problem for the Armstrong children during their adolescence. Armstrong had written to Katharine in Hoddesdon setting out the full details of Pearl's case and telling her what was being done. He told her not to worry about Pearl, but he believed that this event considerably affected her mental outlook.

Miss Sayle's abnormal condition was first noticed on 17 June and as a result her sister, Miss Gladys Sayle, was asked to visit Mayfield. She remained there during Pearl's illness and stayed on after Katharine returned from Hoddesdon. Gladys mentioned to Armstrong that Katharine appeared to be nervous after her holiday and asked him if she could do anything. She further remarked that Katharine talked far too much and was too excitable for average good health. Armstrong replied by saying that his wife's tension would no doubt improve now that Pearl had left.

Katharine remained in this nervous condition throughout July and the early part of August. On 9 August Armstrong returned home later than usual for lunch and Katharine informed him that she had been telling the children that he would not come home as he would be arrested for something she had done. At the time he treated her comments as a joke and passed some remark about it. After lunch he asked her why she had said it, to be told that she had been underpaying the tradesmen, including Mr Jay, and that she thought he would be arrested as a consequence. He tried to comfort her and said he would be home earlier than usual that evening.

During this period in August, Eleanor, who was then 12½ years old was home from school. On 13 August she went to the station to meet another cousin, Agnes Sayle, who was coming to stay at Mayfield to join her sister Gladys. Eleanor recalled the event quite specifically and remembered that when they arrived at Mayfield at about 5 to 5.15 p.m., her mother was in the dining room. Eleanor went upstairs to show her cousin her room and to take off her coat and then went downstairs into the dining room, leaving her cousin upstairs. Her mother was standing by the window with Pearson and Margaret and she turned round to face Eleanor when she entered the room. She recollects her mother making a few remarks and then saying:

'I have done a dreadful thing which will almost kill me and injure your career and your father's life later on if not now. I have taken too much medicine.'

Eleanor replied to comfort her: 'It is nonsense to think you've taken too much medicine.'

Eleanor recalled that after tea on the same day she was standing by the window with her brother and sister in the drawing room and that her mother was sitting down, when she repeated the same thing. She could not recall what she replied but remembered being very upset and frightened, and she waited by the door for her father to come home to tell him what had happened. Her father tried to reassure her and told her that her mother had said that because she was so ill.

It was during this period that Miss Pearce was away on her annual holiday and Armstrong relied heavily on Eleanor to inform him of anything that happened in his absence at work. He realized that Katharine's remarks to Eleanor were similar to those directed at him and he was very disturbed, for he could not account for their origin and was very concerned about what might happen. He dismissed from his mind as unthinkable the question of Katharine considering suicide and at this stage had not even contemplated the thought of her being removed from the house. What he realized, though, was that from the reports he received from his daughter, his wife's delusions most frequently occurred after lunch.

Armstrong was by now desperately worried about his wife's condition. He did not know what was causing it except for his belief that the pressures, worries and deprivations of the war years, coupled with the effect of her change of life, were contributing causes. He also knew that she was worried about money. He could do no more than ask Eleanor to ensure that her mother rested and he asked the neighbours to keep an eye on her and call as much as possible. He told his neighbours, the Southwicks and the new Rector of Cusop Church, Rector Buchanan, about his wife's strange state of mind and asked them to call on her, which they did.

In the days that followed, Katharine's behaviour became stranger and stranger. She would follow Armstrong from room to room and wander about the garden by herself. She became an insomniac and would wake him up, declaring that she would have to go away at once to avoid causing him any trouble. He told her not to be ridiculous as there were no trains running at night and that she had better go back to bed. On Sunday 15 August Armstrong went to church with his three children and the cousins, leaving Katharine at home. When they returned Eleanor stayed in the garden with her mother while her father went to see Dr Hincks to discuss the whole question with him. Hincks promised to come up and see her and prescribe a sedative. Eleanor noted in her diary for that day, 'In the evening I stayed in and wrote letters while Mother rested as I was afraid of leaving her alone.'

Hincks prescribed sleeping sedatives in the form of bromide, but her delusions worsened and her paranoia and feelings of self-loathing increased to the point of breakdown. When the adjoining field was being harvested the threshing machine circled it. She imagined that the noises were Jay knocking on the window asking to be paid. Hincks called and suggested that she should be sent to a home for the mentally ill, as his sister had been cured by a stay at an asylum. He suggested to Armstrong that her condition was probably caused by the change of life. Armstrong immediately wired for Chevalier to come over. He followed it with a letter explaining that Katharine had not been at all well of late and that he wanted to see him. Chevalier replied by saying that he could not conveniently leave Liverpool immediately, but in a second wire Armstrong insisted that he should come as the matter was urgent.

Chevalier arrived on the 7.48 p.m. train and was met by Armstrong at the station. He explained that Katharine was out of health and appeared to be under the delusion that something she had done would bring harm to himself and the children. He told him that Dr Hincks was aware of the problem and was treating her.

When Chevalier arrived at Mayfield he met Katharine and noticed that she had greatly changed in appearance since he had last seen her in autumn 1919. Although she recognized him at once and spoke quite naturally at times, she would break off the conversation and ramble into quite irrelevant matters, usually declaring that she was a wicked woman and blaming herself for things she had not done and things which she should have done. Chevalier formed the view that she was suffering from some form of religious mania that might lead her to commit suicide and suggested that he should visit Dr Hincks with Armstrong to consider his views. They went to see Dr Hincks that evening and Chevalier urged him to come to Mayfield that night and see Katharine for himself. The doctor visited and said that as her mental condition was now decidedly worse he could only advise that she be sent away for a time to an asylum and stated that he would ask the doctor from Talgarth asylum to come over at the first opportunity to give a second opinion.

After Hincks had left, Chevalier warned Armstrong that the nature of his wife's delusions were such that in his opinion she might really try to take her own life and told him that he should remove from his room anything which might make it easier for her to do so. Armstrong responded that this idea had not occurred to him and immediately removed his razors and put them in a drawer in Chevalier's room. He also removed and hid his service revolver. Chevalier kept a close watch on Katharine, especially when Armstrong was away at his office. On one occasion he brought her back from the road, where she had gone (without a hat) with the vowed intention of going to Armstrong's office to tell him something important, but she did not mention to him what it was, and he did not think it necessary to question her further. On several occasions he persuaded her not to alarm herself unnecessarily and not to leave the house. He cautioned Lily Candy to keep as close a watch as she could to prevent anything happening to her.

Armstrong was very averse to Katharine being sent away to an asylum and emphatically expressed that view to both Dr Hincks and Chevalier. He suggested that he could obtain special nursing at home, but Chevalier pointed out that he would need two specially trained nurses, which would mean a heavy expense and which would make his housekeeping extremely difficult. It was Hincks's view that a stay in a mental home would provide the only possible means for a recovery and that Katharine would probably recover in six months. Armstrong finally agreed and Dr Hincks was asked to make the necessary arrangements for Katharine to be sent away.

Armstrong insisted that Bessie should be contacted, as he could not take the responsibility of sending Katharine away without her knowledge and consent. He sent a wire to her and arranged to meet her at Hereford. They travelled back together to Hay on the afternoon train and Armstrong had a long conversation with her, relating everything that had taken place. Eleanor met them both at Hay station at 4.45 p.m. and they came back to Mayfield immediately.

Bessie was greatly upset when she met Katharine and refused to be alone with her unless either Armstrong or Chevalier was present. Although Katharine appeared at first pleased to see her sister, her condition greatly deteriorated the longer Bessie was there. Eleanor wrote in her diary that night: 'Auntie has been sent for because mother is not at all well.'

It was a beautiful mild day on the Sunday. Katharine stayed in bed and her breakfast of a boiled egg was taken up to her by cousin Agnes, who then took the three children to church. Armstrong only saw Katharine in the morning when he was dressing, and after eating his breakfast downstairs he went to see Dr Hincks to help with the appropriate arrangements. He then had to see Mr Tunnard Moore to ask him to sign the committal papers. He returned to the house at 11 a.m. Upon his return Bessie told him that Katharine had been sick after taking her breakfast.

It was Bessie who had to explain to her sister what was happening and why it was necessary for her to go away for a short period to a nursing home for a complete rest. Dr Jayne from Talgarth asylum arrived shortly after Armstrong's return from seeing Tunnard Moore and Armstrong was present during Jayne's conversation with Katharine. Her delusions were readily apparent and Jayne had difficulty in eliciting any meaningful responses to his questions. She stated to him that she had been over-economical and Jayne replied that this was a virtue. Dr Hincks and Dr Jayne conferred and they both agreed that she should be sent to Barnwood House in Gloucestershire. When Jayne left the house Katharine asked why he had been sent for and Armstrong told her that he was there for a second opinion.

Lunch was a sober affair that day and was taken as usual between one and two o'clock. Katharine joined in this family meal. Hincks had ordered a car for 2 p.m. but it did not arrive until 3 p.m. During the wait Armstrong was alone with Chevalier in the library and Bessie remained with her sister. The party left the house at 3.40 p.m. Hincks sat in the front passenger seat and Katharine was closeted between her sister and husband in the back seat of the open car. They had taken a basin with them because Katharine had been sick again before the car arrived.

Katharine was an ill woman before the journey, yet she had been certified as a result of her mental delusions and the papers had been signed on that basis. No one seemed to realize that she was physically ill.

The car had to stop once to allow Katharine to be sick again. It was a painful journey of fifty miles as Katharine, the once-proud lady of the house, was driven to a mental hospital having been certified by two doctors as insane.

6

Upon arrival at the asylum she was helped into the building by her sister, who had taken her arm to help her stumble along. She was in a sorry state. Her heart was pounding and she was tired after her bouts of sickness, both before leaving Mayfield and during the car journey. Dr Townsend, who was the medical supervisor, immediately took her off to be examined by his assistant Dr Janet Smith, who was placed in charge of her new case.

Katharine had no idea where she was or the nature of the institution in which she had been placed. She succumbed to the subsequent examination in a state of shock and lassitude. At first she was placed in a warm bath and Dr Smith noted that she had a few small bruises on her legs. Upon examination she was found to have a pulse of 120 and her temperature was 100. She had sordes round her mouth and looked physically ill. Her complexion was very pale and sallow. Her tongue was fissured and very furred, and although nothing abnormal was found in the examination of her abdomen, she was constipated. Two murmurs were noted in her rapidly beating heart. Her skin was very dry and when she was requested to pass a sample of urine she was unable to do so, and a small amount of urine was drawn from her by a catheter.

Before Armstrong left the institution Dr Townsend told him that it would be better if he did not visit his wife at intervals of less than two to three weeks. When Bessie reappeared after settling her sister, the party travelled back to Hay rather sorrowfully. Chevalier had stayed behind with the children, who had been to tea with the Revd Buchanan that afternoon. In the evening Chevalier accompanied Eleanor to the evening service at Cusop Church. When Bessie and Armstrong returned from Barnwood, all three of them discussed and agreed that there was no alternative to Katharine being sent away. Chevalier could do no more and he left Hay the following morning.

The following few days at Mayfield passed peacefully enough. The children played happily in the garden, which Armstrong tended in the afternoons. They went to tea with the neighbours Mr and Mrs Southwick. Bessie stayed on until the Friday, 27 August and then left for Torquay. It was arranged that Iris Sayle take her place, and on that day Eleanor met her other cousin from the 4.48 train.

Meanwhile, at Barnwood, Dr Smith decided that Katharine should be put to bed and in an attempt to induce sweating wrapped her in blankets and hot-water bottles. She prescribed fluid food with plenty of barley water to drink. Her dry skin reacted well to this treatment and on the second day Katharine passed five ounces of urine. It was noted that there was a slight degree of albuminuria[3] in the urine but no sign of pus or blood or other abnormal constituent.

Katharine then began to menstruate for the first time since 1919. On account of this lapse of time and considering her wasted appearance, Dr Smith decided to conduct a vaginal examination. Her uterus was found to be somewhat small and atrophied but normal in position. There was no roughening or modulation of the cervix to suggest any malignant condition and there was no pain on examination.

Her nervous system was also commented upon and it was noted that she 'showed a fine muscular tremor. Knee jerks were listed and not exaggerated. No babinski sign present and no ankle clonus. There is no squint but she suffers from exophthalmia specially marked on left side and left eye sightless.'

Two days after admission Dr Townsend reported to Armstrong:

> There is no material change in your wife's mental state, her heart is distinctly feeble, and I am sorry to say there is albuminuria, but she is taking all the nourishment ordered, and is having a good amount of sleep. Mrs. Armstrong is very confused, she rambles in conversation, and today there is a considerable amount of difficulty in getting her to remain in

bed, but of course in her debilitated state this is absolutely essential.

Townsend saw her practically every day and discussed her developing condition with Dr Smith, whose notes are revealing:

August 24th – passed about 15 ounces of urine today, temp. 99, pulse 110, slept two or three hours during the day having only fluid food [signed J. Smith].

August 28th – albuminuria practically cleared up and normal quantity of urine being passed. She is in very poor bodily health and had a tiny bedsore over sacrum. Sleeps 6 to 8 hours [signed J. Smith].

August 31st – she is now having some solid food ... She looks better but is still very weak. Pre-systolic murmur in the mitral area, pulse 100 temperature occasionally rises to 99.

September 7th – there is loss of power in hands and feet and wasting of the muscles. Fingers of both hands are highly extended and flexion is difficult. She complains of pains in her calves and is unable to walk. Condition is probably due to neuritis. Patient is very depressed and very despondent about herself and at times she becomes very agitated.

On 11 September Armstrong paid a visit to her. He found that she had lost the use of her hands and feet. He was allowed to speak in private to her but Katharine cautioned him against talking, because she believed the nurses and doctors were listening to their conversation. She had developed a dislike toward all the nurses and especially Dr Townsend. Huddled in her bed, practically unable to move, she must have presented a sorry sight that day. Armstrong spoke to Dr Townsend and received a full report on her progress, but at this meeting her recovery seemed a long way away, as Katharine was not only still deluded, but she had now lost the use of her limbs.

In the following days Dr Smith noted:

September 14th – No change in mental condition; she complains very much at not being able to move her hands. Takes food satisfactorily.

September 21st – no change to record.

Both Dr Townsend and Dr Smith were now concerned about their patient. At first the treatment consisted of enforced bed rest and nourishing food, in the hope that by addressing her physical condition and strengthening her body, her delusions might disappear. However, this treatment appeared to be having a detrimental effect, as the bed rest seemed to have contributed to a near paralysis of all the limbs and a wasting of the muscles. They could not find anything wrong with her physically and could find no sign of organic disease which would account for the loss of use of her limbs. They reached the tentative view that in all probability the problem was psychosomatic – a concomitant of her mental breakdown.

On 3 October they decided to give her a tonic consisting of citrate of ammonia and iron, a hydrochloric solution of arsenic and tincture of nux vomica, three times daily. In effect this meant that she was given $\frac{1}{7}$ of a grain of arsenic per day.

Dr Smith reports:

October 3rd – there is no improvement in the patient's condition; she is having ferrous et ammon (arsenic). Her limbs are massaged twice daily.

On 15 October Townsend reported by letter to Armstrong:

I am sorry we have come to the conclusion that Mrs Armstrong is suffering from neuritis, which is involving both hands, feet and legs. This gives her feelings of discomfort and she has some loss of power and co-ordination. What the exact cause is, it is difficult to say, it is probably toxaemic. Unfortunately the altered sensation is giving Mrs Armstrong the idea that she is being electrified and her attention is abnormally concentrated upon the conditions of her hands and feet, and as a result she is inclined to take an exaggerated view of her condition. There is nothing in this neuritis to cause you any anxiety but I thought it well to let you know, and if there is any further development I shall inform you.

Dr Townsend wanted a second opinion, because there was a divergence of views in the institution. He suggested to Armstrong that Dr Soutar be asked to examine her. Armstrong agreed and on 22 October Dr Soutar reported to

Townsend, 'We have considered today Mrs Armstrong's case, and were in agreement as to the nature of the case, but you may like to have my opinion in writing, so you may let the patient's husband see the report, or a copy of such part of it as you think advisable.' Dr Townsend forwarded Soutar's report to Armstrong:

> ... The subjective sensations of which the patient complains are common in functional disorders, and the distribution and variability of the objective alterations in sensation which are ascertained point to a functional disability. The postures of arms, legs, hands and feet which Mrs Armstrong assumes and her gait suggest functional rather than organic trouble. In her general mental attitude towards her physical manifestations there is that insistence upon them and that concentration of attention towards them which are so characteristic of functional disorders ... No doubt she had discomforts of a neurotic type which may have been the starting point of the functional failure of the limbs, and disuse had in turn maintained and continued there. It was noticeable that, under direction and suggestion, the postures could be readily modified.

When Dr Smith examined her on 3 November she noted that there was a slight improvement both in her mental and physical condition and that although she was 'much given to worrying and fretting' she was regaining the use of her limbs as a result of massage, which helped to restore her muscles. It was decided to discontinue with the arsenic tonic on the following day.

Katharine continued to make progress and on 20 November she got out of bed and managed to walk a few steps with help, but it was noted that she was 'hypochondriacal and self-centred'.

By the middle of December she could walk unaided, although her movements were clumsy. She also began to regain the use of her hands. She was still mentally disturbed, depressed and worried continually. She heard voices and still gave expression to feelings of unworthiness.

At this time Armstrong paid her a visit and found her to be very depressed. She stated to him that it would be quite an easy matter for her to throw herself out of the window to destroy herself, to put an end to all the worry and care which she thought she was causing him. Armstrong said this was the only occasion on which she had mentioned anything of this nature, and that on subsequent visits she never referred to the matter again.

At Christmas he visited again and Katharine appeared much better. He recalled that he was waiting in an outside room and noticed that the nurse had to help her across the ward, but when she saw him she walked towards him perfectly well without aid. It was as though when she thought about walking she found it difficult, but when she forgot about what she was doing she could manage perfectly well, adding weight to Soutar's diagnosis of a functional disorder, and that there was nothing organically wrong to cause her loss of power in her limbs.

By this time Katharine was fully aware of the nature of the institution in which she found herself and asked Armstrong why he had allowed her to be taken in, and why her sister had agreed. She begged him to take her home, as she felt she would be much better at Mayfield. Her delusions seemed to him to be less acute and confined to small personal matters. He believed that her confinement at Barnwood was continually preying on her mind and was convinced that if she remained there the knowledge of her surroundings and her compulsory detention would permanently unhinge her mind. During this visit she told him she still was worried about her will and that she had written to her sister about it.

It was during this period that Katharine wrote a number of letters both to her sister Bessie and to her good friend Chevalier. Her letter of 21 December to Chevalier showed that she was still mentally ill, exhibiting evidence of self-incrimination and self-loathing. She wrote:

> I am filled with remorse at the thought of the indifference which I treated you & your great kindness in Aug. last. I have ever since I came, your face is constantly before me & your words in my ears. I remember my wicked indifference to your health. I cannot think how I could leave thoughtlessly such a husband & children, sister, friend and niece. I did not even take comfort from the hymn E. wrote out & put on my dressing table. She is really a wonderfully good child. Both she & Sonny inherit religious bent & I have shown want of faith

Katharine Armstrong

Chief Inspector Crutchett
and Detective Sergeant
Sharp at Hay

A grave digger exhuming the body of Mrs Armstrong at Cusop
Church under the surveillance of a policeman

Detective Chief Constable
Weaver and Major
Armstrong arriving at Hay
Police Court

Doctor Hincks arriving at
Hay Police Court

Oswald Martin arriving at
Hay Police Court

Constance Martin

Mr and Mrs Fred Davies
arriving at Hay Police
Court

Mr and Mrs Gilbert
Martin arriving at Hay
Police Court

Left to right: Mr R.H. Chivers (managing clerk) and Mr T.A. Matthews arriving at Hay Police Court

Hay Police Court with Armstrong in dock and Mr Micklethwait addressing court

Miss Friend and Miss
Hutchins at the assizes

Sir William Willcox at the
assizes

Mr Webster and Doctor Hincks at the assizes

& so I brought this trouble on them. I am here for Christmas
and I can only wish you & yours all that is good.

I read your charming letter to Margaret. I can never thank
you for all your kindness to us and ours. I am filled with
shame at the thought of the poor requital you have.

I hope you are well, very busy I am sure.

With much gratitude & all kind greetings to all.

Yours most sincerely, K.M. Armstrong.

On the 31st December she posted another letter to
Chevalier:

A huge request! Will you if at all possible come and see me on
urgent business tomorrow or Monday. I never showed you a
document in which your name appears. Oh, do come for love
of my husband and children. I am unworthy.

With kindest regards,

Yours sincerely, K.M. Armstrong.

P.S. I improve but do come without delay.

Upon receipt of this rather strange letter Chevalier wrote to
Armstrong, enclosing it for him to see. Armstrong replied to
him on 2 January:

Many thanks for letter and good wishes. There are no
regulations as to letters at Barnwood Ho. and as far as I know
none are opened. I think I should reply in a cheery strain
without referring unduly to the worries but rather treat them
as retarding her return. I saw her last week and found her
generally better but still worried about her own shortcomings.
I think these will vanish on her return home, as she has too
much time for introspection & most of the trouble
exaggerates her present state. She thinks she will not return &
therefore dwells on the present. As soon as I can persuade the
M.O. that she can be moved I shall have her back as I don't
think she will improve in the least where she is. When she
finds she is really back she will pick up as she is certainly
physically better. It is quite clear the loss of power was
functional & not organic – they had to call it neuritis for want
of a better name. This weather is atrocious & the mild wet
days have rather got on my nerves. I have been very down for
some days & much off colour. You know the feeling when
nothing seems to go right & work is a nuisance. I am longing
to have her back.

With best wishes to you both.
Ever yours H. Rowse Armstrong.

Chevalier replied as requested and explained that it was
not possible for him to come and visit her at such short
notice.

Katharine then wrote to her sister on 11 January, enclosing
the document which she wanted to show Chevalier. She also
enclosed a little note, explaining what she wanted done. The
document itself and the note, demonstrate that she was still
actively deluded at this time. She said: 'Take D. of G. to a
lawyer – ask Miss H. not yourself. She can mention
Nursing H. Sign it and A.K. can ask it to be stamped *at once.
It is serious.*' The document stated:

> I, Katharine Mary Armstrong, hereby renounce all claim to
> my Real & Personal estate, of whatsoever nature &
> wheresoever situated to any that may come to me in Future,
> & assign them to my sister Ida Bessie Friend, Rosary View
> Torquay & to Arthur E. Chevalier, 3 Arnside, Oxton, to hold
> all in trust & administer for the benefit of my three children.
>   (signed) Katharine Mary Armstrong.
> this 1st. day of
> January nineteen
> hundred and
> twenty one.
> Witnessed by (1)
>   (2)

These documents were enclosed in a letter to Bessie dated 11
January:

My dearest Bess,
    I wonder if 'Neale' wd be so exceedingly kind as to come
and see me. Mr. C. can't. I want to see a businessman as well
as my own dear lawyer. B. said her brother would do
anything for us. I forgot to ask where is my original Will. I
think all Executors ought to know. Will you tell Arthur? Is it
with yours. H. has the copy, but original was locked away by
you while he was on service. Hope you are well as usual, post
time – did you hear H. had to sleep in Gloster as there was
break down.
    Your Kitty.

Bessie's written reply has not been retained, but Katharine wrote in response on 17 January:

My dearest Sister,
   I am overwhelmed with all your and Auntie's unfailing goodness to me and mine. The nightdress is lovely and I value all the loving stitches so much. I am afraid Auntie will find the other hard. How good she always is. Our parcels are always opened. I wd never have come had I realised I was losing my liberty. Matt. 10. 20. My dear old boy says he will fetch me this week: The Dr says the 22nd, but I have an awful feeling I shan't get out if he delays till then. You did not tell me the codicil is done, nor did you mention any business except the Will. That is my last, and I should like A.E.C. to know where it is and see it. Do write to him.
   I find the one pr knickers enough they keep me so warm this cold weather, also the lovely stockings. There is an excellent library here, but it is sweet of Auntie to cut out the pretty B.W. stories. H. was detained by a train breakdown, so he spent the night in an hotel. I think it fortunate he is a lawyer and understands business as there are formalities connected with departure. My special love and thanks to A.P.F. I try the piano without much success. Please thank Ida for her lovely letter. Mrs Thorpe's is characteristic, but quite true. I return it. I wish you would wire to H. not to delay in fetching me. I am miserable and aching to go home. He does not realise how every day counts to a mother. I am quite normal and use hands and feet better. This is dreary weather for you all, but you have had a lovely lot of sunshine. My dearest Bess I know you always do your best for everybody especially your own kin. The children love you second only to me. I long to get out that I may have a chance to lead a truer life. I have taught the children to be true. Every term's letter says E is conscientious. Heaps of love to all from
   Your loving Kitty.

In the mean time Armstrong had spoken to Hincks and discussed his wife's removal from Barnwood. Hincks had no objection in helping to secure her release, even though he had not seen her since her certification. He wrote to Townsend on 11 January, saying that he was glad to hear that Mrs Armstrong was improving mentally and physically, and that from what Major Armstrong had told him she appeared to have lost her delusions.

Her principal worry seems to be her surroundings and her
anxiety to get back home to start her household duties again.
The eldest child returns to school next Tuesday. My
suggestion is – if it meets with your concurrence – that he
should take the child back to school by car and bring his wife
home with him. There will be the old nurse at home who may
be trusted to look after her. The two younger children will be
at home.

Townsend wrote back to Hincks immediately on 13 January:

Mrs Armstrong has improved both mentally and physically
and Major Armstrong is now desirous of having her home. In
my opinion she is not yet well mentally, she is constantly
making accusations against herself or having mispent her life
and failed in her duty towards her husband and children, and
she says she has been guilty of selfishness, so you see her
delusions have not gone. Her great anxiety is to return home
and so under the circumstances I think it will be well to get
from the Committee on Monday next a leave of absence on
trial for three months and during that time it is possible that
with the change to home she may return to her normal mental
state, and on the other hand if she relapses and becomes
impossible she can return to Barnwood without recertifi-
cation. We consider that the paralysis of feet, arms and legs
was entirely functional, it is very much better but not yet quite
well.

Hincks showed Armstrong the letter from Townsend.
Armstrong then replied direct for form of application for
release on leave.

After careful consideration I do not wish my wife to avail
herself of this, and prefer that she be released. As far as I can
tell from conversation and correspondence her only trouble is
caused by the knowledge of her surroundings. The original
delusions have absolutely ceased and I feel sure that a return
to her home and light household duties will be beneficial. I am
quite prepared to take the risk and shall be glad if you will
treat this letter as a formal request for release. My eldest
daughter leaves for school on Tuesday and the next child is
with a friend every morning – who teaches him. It will take a
few days to re-arrange matters, but, if regulations permit I
should like to take my wife back on Saturday week the 22nd.
inst. Dr. Hincks tells me he has written to you on the subject.

Armstrong also wrote to Miss Seymour, whom Katharine had last visited in the summer of 1920. She originally suggested taking her home to Blockley, but this could not be arranged. Miss Seymour visited Katharine at Barnwood on 20 or 21 January and then travelled to Mayfield. Miss Seymour agreed that Katharine's removal was the only thing for her, and it was arranged that she accompany Armstrong to Gloucester the next day, remain at the New Inn, and that Armstrong proceed to Barnwood to collect Katharine, and call at the New Inn on the way home.

There was a bit of form about Armstrong. He borrowed a friend's covered Rolls-Royce and travelled in style to collect her. A mental hospital is a depressing place, especially for visitors, who see other mental patients and cannot help but notice their afflictions. It must have been quite unbearable for Katharine, who was a proud upright woman, to be placed in the midst of such people and she was extremely relieved to be collected by her husband on that day. They called at the New Inn and Katharine conversed with her friend Miss Seymour, telling her how lovely it was to be going home. Miss Seymour then made her own way home and Armstrong returned to Mayfield with Katharine, who talked incessantly on the journey, repeating that she could scarcely believe it, asking Armstrong why he had allowed her to go away at all.

There was a welcoming party at Mayfield. Miss Pearce had spruced up the house with the help of Inez Rosser, who had joined the household as a domestic servant just before Christmas. Sonny and Margaret were also there to greet her. The garden was not overgrown in that winter month but in December 1920 and January 1921 the weather had been very mild and the paths were green with weeds. Armstrong had asked Jay about them and had been told that he managed to keep the weeds down with weedkiller quite effectively when Armstrong had been away. Armstrong had written in his diary '3/pt. 2 Gall H20 W.Kill' to remind him of the correct proportions to make weedkiller, modifying the three gallons of water to two gallons as his larger watering-can had rusted away. On 11 January he purchased a quarter-pound of arsenic from the chemist's shop to put on the paths, but had no opportunity to use it before Katharine was brought home, because he was ill in bed on 13, 14, 15 and 16 January.

Armstrong specifically remembered that Fred Davies did not serve him at the time and that the sale of arsenic was conducted by John Hird, the shop assistant. In fact he did not recall seeing Davies in his shop at all that day – nor did he see Hird weigh out the arsenic as he was looking at something else in the shop showcase. However, he did remember that the arsenic was wrapped up in white paper with a label and then rewrapped in another white paper, but he could not be certain whether or not there was a label on the outer cover. The parcel had been handed to him tied up with string.

After making his purchase he returned home and went to the cupboard in the study and took out the two tins of caustic soda. The lids were extremely tight and it required a considerable force to remove them. When he looked in them he discovered in one of the tins that he still had some of the arsenic that he had purchased in 1919. He placed the two tins on top of each other with the unopened packet of arsenic that he had just purchased on top of the upper tin. He did not know at the time that his new purchase contained unadulterated white arsenic and that it had not been coloured. That packet of arsenic was to feature very strongly at his subsequent trial.

Katharine had been in Barnwood for exactly five months. During the whole of her stay she exhibited all the signs of a mentally ill person. She was depressed, introspective, secretive, melancholic and hypochondriacal. She continually blamed herself for her imagined wrongdoings and neglect, particularly in relation to her husband and children. Although it appeared that she had recovered her physical health to a degree when she returned home, she had not recovered mentally. She was not given any medication to treat her depression but she did regain the use and availability of her horde of homeopathic medicines which were stored at Mayfield.

These homeopathic remedies were important to her.

7

Katharine was a believer in homeopathy, and to a lesser extent Armstrong shared her belief, but the practice of homeopathy can be dangerous if too much of the 'similimum' is taken, because the essence of homeopathy is to treat like with like, and too much, too quickly, can trigger such serious side effects that ingestion of the poison taken can lead to greater problems. Arsenic used as a tonic has to be taken in very small quantities at a time. At Barnwood the maximum daily dose was 3/20 of a grain per day. Arsenic is a deadly poison in large doses and two grains is known to have caused death. It is a substance which should be treated with great respect.

Katharine's horde of homeopathic medicines was stored in a cupboard in her bedroom. The cupboard door was never locked, although the key was kept in the keyhole. The servants were not supposed to open the cupboard or remove anything from it without her express permission. It was fixed in place in 1912 when the family moved to Mayfield. Armstrong never went through the cupboard and could not say whether or not there was any arsenic contained in it, but it contained an array of potions, pills and ampoules which were used at times by Katharine. It also contained many homeopathic remedies once belonging to Armstrong's mother, which Katharine had brought back from her Devonshire house after her death. When the stock ran low Armstrong, at Katharine's request, ordered more supplies from Messrs Mac Symons Ltd, Deane Street, Liverpool. There is no doubt that Katharine treated herself and the children of the family on a regular basis with these medicines. She also used to treat herself with her 'after-dinner pills' which she kept in the dining room. Katharine was no stranger to medicines and regular doses of small quantities of poison. She knew the correct measures and would have been aware of what she needed to protect herself from illness – for it was illness that she feared, especially biliousness, even more so in her state of hypochondria.

Arsenic in the form of the homeopathic remedy arsenicum album is obtained by roasting natural arsenides of iron, nickel and cobalt, which are diluted by trituration. It was a known remedy for many ailments and is prescribed for loss of appetite, chilliness, diarrhoea brought on by food poisoning, fear to the point of terror, nausea with burning pains, stomach upset with burning pains and tiredness after diarrhoea or sickness. In homeopathic terms arsenicum 'types' are nervous, unsettled and anxious. They may fear death when left alone. Their complexions are pallid and their skin feels cold to the touch. They demand attention and can be critical of those caring for them. They lack physical resilience and fall prey to other ailments with exaggerated symptoms. They are prone to suffer from diarrhoea, exhaustion, eye inflammation, flatulence, food poisoning, gastric flu, hay fever, headaches, indigestion, insomnia, retention of urine, sore throat and vomiting. Katharine suffered at times from most, if not all, of these ailments.

The evening that she returned home Armstrong telephoned Gladys Kinsey, who was an experienced, professional nurse of eleven years' standing. Nurse Kinsey lived in Broad Street, Hay, and knew Armstrong by sight, if not to talk to, and was interested in the doctor's job offer. Armstrong told her that although his wife did not require full-time nursing care she needed a little assistance in dressing in the morning and undressing in the evening, and that Miss Pearce would be able to look after her during the day.

Nurse Kinsey was a brisk, businesslike woman dressed in uniform with a white starched apron. She certainly looked the part, wearing her hair neatly tied in a bundle, with a flowing headdress. She arrived at Mayfield promptly on the morning of 23 January and immediately realized that her charge was under the illusion that there were people in the house and that there were springs in her feet. She had been asked to stay for about an hour in the morning and return for the same time in the evening. On her arrival on the first day she helped her new charge to dress and bathe, and having seen her safely into the drawing room, left the house. She returned in the evening, helping her to undress and settle down. She then saw her off to bed.

Armstrong had asked Hincks to call when he could, to keep an eye on his wife. He visited on the 25th and, as this was the first time he had seen her since he certified her as insane five months earlier, he was naturally anxious about how he would be received. Katharine was equally concerned to see him because she dreaded being sent back to Barnwood. The meeting was formal and they shook hands. Hincks asked how she was. She thanked him for his attention and replied that she was now quite well. Hincks later stated that he found her to be quite healthy at this visit. Nurse Kinsey called on the following morning and when she was helping Katharine to dress, she was asked by Katharine if she thought it would be sufficient to kill herself 'if I threw myself out of the attic window'. This remark distressed Nurse Kinsey and she went to see Dr Hincks to tell him what Katharine had said and made it quite clear that she should be in the charge of a mental nurse, for she was unqualified to take on those responsibilities. She then found Armstrong and told him the same thing. Armstrong tried to persuade her to stay, but she would not listen to his entreaties, declaring that she was not prepared to continue. Finally she excused herself by saying that she expected to be called away at any time to a confinement. Armstrong realized that he had to get a new nurse, and one who was able to deal with mentally ill patients. He was also aware that his wife now needed to be watched at all times.

Nurse Kinsey continued with her duties until a replacement nurse could be found and that evening she stayed for supper and shared the meal of tinned bully beef with brown bread and postum. Armstrong, his wife and Miss Pearce ate together. Nurse Kinsey then helped Katharine to bed.

When Nurse Kinsey was going up to Mayfield the next morning she met Armstrong on his way to work. She asked him how his wife was and he told her that she had had an attack of vomiting in the night. She enquired what could have caused it and he said he thought it was due to the pills which she had taken. On her arrival at the house Nurse Kinsey found Katharine walking about the bedroom in a depressed state, waiting for her to come. She started to cry when asked about the sickness in the night and said that after supper she had taken two of her pills, but that she now felt better and thought it was indigestion. After helping her to dress, Nurse Kinsey suggested that to take her mind off things, they should go and make some beds.

Nurse Kinsey left the house in the morning as usual, but returned about half-past one and remained with Katharine until the new nurse arrived. Nurse Eva Allen had a kindly face and was not as austere as Nurse Kinsey. She did not wear uniform and was more relaxed in her appearance. Employed by an agency in Cardiff, she was directed to go to Mayfield. She travelled by car to see Dr Hincks and found that Armstrong was already there.

Hincks and Armstrong told her that Mrs Armstrong was suffering from delusions that affected both her arms and her feet, in which she thought there were springs, and was instructed that she had to be with her at all times unless Armstrong or Miss Pearce were with her. She was also directed to massage her feet and arms.

Nurse Allen was then driven to Mayfield by Hincks's chauffeuse in his car. Miss Pearce introduced the new arrival to Nurse Kinsey, who immediately took her to see Katharine, who was in the drawing room.

Katharine looked thin and frail and complained that she should not have been sent to the nursing home and blamed her sister for sending her there. The two women then conferred and Nurse Kinsey explained the nature of the mental delusions and mentioned her conversation with Katharine about the attic window, saying that she thought she might commit suicide. This was the first occasion that the mental delusions were mentioned to Nurse Allen.

Nurse Allen began her duties at the household and as instructed spent all her time with Katharine with the exception of a two-hour break between 2 p.m. and 4 p.m. She slept in the same room and Armstrong moved out into a bedroom across the landing. Nurse Allen found that Katharine had a good appetite, and all meals were taken with the family. She found her to be reasonably well, apart from her delusions, and periods of depression, during which she would often say, 'Oh, I do wish I could die.' Nurse Allen massaged her hands and feet as requested, for Katharine continued to say that they felt odd – a fact she would habitually blame on the nursing home. At night Katharine often got up, saying that there were other people in the house; sometimes she would wander across to Armstrong's bedroom, only to be brought back to bed by the nurse. Katharine continued to take her own pills, to which Nurse Allen had no objection, as they did not seem to be causing her any ill-effects that she could notice. At this period there was no vomiting or other sickness although Katharine often complained that she was nauseous, but the main problem seemed to be the tension and lack of mobility in her limbs.

On 30 January Dr Hincks called to see her again. At this visit he again found nothing wrong with her; but this was only because she would not confide in him, viewing him as the last person in the world whom she could trust. However, she was by now actively complaining to Nurse Allen and Armstrong that she had a loss of power in her hands and feet. These ailments were a continual worry to her and she later remarked to Armstrong, 'I shall never be able to play the piano anymore.' Despite these problems she could still entertain and the Revd Buchanan, Mrs Southwick and Mrs Griffiths came to tea on occasion. Katharine was perfectly able to pour out tea and pass round cups and saucers and could walk perfectly well when she did not think about what she was doing. She consistently stated to Armstrong that she had gone away to the nursing home sound and returned a cripple and that she had been drugged when she was there. She laid all the blame at being sent away on her sister. Armstrong tried to dissuade her from some of her more absurd ideas and delusions. He explained to her that the noise at the window, which she thought was Jay knocking, was the sound of the reaping machine in the adjoining field, and Katharine accepted the explanation, saying how foolish she was. At this time Armstrong was not made aware of any of Katharine's other delusions, such as her belief that there were strangers in the house. He claimed that Katharine never spoke to him about these matters and he believed that it was only a matter of time before his wife would make a full recovery.

Hincks returned on 6 February and again on 11 February. The doctor did not remember anything untoward on the first visit, but on the second he found Katharine to be in a very strange state. She was in the drawing room seemingly unable to walk. He tried to get her to stand up, helping her with his arm, but she was quite unable to walk properly. She complained to him that the curious feeling in her feet had returned and described it using the simile of springs pushing her up from the ground. Hincks decided to make a thorough examination. She was taken upstairs and undressed. He found that the knee jerks were absent, that there was no ankle clonus, that her hand grip was diminished and that she was scarcely able to pick up a pen. She complained to him that she was unable to knit or play the piano. He knew that Dr Townsend had diagnosed a similar condition in Barnwood as functional and not organic and he thus prescribed no medicine. Armstrong had a discussion with him after his examination and asked whether or not the injuries that his wife sustained during her bicycle accident before their marriage could have had any after-effects, but Hincks said that he did not think so.

On Sunday 13 February Katharine had Sunday lunch with all the family and Nurse Allen in the dining room. The lunch consisted of boiled mutton, potatoes and greens and boiled suet pudding, followed by gooseberries and junket. There was a bottle of Burgundy on the table but Katharine did not have any. After lunch Katharine retired to her room for a rest. Neither Nurse Allen nor Armstrong went with her. Nurse Allen withdrew to her own small room. About twenty minutes after Katharine retired Nurse Allen was called by the children, who told her that their mother had been sick. She immediately went into Katharine's bedroom to see her vomit. She noticed that the vomit was like bile and she kept it for Dr Hincks to see. Katharine did not want Hincks to be called, and since she was lying on her bed with her clothes on, Nurse Allen undressed her and put her to bed. After some time she gave her some hot water and a pinch of bicarbonate of soda. About tea-time she gave her some hot milk and then sat with her for the rest of the evening during which time she did not vomit again. Nurse Allen thought that it was a bilious attack. Concerned about the pills which Katharine had been taking and worried that they may have caused the vomiting, she took them all away and hid them, leaving Katharine without the protection of her homeopathic potions. Armstrong had attended church and when he returned, he relieved Nurse Allen who went downstairs for her supper. She retired at about 10.30 and Katharine was not sick again in the night.

The following day, the 14th, Katharine got up and sat in the front porch wrapped in an eiderdown with a hot-water bottle at her feet. Mrs Price, the wife of the bank manager, came to visit her and they spent some time together talking. Katharine told Armstrong about the visit and she seemed better overall. She told him that she had walked about the garden and he expressed the hope that she had not caught a chill. That evening he went to a masonic meeting at the lodge at Hay.

Nurse Allen put Katharine on a light diet, together with water and milk. Katharine was up and out of bed on the following days and continued to give her young son his lessons. These lessons were taken in Armstrong's study, which contained the arsenic. On either 15 or 16 February, there was a discussion at lunch between Armstrong and his wife about the fact that Pearson had mislaid a certain exercise book, later found in the nursery.

On either 16 or 17 February the vomiting recommenced with a vengeance. There is no agreement on the exact day, Dr Hincks and Nurse Allen differing in their recollection. Whatever the day, Nurse Allen telephoned Hincks and told him that Katharine had been vomiting violently. She was told to come to his surgery and get some calomel. On the way to the surgery she met Armstrong and Hincks in the doctor's car. Armstrong got out and Nurse Allen took his seat. Doctor and nurse continued the journey to Mayfield in the car. On their arrival at Mayfield Hincks examined Katharine, who was now very ill and weak from consistent vomiting. She was given a turpentine enema but was spared the calomel. Katharine appeared to benefit from the enema as she had complained of a lot of flatulence. Hincks also prescribed 'a mixture of 4 drams bi-carbonate of soda, 3 of tincture of oranges and 1 of spirits of chloroform, water to 6 ounces.

One tablespoon to be taken in water with half teaspoon full of lime juice until the vomiting ceases.' He may have also prescribed a bismuth mixture on this occasion, although he did not record the fact. In the evening he returned and injected Katharine with morphine to enable her to sleep. From this day onwards Nurse Allen was in constant duty in the bedroom with very little time to herself.

Questions were now raised about Katharine's homeopathic medicines, which she still wished to take. Nurse Allen was suspicious of them and, wanting to know whether or not Katharine could continue to take them, asked Hincks for his opinion. Two bottles, marked 'Ignatia' and 'Brucine', were shown to him. Hincks later believed that it was Armstrong who had consulted him about the bottles. In any event Hincks said that he would look them up and advised that no more should be taken until the following day. He researched the names of the drugs in Martindale's British Pharmacopoeia and on the next visit stated that they were both products of plants from which strychnine was prepared.

Ignatia, more commonly known as St Ignatius' bean, comes from a tree growing in the Philippine Islands and China. The beans contain a large quantity of strychnine. Large doses are fatal but small quantities produce only unpleasant symptoms such as headaches, loss of appetite, trembling, twitching, cramps, giddiness, cold perspiration and nervous laughter. The homeopath prescribes ignatia to deal with mental symptoms such as shock and depression and physical ailments such as sore throats, coughs, fevers, headaches and indigestion. Nux vomica, commonly known as poison nut, is obtained from the seeds of an evergreen tree native to the Far East, North Australia and China. It was also called the vomiting nut, and due to its poisonous nature was at one time considered to be of doubtful medicinal value. In small doses it helps promote the appetite and digestion and increases the flow of urine. Larger doses cause loss of appetite, depression, anxiety, disordered muscular system with trembling, rigidity or stiffness of the limbs and staggering when walking. Even larger doses cause convulsions and death from asphyxia.

Katharine still wanted to take her own pills and Nurse Allen and Dr Hincks only examined the labels on two bottles, disregarding the medicine cupboard alongside her bed and the 'after-dinner pills' that were kept downstairs in the dining room. They were not, of course, aware that pure arsenic was stored in the study, but Katharine was aware of its whereabouts. She had been teaching the little boy in the room where it was kept and had searched the study for his lost exercise book.

Hincks told Nurse Allen that he had no objection to Katharine continuing with her medicines. At this time Katharine was apparently confined to her bed, unable to get up even to relieve herself.

This was the start of Katharine's final illness – one from which she never recovered. Hincks called at frequent intervals. Throughout the following days the vomiting continued, with Katharine sinking deeper and deeper, her body wasting away. She was given light food with bread and milk, but she could not keep it down. Each morning Armstrong would go into her room and ask the nurse how she had slept. He noted in his diary: '17th. K. very ill, 18th. ditto. bad night, 19th. ditto. bad night.' In the evenings he used to read to her. He stated that he never had anything to do with her food, which he left entirely to Nurse Allen and Miss Pearce. He said that he could not understand what had caused the illness, recalling that on the Saturday Hincks told him that his wife seemed to have improved and that she might at last be turning the corner. He spent part of the evening of 19 February reading to her.

Nurse Allen was beginning to be worn down by the sheer amount of time she had to spend with Katharine, and on Sunday morning Hincks advised Armstrong to obtain a relief nurse for that night. Armstrong went into Hay and asked Nurse Lucy Alice Lloyd if she would help. After lunch Armstrong spoke to his wife about the confirmation service which was to be held at Cusop Church by the Bishop of Hereford later that afternoon. He mentioned that unless he could do anything for her at home he would like to attend the service as it was the first one which had been held for six or seven years and that naturally he had several duties to perform as rector's warden. Katharine agreed and said that she would try and get some sleep as she felt drowsy. Armstrong went to the confirmation but afterwards, when the rector pressed him to go to tea and meet the bishop, he declined the invitation saying he wanted to check up on his wife's progress.

Nurse Allen went to bed at eight o'clock and Nurse Lloyd arrived at Mayfield at about nine to ten in the evening. She took her things off and went straight upstairs to Katharine's bedroom. Everything had been put out ready for her and Miss Pearce told her what she should do, showed her where she should sit and instructed her that she should give Katharine her milk food, which had been placed in the room, when she wanted it. Katharine said it was funny that she had not had Nurse Lloyd attend to her before and appeared quite sensible to the nurse. Armstrong came into the room after the nurse arrived, but he left soon after, offering her his help should she need anything.

Nurse Lloyd settled down with Katharine, who was restless in the beginning of the night but at the end had a good sleep. Nurse Lloyd remembered feeding her twice and recollected that she might have vomited twice during that period, but could not recall any diarrhoea. She felt Katharine's pulse throughout the night and considered that it had improved by morning. At 8 a.m. she left the house and did not see Nurse Allen at all while she was there. Armstrong could not remember what she reported to him in the morning but noted in his diary, 'Nurse Lloyd here for the night.'

He sent a postcard to Bessie, saying, 'K. was slightly easier y'day but hasn't had a good night. Slept a bit with an opiate. Complains still of much pain internally and vomits at intervals. Dr H. hopes that latter is under control as not so frequent. Had local nurse last night to relieve Nurse Allen. H.'

Dr Hincks arrived that morning, 21 February, and told Armstrong for the first time that he could lose his wife and asked him to get some brandy and champagne. According to Armstrong he did not explain why he found it necessary to tell him this so soon after telling him that she had 'turned the corner', neither did he comment on the fact. Armstrong got some brandy from the King's Head Hotel in Hay. The hotel was not then open for the sale of alcohol, but as Armstrong knew the licensee he was able to explain his requirements. He rang up a friend of his, Major Booth, of

Brynmelin, Cusop, for the champagne but he was not at home. Armstrong went to the police court, where the Hay Bench was sitting at 11.30 a.m. While he was there he was called out to speak on the telephone to Major Booth, who kindly promised to send some champagne to Mayfield at once. Immediately the Hay Court had finished he went straight home, taking the brandy with him. The champagne had just arrived. He went to the bedroom straight away and opened the brandy and the champagne in the presence of Nurse Allen and Miss Pearce. He poured some champagne and handed the glass to Nurse Allen to add the brandy. Nurse Allen then gave the brandy and champagne to Katharine who brought it back a few minutes afterwards. He went back to his office after lunch and arrived home at about 4.30 p.m. and went to his wife's bedroom. Nurse Allen was there giving her some food. Katharine was very drowsy and he suggested that Inez Rosser, the housemaid, should come up and sit in the room while he and Nurse Allen went downstairs to get some tea. Katharine then said, 'I don't want Inez, I want Nurse to stay.' She made these remarks in such a strong voice that both Nurse Allen and Armstrong commented upon it at the time, thinking that it was a good sign.

Armstrong went downstairs alone and had his tea while Nurse Allen remained with Katharine. He then returned to the bedroom and read to her until she fell asleep at about six o'clock. When Nurse Allen returned to the room, he went to the library, where he spent the rest of the evening reading and smoking until he retired to bed at ten o'clock. Before he went to bed he looked in his wife's bedroom to see how she was, but she was asleep.

Nurse Allen had been told by Hincks to go to his surgery for nutrient suppositories. Nurse Allen gave Katharine these, but they were not retained and she became incontinent. Attempts were made to get her to take milk direct by her mouth but it always returned. At about 4 a.m. on Tuesday Nurse Allen noticed a great change in her. Katharine asked her if she thought she was going to die and said, 'You have such a kind face I will believe you if you tell me.' Katharine added that she did not want to die as she had everything to live for, a nice husband and nice children. She kept saying that she wanted to see her husband and then slept fitfully.

Nurse Allen decided not to wake Armstrong until the morning.

At 8 o'clock she woke him up and told him that his wife was delirious and asked him to go and see her. He went to Katharine's room and sat at her bedside for nearly an hour while Nurse Allen telephoned for Hincks. Armstrong had his breakfast at nine o'clock and Hincks arrived at nine-thirty. After discussing the case with Hincks at Katharine's bedside, the doctor said that her condition was hopeless, although he did say she might last the day out. He suggested to Armstrong that he could do nothing by remaining in the house and that he had better go to the office. He then took Armstrong down in his car.

Armstrong arrived at the office at ten o'clock and at ten minutes past he received a telephone call from Nurse Allen who said that his wife had passed away. Armstrong at once called at Dr Hincks's surgery, but found he was out and left a message for him. He then went straight home.

Armstrong was deeply shocked, but he was not a man to show emotion, and his seeming coolness was later remarked upon by Nurse Allen, who was crying when he arrived home. She said something to the effect that she felt that this was the first case that she had lost. Armstrong went into his study and spent the time before lunch using the telephone, writing and conferring with Miss Pearce. He had a light lunch and then went to meet Bessie from the one-thirty train. He made arrangements for the funeral and discussed with Hincks the cause of death. The doctor agreed that no reference need be made to the fact that she had been in a home for the mentally ill. Hincks said that in his opinion the cause of the vomiting might have been psychological and Armstrong agreed that it might be so. Nurse Allen got up at 5 p.m. and went for a walk. When she returned Armstrong, Miss Pearce and Bessie were having supper in the dining room. Nurse Allen was introduced to Bessie, who appeared to her to be very upset. They then went into the drawing room and Nurse Allen ate her supper alone.

The following day Nurse Allen left the house and on the way to the station she overtook Armstrong walking alone. He was going to meet Eleanor, who was coming home from school. That was the last time Nurse Allen saw Armstrong until the subsequent trial.

The funeral was fixed for 25 February. It was a quiet affair attended by members of the family, Arthur Chevalier and a few other close friends. Armstrong laid a wreath on Katharine's grave marked 'From Herbert and the chicks' and there were floral tributes from Dr and Mrs Hincks and Mr and Mrs Griffiths among fifteen others. The service was conducted by the Reverend Buchanan of Cusop and the lesson was read by their friend the Revd de Winton from Hay. Miss Pearce was too upset to attend the funeral of her mistress, but she did attend the memorial service held on the following Sunday.

Katharine had been buried in the church where she had so often prayed. Her death marked the end of an era for the Armstrong family, which consisted of the three young children who mourned the loss of their mother, and the man who would later stand trial for his life. As events unfolded, not one person who knew them could suggest that they had been anything but a devoted and affectionate couple, a matched pair, despite their incongruous size and style.

8

Either on the day of or the day after the funeral Armstrong told Chevalier that Katharine had made another will, in which he (Armstrong) had been appointed sole executor and sole beneficiary. He explained to Chevalier that his wife did not consider it necessary to appoint trustees as he intended to use all her money for the children. Chevalier did not ask to see the will and Armstrong did not consider it necessary to show it to him.

Chevalier privately expressed some surprise at this news and decided to mention the conversation to Bessie on the morning of his departure from Mayfield. Bessie then showed him a rough draft of the 1917 will that she had found in a drawer in Katharine's bedroom and told him that she had the original at her home. Chevalier told her to put the rough draft back where he found it and later that morning caught the train to Liverpool.

Some weeks later Bessie sent him the original of the 1917 will. Chevalier read it and returned it, pointing out that the value of the document depended entirely on whether or not it could be suggested that the later will was obtained by undue influence or when Katharine was not competent to make it. He asked her if she proposed to take any steps in the matter, since personally he had no knowledge of Katharine's mental condition during the previous summer, when she had made her second will. Later on, Bessie asked Chevalier if he would obtain a copy of it. This he did and he received a reply from her that she had decided to take no further action as she had nothing to go on. The reason she gave to Chevalier for being upset that her sister had left her money entirely to her husband was that she thought that he was inclined to make risky investments and also that he was rather extravagant in his expenditure. Ultimately she feared something might happen which would deprive the children of their mother's money.

Bessie also wrote to Armstrong about the will and he replied that he knew nothing about the first will except what Katharine had told him.

Armstrong proved the second will in the normal course of business in his office and swore the oath of executors in front of Oswald Martin without secrecy. He obtained the grant of probate in March: the gross estate amounted to £2,419.18 gross and £2,278.3.0. net. With the exception of a mortgage due from Miss Friend, which was paid off by her, and which was used partly by Armstrong for duties, the estate was not touched at any time. Armstrong continued the account at Teignmouth and there paid in the dividends from the estate. Various payments from this account were made for the children's education alone.

In May 1921 Katharine's aunts left Armstrong's birthday unnoticed. He could not understand what was wrong and asked Miss Pearce, who intended to pay them a visit in June, to enquire why they had taken umbrage. Miss Pearce told him that they were upset about the will. Armstrong then received a letter from Miss Farley reminding him that dividends from certain shares owned by Katharine had always been paid to her and asking him to do the same. Armstrong readily agreed and also agreed to pay a sum equal to the interest on some war loan to Mrs Short, who continued to live with Miss Farley.

Before this was resolved Armstrong had begun to feel unwell after the strain of Katharine's illness and death – a strain aggravated by the extreme pressures of business. He consulted Dr Hincks, who gave him a sedative and advised him to go away for a change of air or he would have a breakdown; a barrister, Mr J.H. Watts, also offered him the same advice.

Before going, he had to inform various people that he would be absent and a flurry of letters were written to various parties on 16 March. To the solicitor Lewis Jones, with whom he was not in dispute, he wrote: 'I have sent your drafts for approval to Jeffreys & Powell and expect them back any day. I am sorry to say that my Doctor has ordered me off as my nerves have gone rather wrong. I shall be away for a month but on my return the matter will be completed.' On the same day he wrote to the solicitors acting for William Morgan, 'We regret that owing to the absence of the writer through a personal bereavement your letters have remained unanswered.' And to Tom Morgan, the brother of William Morgan, he wrote demanding that he pay his brother's rent that was due to Williams Vaughan ' ... As we understand he is at present laid aside, will you let us know whether you are in a position to settle this matter, as we do not wish to have to take proceedings which we shall be bound to do unless a settlement is arrived at.'

No doubt Armstrong was greatly relieved to be getting away from it all. This was to be his first holiday since 1914, and as he considered that the rate of exchange was favourable and thinking that it was the only convenient place he could go, he left England for Taormina in Sicily on 18 March 1921.

Armstrong wrote, 'I got both sun and sea breezes and after about a week I began to feel better. The trip cost me altogether about £60 and the suggestion that immediately after my wife's death and presumably having obtained her money I lived a gay life on the Continent is absurd.'

In any event his wife's will had not been proved until after he left England and he could not have realized her estate until his return.

Armstrong kept a diary, certain entries in which have given rise to speculation about his behaviour on this trip abroad. Some leapt to the conclusion that he was living the life of a merry widower. The recorded entries were often in any event mistranscribed.

28th March 1921: Concert (Nopley Excelsior Mrs. Magiore [sic]) Hotel Metropole.

He attended a piano recital at the Excelsior Hotel Taormina, mounted to raise money for an ex-serviceman. Armstrong states that he met Mrs Macguire in the train between Turin and Naples, but had nothing to do with her, that she did not come to Taormina and that he had never seen nor heard of her since the train journey.

29th March: G & M with Seymour and Ingles 11

This referred to a visit to Gardina and Modena, Sicily, with Symons, an Air Force officer whom he had met, and Inglis, an American.

30th March: Leave for Malta

On this date he left Syracuse for Malta, as Symons suggested that he could obtain a passage for him on the trawler *Ouse*, commanded by Lieutenant Joliffe RN.

Symons knew that Armstrong had lost his wife and suggested that he should travel on to Malta where the change of scenery would do him good. Symons was a married man and he was with his wife at Taormina. He arranged for Armstrong to stay at his club at Valetta and then arranged for him to stay at the St. James Hotel, where he introduced him to many of his friends.

1st April: Rigoletto with Susan

This wrongly copied passage referred to *Rigoletto* with Symons, not Susan.

4th April: Joliffe to dine at Club Lorfe James 7.30 Aldwyn tea

On 2 April Armstrong had dined with Joliffe at his club and had arranged for another dinner on the 4th which was cancelled. Armstrong said that the other entry should have read 'Lunch James 7.30' and 'Aldridge – tea'. James was an Ordnance Officer and a friend of Symons; Aldridge was another friend with whom he had tea. Symons had introduced both men to Armstrong. They were all Freemasons.

There were other entries in which the names of Miss B, Miss Buchanan and Miss McRae appear, from 4 to 16 April. Armstrong explained them by saying that Miss B was Miss Buchanan, who conducted dancing lessons at the hotel where he was staying and Miss McRae was her assistant. He had had no opportunity to dance for some time, and wanting to go out with some of his friends, such as Symons, Joliffe and Aldridge, he decided to take lessons. The diary entry,

'10 a.m. Miss Buchanan', referred to the time that the classes were held.

Armstrong was very fond of music and during his stay in Malta attended the opera quite frequently as the prices were low, the stalls only costing three shillings and sixpence. He went to *La Traviata*, as well as *Madame Butterfly*. The only public dance he attended in Malta was rather a special occasion organized by Miss Buchanan for her present and past pupils, and Prince George attended.

14 April: 19.15 Boden Deve Chch 20.30 Pccceptory

This should have read 'Bodell-dine Club'. Commander Bodell, RN, was master of a lodge of Freemasons while in Malta and was later seconded to the Admiralty. Later in the year he sent a Christmas card to Armstrong. A Knight Templar and Knight of Malta, Bodell had at Armstrong's request arranged for him to acquire the same honours. It was necessary for Armstrong, before being 'exalted', to cable to a prominent Freemason in Hereford and ask him to vouch that he was a lodge member. With all formalities over Armstrong was made a Knight Templar and Knight of Malta at the Preceptory on 14 April. Thereafter the solicitor spent a good deal of time in the company of Bodell and they became great friends.

15 April: 'Billeted' with Miss B.

This entry referred to a play, *Billeted*, which Armstrong attended with Miss Buchanan. Colonel Russell, a Chief Ordnance Officer of his acquaintance, asked him if he would make up a party of four that day to attend the theatre and dinner. The party comprised Armstrong, Miss Buchanan, Colonel Russell and his ward. They dined at St James Hotel and then attended the play. Afterwards Colonel Russell and Armstrong had supper together at the club. The play was a rather special affair, according to Armstrong, in that it was in full dress and attended by the governor of Malta. Armstrong took a singular interest in it because the stage manager was an old friend of his who became aide-de-camp to the governor himself.

Documentary evidence supports the contention that

Armstrong was not living a riotous life on the Continent. On 9 February 1922 the following letter was sent to Armstrong's solicitor. It is worth setting it out in full.

We understand that you are acting on behalf of Major Armstrong in connection with the serious charge against him which has been noticed by our Client, Mrs. Ann Ryle of Parnham, Beaminster, the Wife of Mr. Edward Hewish Ryle who is a son of the Dean of Westminster.

Mrs. Ryle noticed in the opening Speech for the Prosecution that stress was laid on the fact that Major Armstrong had gone abroad in March and was enjoying himself, apparently callously in Italy. Mr. & Mrs. Ryle were staying at the Hotel San Domenico, Taormina, Sicily, during March 1921 leaving there on the 28th and they remembered seeing Major Armstrong in the Hotel – in the course of collecting subscriptions from visitors for a local charity, they obtained one from Major Armstrong and in consequence became on speaking terms with him, and they conversed with him on several occasions. They understood that he had recently lost his wife and the opinion they formed was, that he was depressed, lonely and in low spirits, in fact the whole of his conduct was such as was to be expected from a man who had recently suffered a heavy bereavement – he seemed to spend most of his time alone or in company with one other man.

Prosecuting Counsel appears to have referred to an entry in Major Armstrong's diary from which it was deduced that on Easter Sunday he had participated in a Fete – Mrs. Ryle says that this Fete, or 'Fiesta', was merely the local method of celebrating Easter Sunday – the Roman Catholic 'Fiesta', which consists of processions through the streets from one Church to another and was of purely a religious character. All the Inhabitants and Visitors spent most of the day in the Streets watching the ceremonies, which at no time degenerated into anything approaching what in England would be called a Fete.

The Concert referred to as being attended by Major Armstrong on Easter Sunday was a small one given by an English visitor – all members of the English Colony had been pressed to attend as being in a good cause. It was a serious concert and in no way a frivolous affair.

Although Mr. & Mrs. Ryle left on the 28th March the Dance on the following day was, they know, got up in aid of the same charity to which Mrs. Ryle had already asked Major

Armstrong to subscribe and all the visitors were begged to attend to it.

Mrs. Ryle asks us to inform you of the above and we need scarcely say that she has no desire to be called as a Witness; but she considers it her duty that these facts should be known to disprove the impression given by Counsel, that Major Armstrong was behaving himself in any way different from the most staid visitors residing in Taormina during her stay there, or that he acted in any way other than a man labouring under a family bereavement would do.

Yours faithfully,
Kitson & Trotman,
Solicitors of Beaminster, Dorset.

With such a testimonial in mind the remaining entries of Armstrong's diary do not represent anything but a reserved man's brief account of ordinary engagements, such as:

17th April: Lunch Vella

Major Vella was in the Royal Malta Regiment, and Armstrong had lunch with him.

18th April: 7.45 Appleton Club

Appleton was the aide-de-camp to the Governor of Malta and dinner was spent in the club with him.

On 20 April he left Syracuse for Rome where he spent two days. He then travelled to Paris where he stayed for four days, leaving on 28 April. He returned to England the next day and travelled to Bournemouth to meet his old friend Marion Gale with whom he had corresponded when he was on the Continent.

At first instance it is easy to read into Armstrong's diary the record of a debauched middle-aged ex-Army officer living the life of a merry widower on the Continent having just got rid of his wife in England; but to do so is unfair to the recorded facts and the memory of the man. There is no evidence to support such imputations and assertions.

The later statement of the Crown that 'on 28 April Armstrong returned from abroad, and within 24 hours of arriving in this country was discussing the question of marriage with another woman here' was again untrue.

His friendship with Marion had begun in the autumn of 1915. He had met her through Mr and Mrs Tanner, with whom he and other officers attached to the Royal Engineers Camp at Christchurch, Kent, were billeted. Marion Gale lived with her elderly mother, Mrs Roberts, and her niece Eleanor. She also let furnished apartments to people whom she knew. During the war years Armstrong's duties took him away from Christchurch from time to time, but he invariably returned there for duties at the camp until 1918 when he was posted to France. He was always a welcome visitor at Marion's house, but he was also on friendly terms with other members of Marion's household. Marion used to visit him at the Camp with her aunt, Mrs C.C. Trees, of Cheltenham. Armstrong spoke quite freely of his marriage and his three children, making no secret of the fact. Marion remembered Armstrong telling her that his wife had visited Christchurch but that this trip had taken place before having met him. Katharine knew of his friendship with Marion and her family and he often talked to his wife of the hospitality and kindness which Marion had shown to him.

In the last week of July 1920 Marion was staying with her friends Mr and Mrs Rowland at Catford Hill. Armstrong had previously written to her saying that he had business in London and they arranged to meet for dinner. He stated that his wife knew of this meeting. After dinner he saw her off from either Charing Cross or Victoria Station on a train bound for Catford, where she arrived between ten and eleven o'clock.

Armstrong wrote and told her of his wife's death and both Marion and Mrs Roberts expressed their sympathies. Marion also wrote to Mrs Trees and at her request passed on her condolences.

Armstrong paid a visit to her house when he returned from the Continent and gave Marion a small mosaic brooch and her niece a cigarette case, but neither had any intrinsic value. He stayed the night at Ford Cottage and travelled home the following day.

Armstrong took his son back to Monkton Combe School at Bath on 13 May 1921 and then travelled on to Bournemouth the next day. On Sunday 15 May he visited Marion for tea and stayed for supper. On this occasion he insinuated to her that if she ever wanted a second home there was one waiting for her at Mayfield. He knew that she had had an unfortunate married life and very trying domestic affairs and in his own way this offer of another home was his way of a proposal of marriage.

He did not see her again until 27 August, when he had travelled to Swanage to collect Eleanor, who was spending a part of her holiday with friends. Owing to an illness in the household, they could not invite him to visit and so Marion had dinner with him at Bournemouth. He escorted her back on the tram and she left him about 9 p.m. She saw him again the next afternoon but was unable to see Eleanor due to the illness in her house. On this occasion they discussed marriage and informally agreed that they would wed, but each acknowledged that nothing definite should be fixed until February 1922, that is, after a year's mourning, and that in any event marriage could not take place before the summer of that year. Armstrong did not tell his children of this intention.

In October 1921 Marion arranged to visit Mrs Trees at Cheltenham and at Armstrong's request she came to Mayfield to see how she liked it, for she had expressed doubts at being able to settle down in a country district. On the night of 14 October Marion stayed at Mayfield and on the following morning they walked to his office, had lunch, and he then took her to Hereford, leaving her to proceed on her own to Cheltenham. During Marion's visit, Miss Pearce was at Mayfield with Inez Rosser and Margaret. Armstrong said that he told Miss Pearce of his intentions as he thought it only fair to do so. If he did, Miss Pearce forgot all about it.

Marion wrote to Armstrong after this visit and Armstrong replied. Nothing definite had been fixed between them and the matter of the proposed marriage and its final arrangements was postponed to a later date.

Marion never saw Armstrong again until his subsequent trial.

Theirs was hardly an improper courtship, smouldering with passion and uncontrolled abandon. On the contrary, it was conducted in a perfectly orderly way. Marion, by this time, was fifty-three. She had had an unhappy marriage and had been left with an elderly mother and limited means. Her life was one of unending drudgery and it is not difficult to see that a future as a solicitor's wife with a ready-made, well-set-up family, in a grand house with servants, would have been attractive to her, despite the fact that she was faced with the difficulty of having to leave all she knew. She was an eminently respectable and sensible woman. She did not want to rush into things and at all costs wanted to ensure that a decent time elapsed after Katharine's death before contemplating the announcement of a formal engagement. She would not have dreamt of conducting an affair with Armstrong, or any other man for that matter.

As for Armstrong, he had returned from the Continent with a new lease of life and had overcome his depression and anxiety after his wife's death. He needed a housekeeper to help with the children. He had written to Chevalier in May of 1921 and told him that he could now face the future with a correct sense of proportion.

> I don't know how it was but my nerves gave out and everything seemed to be in a dream, then my sleep went off so I thought it was time to get right away. You will have heard from me at Malta and how I got there. I put in 3 weeks with a continued change of social life and exploring a most interesting place ... I am glad to say a lot of fresh work came in while I was away and I am very busy; enough to keep me going at full pressure for months and keep my mind from dwelling too much on the past. I want someone to come and keep house for me during June as my guest while Miss Pearce goes to T'mth with Margaret. Do you know anyone as I am at my wit's end?

In May 1921 the weather was fine and hot and an early drought had set in. It was not a good time for applying weedkiller, as without rain the gravel on the paths would not absorb it. In some frustration Armstrong went to the cupboard in his study to look at the arsenic that he had purchased in January even while he realized that he could not use it. He noticed that the packet, which was still on top of the tin of caustic soda, appeared to have been opened. His recollection was that 'the string had been taken off, and the outer wrapper opened. I do not remember the string at all. The impression left on my mind was that the packet had been opened but my remembrance of the details is not now clear.'

Armstrong said that as far as he knew no one used the cupboard except him, although Katharine and probably Miss Pearce knew that arsenic and caustic soda were kept here. 'Had Mrs Armstrong gone to the cupboard for anything between the date of the purchase and the date of her death she must have seen the packet of arsenic as it was in a conspicuous place in the cupboard.'

What really caught his attention when he opened the packet in May was the fact that the arsenic was white; Hird had inadvertently forgotten to add soot or charcoal. He transferred the arsenic into the central drawer of his bureau, which was in his study, and locked it.

In June Miss Pearce had taken Margaret to Teignmouth and the other children were away at school. Mayfield had been locked up and Armstrong was staying with his neighbour, Tunnard Moore. He was at a loose end during the period between his return from the office and dinner, and as the dandelions and plantains on his lawn were assuming enormous proportions, he decided to do something about them. He went to Mayfield and took the packet of white arsenic out of his bureau and divided it into roughly two equal parts. He secured one half in the inner wrapper, folding it up again in a piece of blue draft paper, and replaced it in the drawer in his bureau. He took the other half and made up a number of small packets, each containing about four to five grains of arsenic, and placed them in his pocket.

He used an old chisel to make holes in the roots of individual dandelions, into which he poured the arsenic from each packet adapting the method promoted by the Boundary Chemical Company, which supplied a boring instrument called a kilm for such a use. He had purchased a kilm before the war but had found that its cardboard wrapping had been destroyed by damp and was useless. The beauty of the method was that the surrounding grass was not destroyed as with liquid weedkiller; the powder acted only on the root of the plant in question, thus destroying it individually.

Armstrong thought at the time that he had utilized all these packets in this way, only to realize much later that one had not been used.

He used the remainder of the half packet of arsenic to conduct experiments into its solubility with caustic soda, using a gas ring in the nursery and a little glass jar. He put a portion of the arsenic and caustic soda into the test tube and added a quantity of boiling water to test the solubility of different proportions of arsenic to caustic soda. He wanted to find the correct ratio, as he was unable to determine whether or not a proper solution had been made in the closed petrol tin that he had used before. He found that by reducing the proportion of caustic soda to arsenic a higher degree of solubility was reached. In this way all the arsenic that he had taken out of the drawer was used up and only the packet that he had wrapped in blue draft paper remained in his bureau.

At the office the fresh work that he had taken on was the Clifford sales on behalf of Captain Hope. These sales were to dwarf the Velinewydd sales in their complexity, comprising eight farms, numerous smallholdings, cottages, accommodation lands and several miles of salmon fishing in the Wye, comprising 2,008 acres and split into fifty-two lots. Armstrong's practice had by now stabilized and was beginning to grow. He had been hard at work before Katharine's death and upon his return from the Continent found that he could cope with even more work. He was now beginning to profit at the expense of his rival Oswald Martin.

9

By the time Armstrong returned from abroad Oswald Martin had been in Hay for just over twenty-four months, and after the death of Robert Griffiths in November 1920 had been practising on his own account for the last five of them. No doubt he contemplated with satisfaction his impending marriage to Constance Davies, the cherished only daughter of Fred Davies, and the impending publication of his Tax Book for farmers.

On 20 September 1921, three months after Martin's marriage, the local postman dropped an innocuous-looking little parcel through his letter box.

This box of chocolates is the real key to the whole story – a key of fondant and pistacchio noisettes, of Turkish delight and nougat – esoteric tastes to restore a jaded palate, wrapped up in a box and tied with an orange ribbon. But could anyone have known that this harmless little box of chocolates, wrapped in brown paper and innocently delivered by the local postman, was destined to determine the course of a man's life?

The exquisite tastes in this box were sampled on its delivery by both Mr and Mrs Martin, a couple not long married and still wrapped up in post-nuptial bliss. They ate a few of the chocolates without any ill-effects and put them away in a drawer containing soda-water sparklets.

'On September 20th, 1921,' said Oswald Martin, when questioned later, 'I received by the morning's post a parcel wrapped up in brown paper, addressed to me at Bredon Hill, Cusop, Hay, Herefordshire.'

'How was it written?'

'It was printed in Roman letters.'

'Was it in ink?'

'Yes – it was in ink.'

'Did you keep the wrapper?'

'No, it was destroyed. I cannot find it.'

'Inside the wrapper, what did you find?'

'There was a box of chocolates.'

'Look at this box of chocolates. Can you say that is the same or a similar box?'

'So far as I can tell, that was the box I received.'

'Can you tell where it came from?'

'The postmark was obliterated, that is, indistinct.'

'Was there any indication of when it was packed – any packing label?'

'No.'

'Was the box full of chocolates? Did you open it?'

'I opened it myself. It was tied with a red ribbon, I believe, sideways. There was a layer of white paper on top of the box, which was full of chocolates, and they appeared to be stale. There was a "whitish" powder on the box.'

'What did you do?'

'I left them with my wife.'

'Did you eat any?'

'We had some that evening, two or three, no more.'

'Any ill-effects?'

'No, and we found the chocolates were not stale, though they appeared to be.'

'Was there anything to indicate to you who sent it?'

'Nothing whatever.'

'What did you do with them?'

'They were put by.'

'When you received the box of chocolates and opened them you were suspicious of them?'

'I was not suspicious about them. I was merely curious to see who sent them.'

'The ribbon was tied in a different way?'

'Yes, different from the usual way they are tied.'

'And when you opened them they appeared to be stale?'

'They appeared at first glance to be stale, and the packing label had been removed.'

'And you were curious as to where they came from?'

'Yes: I thought at first they were from a friend who had

been playing a practical joke.'

'Although it was something to excite your suspicion and curiosity?'

'It could not excite my suspicion – it excited my curiosity.'

'Your suggestion is that Major Armstrong sent the chocolates?'

'It is not my suggestion at all.'

'Do you, or do you not, suggest that Major Armstrong sent those chocolates?'

'I refuse to answer.'

'That will not do, Mr Martin. Do you suggest that Major Armstrong sent you that box of chocolates?'

'I do not suggest it.'

The chocolates reappeared next month. The Martins had arranged for a little dinner party at their new home and had invited Oswald's two brothers and their wives. The date was 8 October, eighteen days after the receipt of the innocuous little parcel at their home. Constance had prepared the table for the meal and had set out two dishes with sweets on them along with apples in a fruit bowl. She found that she did not have quite enough sweets to fill both dishes and placed about six or seven chocolates from the box on to the second sweet dish. The meal consisted of fish cakes made from tinned lobster, flour and potatoes; followed by bread, boiled beefsteak pudding with an ordinary suet crust, potatoes and other vegetables; the sweet consisted of junket and cream; a platter of cheese was finally rounded off by a glass of sherry. All the guests ate a hearty meal before retiring to their lodgings in a nearby guesthouse.

Later that night one of Oswald's sisters-in-law, Dorothy Martin, suffered attacks of diarrhoea followed by vomiting. In the morning her worried husband went to Fred Davies for a thermometer to see if her temperature justified a doctor being called. The one supplied was broken and he was forced to go back for another one. Her temperature was taken and found to be 99.5 and her pulse was beating more rapidly than usual. She stayed in bed for a few hours and was taken back to Bredon Hill, where she lay down on the sofa. Dr Hincks was not called to see her, although Fred Davies visited and advised her not to return home until the following day. As she was prone to attacks of diarrhoea, her illness was put down to biliousness after taking a full meal.

Dorothy's sickness ruined the weekend for the Martins. Constance was upset because Dorothy had been ill after a meal at her house and was especially attentive, visiting her personally in her bed in the lodging rooms where the couple had spent the night, and it was Constance who took Dorothy's temperature when the thermometer had been obtained from her father. On such occasions everyone wants to know the cause of any unexpected illness. Fred Davies, who was asked for his opinion, could not have suspected the chocolates, because he was not told about their receipt. A more important reason why the chocolates were not questioned was that Dorothy was not the only one who had eaten one of them. This became clear at the police court:

'You would not like to be certain that it was only you who ate any of the chocolates?'

'No, I should not like to say that.'

Even Constance herself believed her other sister-in-law, Mrs John Martin, had eaten a chocolate.

'Can you tell me who had any, can you recollect?'

'I think my sister-in-law had one, and I think Mrs Gilbert Martin had one.'

'Anyone else?'

'I do not know whether the other people had sweets or not.'

'You would not like to swear how many people had chocolates and how many people did not?'

'No.'

After the dinner party Constance replaced the remaining chocolates from the sweet dish back into the box and put the box back in the drawer. Nothing more was heard about them for a further twenty-one days.

Martin's actions that day bear out his evidence that he was not suspicious about the chocolates. If he had been he would not have sampled them and allowed his wife to try them. If his evidence is to be believed, he was merely curious to know who had sent them and had no thought whatsoever at that time that someone, least of all Armstrong, intended him or his wife harm.

However, if it is considered that his statement that he was not suspicious is odd, and that normally a recipient of a box of chocolates sent by post without a message or a card with its packing label removed and its outer ribbon retied in a different way to normal would be wary, can he be believed when he said that he knew nothing about the box of chocolates?

The problem about the box of chocolates is that their very existence is scarcely believable in itself. Who would send a box of chocolates anonymously? Martin's statement that he thought it was a friend playing a practical joke might be near the truth. A practical joke is an attempt to cause mischief. What is the effect of such a joke apart from making Constance think that the sender of such a gift was a woman friend with whom Martin had previously been intimate? Imagine the effect of Constance having received a bunch of flowers anonymously. In such a case Martin would have wondered who the sender could possibly be and question Constance. It is very probable that even if the sender had disclosed her identity (the sender is unlikely to have been a male friend) Martin would not have revealed it to his new wife.

It is possible that Martin knew who sent them. There is only his word that no card was contained in the packet to indicate the identity of the sender. Martin must have known the brand of chocolates in order to recognize the way that the ribbon was tied. He was not long married and the gift could have been from one of his admirers, as it was not addressed to both of the Martins, which would have been the case if the gift had been a late wedding present. It would have been undoubtedly prudent for him to have said to his wife, when she asked who had sent them to him, that he did not know, and it would have been an easy task to remove the message or card, if one had been sent.

The chocolates are an enigma.

Firstly there were thirty-two chocolates in the box in two layers. Only two were found upon subsequent examination to contain just over two grains of arsenic. If Dorothy Martin had actually eaten another poisoned chocolate which caused her sickness, the tally was three. If the intention was actually to poison the recipient, namely Martin, all the chocolates, or at least some of those in the top layer, would have been poisoned to guarantee success and more than two grains would have been used. Furthermore it would have been far more expedient to tamper with a box of cigarettes and insert arsenic into them to ensure that the recipient, namely Martin, smoked them.

Secondly the chocolates, although addressed to Mr Martin, were received at Bredon Hill, a household consisting of Mr and Mrs Martin and a maid. Chocolates are more often than not a gift for a woman. Therefore it was highly likely that Mrs Martin would eat one of the poisoned chocolates rather than Mr Martin. If, then, this was indeed an attempt on Mr Martin's life, it was poorly worked out from the start.

Thirdly when the chocolates were examined by Dr Hincks, he could see that two of them had been tampered with. He said that this could be seen with the naked eye. This presupposes that the two chocolates had not been disguised with any care and that the gouging was designed to excite suspicion that it had been tampered with, as opposed to it being mistaken for a normal chocolate.

Fourthly if Dorothy Martin had eaten a poisoned chocolate containing over two grains of arsenic at the dinner party on 8 October, full stomach or not, she would have been desperately ill and certainly would not have recovered so quickly the next day.

Fifthly Armstrong could prove that he was never out of Hay on the key dates between the packaging of the box and their receipt by the Martins.

Sixthly the alleged motive for the attempt on Martin's life on 26 October had not arisen on 20 September and, if anything, it was in Armstrong's interests on 20 September to keep Martin alive, in order that he could complete the sales of the two farms to Martin's clients. He had a vested interest: negotiations were well under way with the Yorkshire Penny Bank to arrange for partial releases of the mortgage to allow the sale to go through.

Whoever sent the chocolates did not come forward at the trial. But this is hardly surprising as they were found to contain arsenic, and no one, however innocent, would have dared to suggest that they were the originators and possibly face an attempted murder charge.

As for Armstrong, he was busy at this time setting up the completion arrangements for the Clifford sales as well as earnestly trying to expedite the sealing of the Velinewydd contracts – this in readiness for the completion date, which had been arbitrarily fixed by Martin for 20 October.

After the Velinewydd fiasco in November 1919, Armstrong had tried his best to sell the mansion, firstly to Breconshire County Council and then to a private buyer, who dropped out at the last moment because of the Government's policy on capital taxes. In the middle of 1920 Armstrong was advised by the selling agents that a realistic price was £7,500, which was much reduced from the reserve of £12,500 fixed at the time of the auction. Clearly land prices were dropping fast. However, despite the uproar at the auction, three farms had been sold to sitting tenants. Although the contractual date for completion had been fixed for February 1920, these tenants were not over-anxious to pay the balance of the purchase money and complete as they continued in possession without having to pay any rent. Two of the tenant farmers had employed Lewis Jones, a solicitor, to act for them, but he died in the summer of 1921 and the farmers transferred their business to Oswald Martin. By this time the price of land had fallen well below what they had agreed to pay at the auction, nearly two years before, and they wanted to get out of their contracts. As soon as Martin received his clients' instructions he asked Armstrong to explain the reasons for the delay and was told that there were difficulties with the bank. He then wrote to Armstrong on 29 September saying that unless completion took place by 20 October and his clients received a sealed reconveyance from the bank his clients would rescind their contracts and demand the return of their deposits. Armstrong immediately contacted the bank's solicitor, a personal friend of his, and explained the position to him. The bank's solicitor then forwarded the reconveyances to London which they sealed on 19 October. The next day Armstrong explained to Martin that the reconveyances had been sealed but that he could not personally hand them over as they were in London. Martin refused to accept the position even though Armstrong produced a telegram from the bank informing him that the reconveyances had in fact been sealed. Armstrong requested a meeting with Martin's clients. Once gathered together, he told them that they could purchase the standing timber at the present valuation – well below the contract price – and that he would forsake any rent due from that day to the day of actual completion. This would take place a week later, as the reconveyances had to be sent back to the bank's solicitors in Leeds before they could be delivered to him in Hay. The farmers said they would consider the matter. Next afternoon Martin told Armstrong that on his advice his clients refused to accept the offer and that the notice of rescission would stand. Armstrong then invited Martin to tea – just seven days after he had spent a pleasant two days at Mayfield with Marion Gale, who liked what she had seen.

There had to be a link between Armstrong's invitation to tea at his house and the disputed Velinewydd contracts, despite the fact that both men had a great deal of additional work on during this period. The completion date for the Clifford sales was 2 November and Martin was acting for several purchasers. Apart from Hope's annoyance at Martin's statement at the auction, the Clifford sales were not contentious and the conveyancing was routine, but draft conveyances still had to be supplied and agreed. There was probably more communication between the two Hay firms at this time than at any other. Constant messages and consultations were passing between the clerks as well as the principals.

If Armstrong was more concerned about completing the Clifford sales on time and being accountable to his principal, Captain Hope, through the formidable Moyse, Martin was obsessed by the Velinewydd fiasco. He had set a date for completion and that date had passed. On 20 October Martin attempted to rescind the contracts by letter of that date. Martin must have researched the legal effect of his action but he never delivered writs of rescission, demanding the return of the deposits, interest and costs.

Armstrong first asked Martin to tea on 21 October. Martin felt unable to accept the invitation for that day and was invited to attend the following day. That day, too, was unsuitable for Martin who said he could make it on the Monday (the 24th). The arrangement was again postponed by Martin who finally said he would come on the Wednesday (the 26th).

Armstrong returned to Mayfield on the day of the tea party

on foot. He had spoken to Martin in the morning and Martin had offered him a lift in his car to enable them both to travel to Armstrong's house together that evening. Armstrong declined, however, saying that he had to be home earlier than usual as he had to speak to one of his gardeners.

Armstrong had spoken to Miss Pearce at lunchtime and had told her that Martin was coming for tea. Could she please make arrangements for it in the drawing room. She asked him what she should get and he suggested bread and butter and currant cake or something similar, leaving the details of the light meal to her.

The food had already been brought into the room by the time the two men entered the room. All of it had been placed on a three-tier wicker cake stand, which was tall enough to be placed on the floor. Armstrong rang the bell for the tea to be brought in and the maid, Mrs Price, brought in the silver teapot and placed it on the table, which was just big enough to take the pot, plus two plates, two cups and saucers, a bowl of sugar, a jug of milk and an old-fashioned cream jug. Armstrong then sat down with his back to the desk facing the door and Martin sat in an easy chair practically within the window recess, with another small table beside him.

On the three-tier wicker stand were three plates containing, respectively, bread and butter, sliced buttered currant loaf and some scones. The scones were on the top tier. Armstrong poured the tea, handed Martin a cup and took one himself. Armstrong then handed Martin a plate which he put on the table by his side.

Armstrong says that he rose to his feet, lifted the cake stand and held it towards Martin so that he could help himself. The cake stand was closer to Martin and fully visible. There was no tea cosy on the table to obstruct the view and the top of the cake stand was about level with the top of the table.

Armstrong says that as the scones were on the top plate of the cake stand Martin helped himself to one and put it on his plate. Armstrong then placed the cake stand on the floor and reached across the table to help himself. He says that he may have said 'Please excuse me', as he reached across. After Martin ate the scone, Armstrong says he took the currant loaf out of the tier and left it by Martin on the small table, so that he could help himself – which Martin did, saying he was very partial to currant loaf.

When the pair started the meal it was light outside. Martin was sitting with his back to the window and Armstrong was in full view of him. As it started to grow dark, Armstrong had to light the gas; unfortunately as he lit the mantle, the globe broke, scattering glass over his guest. It was not an incident that Martin would readily forget. The rector called by and Armstrong went to the hall to see him, resuming his conversation with Martin afterwards.

Having finished tea, Martin moved to an easy chair, and said that he would smoke a cigarette as opposed to his usual pipe. Armstrong apologized for having no cigarettes and Martin smoked one of his own.

After tea the two men conversed generally about work and the high pressure they were both under. They also discussed the lodge, as Martin was a member too, albeit not of such an exalted rank as Armstrong; but at no time did they discuss Velinewydd. Martin excused himself at 6.30 p.m. and left the house. Armstrong left the house, too, and went back to his office to draft a partnership deed for a farmer. The tea party was over.

If Armstrong had wanted to murder Martin, he had the opportunity at the tea party. According to Martin, Armstrong handed him a buttered scone with the words, 'excuse fingers', and he had eaten the proferred scone without thought. Yet the very suggestion of an accusation seems outlandish. According to Mrs Price, who collected up the remnants of the uneaten meal, the scones had not been cut or buttered in advance. Several of the scones were uneaten, and after the meal she placed those that remained in a tin – they were eaten later by the maids without any ill effects. If Martin was telling the truth about being handed a buttered scone, it would have been the only one on the wicker stand prepared that way. Armstrong would have had to enter the house, take a scone, go somewhere to butter it, adulterate it, and somehow place it on the stand in readiness for the deed. The facts revealed by the gardener McGeorge were that he met Armstrong going into the house and, on walking round to the side, met him again coming straight out of the side door. In that intervening period Armstrong would have had to acquire a scone, butter it, poison it and replace it. The evidence is that when Armstrong entered the house the meal had not even been laid. If that evidence is correct, Armstrong would have had to go into the kitchen to get a scone. There is no evidence that he did, and strong evidence that he did not. The other alternative is that he purchased a scone from the town and had it ready to put on the wicker stand. Again there is no evidence that he purchased any such item, despite the most extensive police enquiries. In these circumstances the Martin evidence concerning the buttered scone is suspect. In point of fact it would have been far easier for Armstrong to sprinkle arsenic on to the buttered currant loaf, or the bread and butter or even into the tea cup that he later handed to Martin (the tea cups had already been laid when Armstrong popped his head round the door earlier).

The link between the invitation to tea and the time of the disputed contracts was because Armstrong wanted to demonstrate to Martin outside the office his worth and standing; in this way he hoped to influence Martin, to assure him that whatever the differences between their clients they should co-operate. Armstrong showed Martin the utmost civility and tried to impress him. If anything, he was trying to indicate to him how a gentleman should behave in his own home with tea prepared, and brought in, by staff at the ring of a bell. Armstrong's home was an impressive one. The conversation was polite and proper and centred on matters of common interest, such as their pressurized working lives, the nature of the Clifford sales and their Masonic business. In this connection, they discussed a future meeting of the lodge where a drinks licence had to be obtained. There was no reason to mention the contentious issue of the disputed contracts. Armstrong merely wished to demonstrate that home life was distinct from office life, and he went to pains to say that he never brought work through his front door. He wanted to show Martin another way of life, that of the gentleman who courteously invites business contacts to tea. Armstrong stated that he would never, under any circumstances, pick up a scone in his own fingers and place it on a guest's plate. The very thought was an outrage to Armstrong's sense of decorum and etiquette. Whatever the truth, and however hard Armstrong tried, there was an incredible gulf between the two men, one that a tea party could never bridge. Martin was not a man to be impressed by Armstrong or his way of life: indeed he despised the man, his background, his manners and everything about him. When he left the house, he had no idea why he had been invited. If anything, the tea made him more wary of the man, perhaps with good reason. For it was on that very day that Armstrong wrote to Martin refusing to accept the notice of rescission of the contracts. In the same letter Armstrong demanded a year's rent, which was still owing by Martin's clients.

10

Martin left Mayfield at 6.30 p.m. He drove the short distance home, turning left at the Slate House and arriving at Bredon Hill only minutes later. He had previously arranged for his clerk, Alan Preen, to call at his house to take some letters.

He dictated to Preen for about an hour and then went for his supper, leaving his clerk alone. The supper consisted of jugged hare followed by coffee cream. Martin professed to his wife that he was not feeling up to a meal, but ate it nevertheless. He then resumed his dictation at about half-past eight, but after a short time declared he was feeling sick. Preen was dismissed and at about ten past nine Martin ran upstairs and vomited.

According to Martin the vomiting was extremely fierce: 'The colour of the vomit was very dark and its smell was very offensive.' He continued to be sick throughout the night, but as time went on the colour of the vomit became lighter. He then suffered from diarrhoea, and as morning approached he found he could not bear the light and noticed that 'the beat of my heart was very rapid'.

Constance was concerned. After all he had just had a meal from her kitchen. However, as a former nurse she felt perfectly capable of managing a bilious attack, and did not call the doctor that evening. However, she summoned Dr Hincks the next day. Hincks considered that he was suffering from a normal bilious attack and as such attacks had been common in the neighbourhood from August onwards, prescribed accordingly.

That morning, 27 October, was a Thursday. Laura Davies visited soon after Hincks had left: she went upstairs and entered the bedroom where Martin was lying, with a bowl of vomit beside him. She talked to him and told him that her premonitions – that Armstrong would try and poison him – had proved correct.

Later that day Fred Davies saw Hincks and told him that in his opinion his son-in-law had been poisoned by Armstrong. Hincks told him that Martin's illness appeared to be a bilious attack but that he would visit him later that evening and keep in mind what he had said. Privately Hincks thought that Davies's statement was absurd. Hincks saw Martin that evening, and even though he was shown the offending vomit and despite being warned of Davies's suspicions, he did not believe a word of it and continued to treat the illness as gastric flu.

Hincks saw his patient on the following morning and prescribed bismuth. He visited again on the Saturday when Martin appeared to be improving, although 'his bowels had not been moving'.

In the mean time the suggestion made by Laura that Martin had been poisoned was gathering strength. Both she and her husband Fred were quite convinced of the fact but they had been unable to persuade the doctor to take them seriously.

Fred visited Martin for the first time on the Thursday evening after he had told Hincks of his suspicions, and watched Martin be sick. They both talked about the possibility of poison and Martin stated that he had been passed a scone in Armstrong's hands, which, by naming the supposed vehicle for the poison itself, added credence to the rumour. Despite Fred's conviction he, like Hincks, did not take away the vomit for analysis.

What happened next was banal. On the following day, Friday, Fred called again at the household. Laura had made the invalid some port wine jelly which was administered to Martin along with Hincks's bismuth mixture. He was now downstairs on his way to a full recovery. Fred repeated his suspicion about poison and ventured a remark that if he was right Armstrong might try again. He warned his son-in-law and daughter to watch out for anonymous gifts 'such as chocolates' being sent through the post. At this Martin and his daughter exclaimed in unison, 'We have already been sent some chocolates anonymously through the post.' Fred answered: 'You had better bury them.'

Later that night when the Davieses returned home, Fred said that he had reconsidered his advice to his daughter to bury the chocolates and asked Laura to go and retrieve them. Dutifully Laura went to Bredon Hill next morning and brought the chocolates to her house. She said to the police later:

> On the following day, my husband told me he thought he would like to analyse the chocolates, and as I was going to Bredon Hill that day, he asked me to bring the chocolates down with me which I did. When I arrived home my husband wasn't there so I opened the chocolate box and looked at the chocolates with a magnifying glass that was lying on a table. As soon as my husband arrived I handed the box over to him.

In the words of Fred Davies's statement to the police:

> I examined them as they were in the box. I did not handle them but turned them over with a pencil. It seemed to me that two of the top layer had been tampered with at the ends. The ends looked as though they had been gouged out, and I noticed minute particles of white powder adhering to them. I thought I would not analyse the chocolates myself, so handed them over to Dr Hincks to be analysed.

This examination was made by Fred Davies on the Saturday. He waited a further twenty-four hours before showing the box to Dr Hincks. In the face of this evidence Hincks agreed that Martin's illness deserved to be investigated.

Two chocolates from the box contained arsenic and a dinner guest who had eaten one of the chocolates from the box had displayed symptoms consistent with arsenical poisoning. Martin displayed similar symptoms after having a meal at Armstrong's house, and his urine contained arsenic. Armstrong was in possession of arsenic which he had purchased openly from Davies's shop. Katharine had died from an acute sickness which bore similarities to arsenical poisoning. If Armstrong had sent poisoned chocolates to Martin and if he had tampered with the scone at the tea party, it was likely that he had also murdered his wife in the same way. It followed that if his wife's body contained arsenic, he had also poisoned her. The logic was sweet, as night followed day.

Such logic is, of course, flawed. It does not follow that if Katharine's body contained arsenic, Armstrong had to have administered it to her: she could have ingested it in a number of ways. It does not follow that because Martin's urine contained arsenic a strong dose was administered to him at the tea party: the minute trace of arsenic could have originated from a number of sources. Nor, finally, does it follow that the arsenic actually found in the chocolates came from Armstrong's hand, for someone else could have tampered with them. If all these instances are taken separately a number of alternative explanations are plausible and possible, but when taken together, there is a coincidence of suspicion leading to the almost irresistible conclusion that Armstrong was guilty of all these acts. Yet if any one of these incidences is false, a vital link in the chain of suspicion snaps and the whole edifice begins to collapse. This is the danger of circumstantial evidence.

There is always a central, pivotal point in any story which helps to unravel the truth. That point is the chocolates, their purchase, their receipt and the fact that two of them contained arsenic. Fred's statement to his daughter and son-in-law on the Friday, two days after the tea party, that if he was right Armstrong might try again and 'you better be on your guard for anonymous gifts sent through the post such as chocolates', is profoundly hard to swallow. Why should Davies warn Martin against anonymous gifts, unless he knew that Martin had already received such a gift? And in particular why mention chocolates, as a likely anonymous gift, unless he knew that a box of chocolates had been sent to Martin anonymously? Why should anyone conceive that a man would be sent chocolates? Basically the whole scenario at this stage begins to smell as much as Martin's vomit; it positively reeks of complicity. Even more so when the timing is examined in detail.

The tea party was on Wednesday (the 26th). Martin was ill that evening. Hincks visits on Thursday (the 27th). Fred, before he has even seen Martin, tells Hincks of his suspicions. Fred calls on Martin that night and again on Friday (the 28th), when he warns Martin and Constance about anonymous gifts such as chocolates and then tells his daughter to bury them. Laura calls on Saturday (the 29th), picks up the chocolates and hands them over to Fred, who then waits a further day before disclosing them to Hincks.

There was plenty of time for Davies to adulterate the chocolates. Why, if the examination by the Davieses was made on the Saturday, did Fred delay a further day before handing them on to Hincks? They were, after all, next-door neighbours.

It beggars belief that when Fred's warning about anonymous gifts was proven so incredibly accurate, he should not want to see the box there and then. What was in Fred's mind when he warned Constance, and why did he tell her to bury them and not look at them immediately in front of everybody? They were there in the house and could have been examined.

It must follow that he wanted time to examine them in his own home or in his dispensary. That he did not examine them there and then exposes him to the accusation that he wanted them for some other purpose. Fred, Laura, Oswald Martin and Constance were all in the sitting room at Bredon Hill when they had the conversation about the chocolates. The chocolates were in the drawer in the room, having been put there by Constance after the dinner party of 8 October. Surely, if there was no complicity in the whole business Fred would immediately ask to look at them. The fact that he did not implicates him in a plot of major proportions. If he had examined the box there and then, all of them would have noticed that two of the chocolates had been interfered with, as the tampering was visible to the naked eye. No proper attempt at concealment had been made – the hole that had been drilled in one of them was the diameter of a pencil.

Instead of examining them Fred tells Constance to bury them. Why? The act of burial means that they can be retrieved later. Why did he not advise her to throw them away? The answer must be that he wanted to recover them at some future time. Why?

Even at this late stage he wanted to force Hincks to take a urine sample from Martin and have it analysed. Hincks had refused to consider that Martin's illness was anything other than a normal attack of gastric flu, whose symptoms bear a resemblance to those of mild arsenical poisoning, and he would not listen to his junior cousin in trade. For this reason

Davies must have wanted to demonstrate that there was other evidence apart from Martin's actual sickness to give credibility to his theory. After all when Hincks was faced with the unassailable evidence of the chocolates, he was forced to do something.

If there was a conspiracy in connection with the chocolates, it is clear that Constance had no part in it. She must have been an innocent party. Later in evidence she contradicted her husband and told the court that the ribbon on the box had been tied diagonally and not crosswise and said that she was not certain who else ate any of the chocolates at the dinner party. It was Martin who categorically stated that only Dorothy Martin had eaten a chocolate.

Fred was clever. He asked his wife to collect the chocolates in the morning. He distanced himself from the examination by saying that he did not 'take them in my fingers', and 'there were certain reasons in my mind why I should not handle them'. Those reasons must be obvious. He did not wish to lay himself open to a charge that he had injected them with arsenic. He was a chemist, he possessed arsenic and he had the means and skill to administer the powder.

Chocolate has a low melting point and will easily dissolve in a person's fingers. If someone really wanted to tamper with them, by drilling and inserting poison into them, it is a simple matter to ensure that the outer coating of chocolate would fuse over the hole, ensuring that the interference would not be noticed by the intended victim. Yet in this case the two offending chocolates were transparently tampered with and that fact was clearly designed to be observed. When Hincks was shown the box on the Sunday, he had no difficulty in being convinced that that was the case. Indeed he had no alternative but to accept the suggestion that the white powder, clearly visible in the holes in the two chocolates, might be arsenic. Once this was accepted, he had to go along with Fred's suggestion that Martin's urine should be tested for arsenic – which Hincks had dismissed as absurd four days earlier.

If it is a fact that Davies inserted the arsenic in the chocolates to force Hincks to take a urine sample, a chain in the link of the circumstantial evidence against Armstrong breaks. The edifice against him begins to collapse. If Fred and Laura really believed that Armstrong had poisoned his wife, why stop at a mere adulteration of the chocolates? Why not tamper with the urine sample as well?

Such a scenario is conceivable. Davies had the means and the motivation and he would have looked very silly indeed if the urine had been found to be arsenic-free. But the vital question remains: Why did Fred and Laura consider that Armstrong had poisoned his wife? Why should anybody harbour such a thought?

This question may be easy to answer. Small towns like Hay thrive on gossip as if it were currency, with information being traded on street corners and in the town's shops. Earlier that year another case of poisoning had hit the national and local headlines and was the subject of discussion in Hay and the surrounding villages for months. That case also involved arsenic, and also involved a murder charge, with the victim being the man's wife. The defendant was also a solicitor with a country practice similar to Armstrong's. The death had taken place only fifty miles away and the man, Harold Greenwood, had been tried at Carmarthen Assizes. As a result of the brilliant advocacy of Sir Edward Marshall Hall, Greenwood was acquitted and walked away from the dock a free man.

Laura had spoken to her friend Mrs Price, the wife of the local bank manager, who had been with Katharine shortly before her death. Katharine's illness was consistent with a poisoning. Armstrong had openly purchased arsenic from her husband. Laura was convinced that Armstrong had in fact poisoned his wife, and she wanted him exposed. Fred did too.

Greenwood had been acquitted on 10 November 1920, during the period when Katharine was in Barnwood. His wife's body, like that of Katharine's, was disinterred for analysis, but in her case the exhumation took place in April 1920. The unearthing was widely reported and achieved local notoriety.

Greenwood's wife, Mabel, was a wealthy, religious woman and well liked. Greenwood on the other hand had few friends and was a notorious womanizer. In this case local opinion went very much against him, especially when he remarried a mere four months after his wife's death. Rumours abounded and there were hints of foul play, particularly in the signing of the death certificate, which stated that the cause of death was heart disease. Eventually the authorities felt that they had to take some action and quite openly exhumed her body and had her organs analysed. An inquest was convened and the coroner's jury returned a unanimous verdict that Mabel's death was caused by acute arsenical poisoning, even though a fatal dose was two grains and the body was found to contain a minute dose of arsenic, between a quarter and a half of a grain. The verdict at Camarthen was greeted by loud applause in the public gallery. Indeed so great was the public feeling against Greenwood that he was arrested, ostensibly for his own protection.

Mabel had for some months prior to her death complained of fainting fits and pains around her heart. Her friends had noticed that she was shedding weight and that she suffered from consistent attacks of sickness and diarrhoea. On 15 June 1919 she had a Sunday roast followed by gooseberry tart, with Burgundy to drink, and very shortly afterwards had an attack of diarrhoea which she attributed to the fruit. In the afternoon she had bread and butter for tea and in a matter of hours complained of pains around her heart. Greenwood and her daughter then put her to bed. The family doctor was called and prescribed a mixture to settle her stomach. He considered before he left her bedside that she was improving, but at a visit later that evening he realized that his patient was desperately ill, vomiting frequently. At 3 a.m. she died, approximately fourteen hours after she had taken her lunch on the previous afternoon.

The case against Greenwood was a simple one. He had purchased some Eureka Weedicide, which contained arsenic, and the prosecution alleged that he had poured some of the mixture into the Burgundy bottle that Mabel had drunk at lunch.

The case was going well for the prosecution, which suggested to the jury that the motive for the crime was Greenwood's desire for his wife's money and his wish to marry his mistress. Marshall Hall made serious inroads into the prosecution case by citing evidence that her final sickness, including the diarrhoea, was caused by the gooseberries that Mabel had eaten at lunch. He was ably supported by his team of doctors led by Dr Toogood. Sir William Willcox persuasively argued that this could not explain the arsenic found in her body. The case was finely balanced until Greenwood's daughter gave her evidence.

The prosecution had pinned their whole case on the bottle of Burgundy being the vehicle for the poison, but had negligently failed to interview Greenwood's daughter Irene. The prosecution simply collapsed when Irene gave evidence and told the jury, 'Mother and I had Burgundy,' adding that she also drank wine at supper from the same bottle.

Fred and Laura Davies did not know the Greenwoods personally, but they knew of the rumours against him. In turn they did not like Armstrong and had nothing good to say about him. Armstrong said that he could never understand the degree of animosity shown towards him by Fred (he did not know Laura), and why Fred should tell Hincks 'that he could never trust him a yard', because he had acted for him in the past, prior to Martin's courtship and marriage to Constance, and always thought that he had a cordial relationship with him.

There may have been a reason all the same. In 1914 there were two chemists in Hay, J.F. Davies and T.J. Stokoe. Armstrong had always acted for Davies until his daughter became acquainted with Martin. In 1920 Stokoe retired and closed down his shop. Stokoe had an assistant working for him called Mr Sant, who was thrown out of work as a result of his boss pulling down his shutters. Shortly afterwards he asked Armstrong for advice in setting up on his own. Sant and Armstrong worshipped in the same church, where Sant was a sidesman and Armstrong a rector's warden, and had known each other for some years. Armstrong helped Sant to open a shop known as Sant's Drug Stores at different premises and although Armstrong advised him that he could not sell poisons or do anything that brought him within the Pharmacy Acts, Sant managed to do rather well.

This may have been the real seed of Davies's hostility towards Armstrong and could explain Davies's statement that the solicitor could not be trusted. No doubt when Stokoe closed down Davies thought that he would have a monopoly of the chemist's trade in the town. It must have been galling to find an unqualified chemist set up in opposition, selling everything that he sold with the exception of regulated drugs. Armstrong's actions clearly affected his pocket and his prestige in the town which he so dearly cherished. It was music to his ears to hear that a solicitor had actually been arrested for the murder of his wife and, when he considered the evidence unfolding as it was reported daily in the newspapers, the resemblance to Armstrong's own actions appeared commanding.

In Greenwood's case the prosecution suggested that the poison used was weedkiller. Armstrong's gardener had purchased weedkiller, but Armstrong had purchased pure arsenic. Greenwood's wife had been long buried before her body was exhumed and the authorities only acted as a result of local pressure. If Davies was right in his suspicion that Hay housed a true poisoner, it was important to expose him. Yet how could he prove the case and force the authorities to take action? Unlike Greenwood, who was universally despised, Armstrong was popular and deemed morally pure.

Martin's vomiting was severe and Fred and Laura believed he had been poisoned. An attack of gastric flu can be brutal and, if acute, requires hospitalization, because the patient becomes dehydrated so rapidly. In the case of children such attacks can be extremely dangerous. Hincks considered the illness to be similar to those that he had treated in many homes. There was nothing in the symptoms to suggest anything but a routine sickness. Fred was not satisfied and felt he had to do something about it. Time was slipping away, and by the Friday Martin was well enough to be able to go downstairs.

There was little that Fred could do to convince anybody that Martin had been poisoned. Martin had stopped feeling sick and was on his way to a full recovery. Soon he would be back at work and Armstrong's supposed murder attempt would remain undiscovered. Moreover Fred would have lost a great deal of credibility in the eyes of Hincks and his accusation was a very serious one to make against anyone. Hincks and Armstrong were professional people with positions in the town and fellow Freemasons. Davies's accusation would be bound to get back to Armstrong. Davies had to do something to justify himself – and quickly.

Davies did not know about the chocolates at the time of

Dorothy's illness. Clearly he did not know of their existence at the time of Martin's sickness on 27 October or he would have mentioned them then. On 28 October he must have known about them or he would not have issued his warning about 'anonymous gifts such as chocolates' on the evening of that day. So who told him of their existence? It cannot have been Constance, otherwise her exclamation of surprise when her father mentioned the danger would have been rehearsed. Equally it cannot have been Martin, because it is recorded that both he and his wife responded in unison to Fred's comment with equal amazement.

As Fred must have known about the mysterious arrival of the chocolates, why did he warn them to be on the look-out for the arrival of such an anonymous gift? Why did he pretend that he did not know about them already, and why did he tell Constance to bury them, when finally he had elicited that they existed?

Fred wanted to distance himself as much as possible from the chocolates. What better than to be told officially of their existence by Martin and Constance, so that no suspicion could possibly fall on him. Likewise he did not want to examine them in the living room of Bredon Hill, when everyone else would look at them, for if no irregularities had been noticed, it would have looked very suspicious if he had taken them home and they were later found to have been doped.

His plan was a simple one. All he had to do was to suggest that a box of chocolates might be sent anonymously through the post. He knew that Constance would state that one had already been delivered. He then had to ensure that the box itself would not be destroyed and be saved for future retrieval. He could then ask his wife to collect the box in the morning, examine it at his leisure, salt it and deliver it to Hincks.

As contrived, he did ask his wife to collect the box the following day, and at last he had what he wanted. When he had finished with them, the chocolates were clearly tampered with and that white powder resembling arsenic had been placed in two of them. Hincks had to act and do something. He readily agreed that a test should be made on Martin and without hesitation agreed to take a sample of urine.

However, he did not take it himself and asked Davies to provide an empty bottle. Davies took the bottle to Martin and left it with him overnight. Hincks collected the bottle and took it back to Davies, who corked it and dispatched the chocolates and the urine sample to the Clinical Research Association. Could anyone believe the chocolates and the bottle of urine would not contain arsenic?

If this scenario is correct, Martin had no part in Davies's convoluted plan to tamper with the chocolates and like Constance cannot have been part of any conspiracy. Likewise Laura need not have been involved. Admittedly she scrutinized them first, but she did not see any white powder in any of them, despite examining them with a magnifying glass. Fred had asked her to collect them to allow him to undertake an analysis. Can he be believed when he says he never took any chocolates out of the box to look at them? What did he do with them, before he showed them to Dr Hincks the next day?

All the while Armstrong was blissfully ignorant of what was happening behind his back. Little did he know that in two months' time, on New Year's Eve, he would be lying on a hard bed in the police cell of his own court and that he would never walk home again.

11

Martin's illness was a potential nightmare for Armstrong. Completion of the Clifford sales had been fixed for 2 November, and with Martin unwell there was every chance that something would go wrong with these contracts.

On 27 October Armstrong went to work as usual. He called in at Martin's office at about 9.45 a.m. and was told that Martin had not yet arrived. Returning about two hours later, he was told that Martin was ill. Later that morning Martin's office asked Armstrong if he would take a sale for him later that afternoon. Armstrong called again at Martin's office and obtained the necessary details of an auction sale, which he attended on his behalf.

The following day Armstrong called at Martin's house and spoke to Constance to enquire how he was. He also called on Hincks, and after apologizing for asking about a patient, explained that they were crucially involved on a number of pressing business matters, and he was anxious to know whether Martin would be able to attend to them next week. He was assured by Hincks that he would be. Armstrong said that he was on very good terms with Hincks, otherwise he would not have asked him about one of his patients.

On the Sunday Armstrong attended church and on his way home called at Bredon Hill and saw Mrs Martin, who told him that her husband was better. He said that he did not express any surprise as he knew from Hincks that he was on the mend and that in the circumstances he should hardly be likely to do so.

Martin returned to work next Tuesday and spoke to Armstrong, informing him that he had a 'thorough clean out and was now better'. On the Wednesday the Clifford sales were completed without a hitch. Some time later Armstrong remembered 'chaffing' Martin about his driving, saying that if he did not take more exercise he would have another attack soon.

Sometime in November one of Armstrong's clerks, Una Baker, started work in an office adjacent to her boss's room. An oil stove was installed and she found that it made the air very dry. She suggested to Armstrong that it would be as well to have a kettle of water on top of the stove to humidify the atmosphere. He replied that since she would always have a kettle on the boil, she might as well make tea in the afternoons. The kettle was purchased on 25 November and on that day Miss Pearce brought down some tea things from Mayfield.

It was shortly before this date that Armstrong asked Martin to tea again, firstly to Mayfield and then to his office, and according to Martin the invitations were repeated many times. Martin said that he was asked about twenty times and found it very difficult to find suitable excuses for not going. Una Baker remembered Armstrong asking Martin to tea openly on the telephone on about three occasions only. Armstrong said that he did ask Martin on quite a few occasions adding that, 'I am afraid that perhaps in this respect I might have been somewhat persistent', and that when he rang him up he may have said 'When are you coming along?', or words to that effect. Armstrong claimed that the reasons for the invitations were that a Masonic installation was due to take place in December and he wanted to discuss licensing matters and some business connected with the water supply for the Clifford estate needed to be ironed out between them. Martin was, of course, determined not to accept the invitations as he now believed that Armstrong was trying to poison him. Martin failed to attend any meetings of the lodge and when he failed to materialize on 13 December Armstrong never asked him to tea again, despairing of the man.

It is quite possible that Martin did not exaggerate the number of invitations offered to him. Equally Armstrong may have unduly pressed Martin to come to tea, and these continued invitations might well have appeared very suspicious to Martin. Tom Stokoe, who had retired from his chemist's business a year before, explained something of Armstrong's character in a letter to his solicitor, after his arrest.

There is no point in the fact that Armstrong was persistent in asking Martin to tea, whether at home or in the office, because he has been just the same to several of his friends, and always looked for a man's company. I think that, living by himself, he has been lonely during the last twelve months and Army life had made him fond of men's company for a good old 'jaw'. At any rate his insistent invitations to Martin to tea is quite familiar to many of his friends. He asked me three or four times to call and have a talk about the Masonic licence affair, and during 1921 he must have asked me thirty times to call at Mayfield in the evening or at the office in the afternoon. I always dodged the matter because I hate visiting people and he was often so keen that it was quite embarrassing.

To illustrate – the last time I saw him was last Friday week (the day before the arrest) in the King's Head. We discussed books and he asked me to go up and spend the evening with him. I excused myself, as I had a committee meeting on. He said 9 o'clock would do and I said the meeting would not be over. He then said he would wait for me to come at 10 o'clock and I had to stretch the truth and say I had a girl to meet as well in order to give the matter a miss. He was bound to accept this, but made an appointment with me in his office for the week next Monday morning, to arrange an evening that week.

Many times, to avoid a visit, I had to put up a silly excuse to the point of rudeness. He has been just as insistent to other men who have been there once or twice and urged to come again. If the prosecution seeks to place a significance on his repeated invitations to Martin there is *nothing in it*, because Martin was only one of several who had these persistent invitations. He cannot have wanted to murder the lot of us!

In our business relations he has always been very kindly disposed to me. If Armstrong had found a man who would (or could) think out every argument to the last thread of detail, I believe he would have asked that man to live with him free of charge!

In November Trevor Griffiths passed his law finals and Armstrong went to tea with his mother to celebrate the occasion. On 10 December he issued high court writs against

Martin's clients seeking an order of the court forcing them to take over the farms and pay the balance of the purchase price to Williams Vaughan as well as claiming interest on the outstanding purchase price, damages and costs.

Mayfield was now preparing for Christmas. Marion Gale wrote regularly after her pleasant stay at the house in October, giving Armstrong her news, and in a letter that was found in his pockets on his arrest she wished him all the luck for 1922. Neither of them knew that he was under the close scrutiny of Scotland Yard detectives, two of whom were practically living in the town, scouring it for any information that would help their case against him.

On 23 November 1920 a sore had appeared on Armstrong's foreskin after he returned from London, where he was attending the high court in the action for conspiracy and damages against William Morgan. He did not seek medical advice and treated it with boracic ointment, speculating that it had been caused by the friction of a new pair of underpants that he was wearing.

The sore did not get better and on 9 December he showed it to Dr Hincks, who was treating him for a rather severe cold. Hincks examined his penis and said that he thought the sore was syphilitic; Armstrong replied that it was impossible as he had not had any connection with a woman. He asked Hincks if syphilis could be contracted through an infected lavatory, or something of that kind, and Hincks replied that it was perfectly possible to contract the disease in such a way. Hincks gave Armstrong some ointment and the sore disappeared within three days. Armstrong's opinion was that the sore was associated with the severe cold from which he was suffering, caused in turn by his being very run down due to the pressure of his business. He commented that he frequently suffered from irritation and soreness of his private parts as a youth, although he never had an actual infection before and had never required treatment.

Hincks was very doubtful about the case and at his request Armstrong was examined at the Hereford General Hospital by a Dr Edgar Morris, who took a blood sample. The results of this test were transmitted to Armstrong as 'minus-plus-minus', which, Hincks explained, signified that it was necessary for Armstrong to undertake a course of treatment for syphilis. Apart from the one time that Hincks had been shown the sore he never asked to see Armstrong's penis again, and beyond asking Armstrong if it had healed up, he paid no more attention to it.

On 17 December 1920 Armstrong was given an injection in the Herefordshire General Hospital.

On 23 January 1921 (the day after Katharine returned from Barnwood), Hincks gave him another injection at Mayfield. Hincks had difficulty in finding the right place to insert the needle and made several attempts before stabbing him with it. The injection was indescribably painful and resulted in considerable soreness of the muscles in Armstrong's legs and buttocks and he was unable to walk properly for three weeks.

In February he developed a rash which affected his hands, arms, buttocks and thighs. This rash continued during March and April lasting into the middle of May, before gradually subsiding and leaving no marks.

In the middle of May Hincks prescribed a course of mercury tablets and a potash gargle, and as he was uncertain about the nature of the rash he arranged for Armstrong to be examined by two Herefordshire doctors who were attending a meeting in Hereford. One of these doctors Armstrong believed to be Dr Steed, of Staunton-on-Wye, who was later to give evidence on his behalf at the trial. Armstrong was never told the outcome of this meeting by Hincks and never received the doctors' opinion.

In the middle of June Armstrong's gums became very sore, and as they started to bleed, he discontinued with the mercury treatment.

At the end of June he suffered from considerable irritation in the palms of both his hands and subsequently the skin peeled off them, this condition continuing until the end of September, causing him great irritation and sleeplessness at night.

At the beginning of August he suffered from an ulcerated throat, for which he was given a throat spray and a gargle, with very little success.

In October 1921 Hincks said it would be necessary for him to have intravenous injections in his arm, but before beginning this next course of treatment he said that he would like him to be examined by another medical specialist.

Hincks had kept no notes or records of the case, and asked

Armstrong to prepare a memorandum of his symptoms suffered over the previous year to give to the specialist, Dr Heath, of 41 Newhall Street, Birmingham. On 11 October Armstrong was examined by Dr Heath, who tested his urine and explained that it was quite in order. Heath told Armstrong that he was very doubtful that the rash he suffered from was syphilitic in nature and that he was quite definite that the peeling of his palms was not a symptom of the condition. He expressed surprise that there was no sign of a scar from the sore on his foreskin. He told Armstrong that he would communicate with Hincks, but that he was unable to give a definite opinion.

After this consultation Hincks gave Armstrong repeated injections of arsenic in his right arm and told him that he would derive much benefit from them. Generally they were given by Hincks on a Sunday in Armstrong's bedroom at Mayfield and he used to leave the empty packet of Novarsenobillon on the dressing table, which Armstrong used to throw into his grate in the morning.

Armstrong particularly remembered one Sunday, which he believed to be either 20 or 27 November, when he had a conversation with Hincks while the latter was preparing the injection of arsenic. Hincks had asked Armstrong a few moments before whether or not he felt any reaction from the injections as 'you cannot pump big doses of arsenic into a person without feeling some effect'. Armstrong replied by asking him the nature of the drug. Hincks replied that he did not know, as 'I am no chemist.' Armstrong asked if he could see the formula and explained that he had done a considerable amount of chemistry and had seriously contemplated taking it up as a profession. He remembered laughing at the very long name of the chemical which Hincks referred to as 'A.S.' and which apparently contained an oxalate of arsenic. In the course of this conversation Armstrong quite casually and naturally asked Hincks what a fatal dose of arsenic was. Later, in evidence, Hincks said he was flabbergasted by this question, but when taken in context it seems a perfectly reasonable enquiry.

Both prosecution and defence doctors examined Armstrong for traces of syphilis, concluding that he had not been suffering from this disease at all. As for Armstrong he complained that a fresh symptom arose after each new treatment prescribed by Hincks and in this respect it seems he deserves some sympathy.

The arsenical injections continued into December, but were peremptorily stopped due to circumstances beyond Armstrong's control.

On Wednesday 28 December Armstrong walked into Martin's office and asked him if his wife played bridge. He then said something to Trevor Griffiths that caused him to roar with laughter, before saying to Martin 'What about Friday for short notice? If you let me know I will try and fix up a fourth.' That evening he received a short note from Martin declining the invitation. On the Friday he again saw Martin and said, 'What about a day next week? I will leave it to you to fix it. It was perhaps as well that you could not come today as Talbot [the inspector of taxes at Brecon] was engaged.' Oswald made no reply because he knew that on the following day Crutchett of the Yard was going to arrest him. Armstrong walked home that evening completely oblivious of what was going to happen on the last day of that year.

12

New Year's Eve in 1921 fell on a Saturday. Armstrong intended to do some work in his garden that day, and after pulling on his riding breeches and long brown boots, he put on his Norfolk jacket, which he used for gardening work. He transferred some items, which consisted of both business and private letters, from his normal work jacket into his pocket, had his breakfast with Miss Pearce and his three children and went to work.

He walked down Pig Lane to Hay as usual, past Martin's office and across Broad Street to his own office. Arthur Phillips and one of his junior clerks, Amy Jay, the daughter of his gardener, were already at work. He wished them good morning and went upstairs to his desk on the first floor. He took off his hat and sat down. The time was shortly before ten.

A few minutes later he heard heavy footsteps on the stairs, and without being announced, three men walked in. One of them, whom he recognized, introduced himself as Deputy Chief Constable Weaver, and then presented his two colleagues, Detective Inspector Crutchett and Sergeant Sharp. Armstrong was surprised to be faced with three officers barging into his private office in this way, and considered that they must have come on urgent police business.

Crutchett explained without ceremony the reason for his visit. He said:

Inquiries have recently been made concerning the sudden illness of Mr Oswald Norman Martin after his taking tea with you on October 26th last at your house at Cusop. He was

127

taken ill soon after he left you on that date, and was later seized with sickness and purging. A specimen of urine was taken on October 30th, and arsenic was found in it. These symptoms point to arsenic poisoning. It is known that you have purchased arsenic, the last occasion being on January 11th 1921. It is therefore necessary to enquire whether, and if so, how and by whom, arsenic could have been introduced into the food taken at the tea party. I would also tell you that on the 20th September Mr Martin received by post a box of Fuller's chocolates, and on examination it was found that some of the chocolates had been tampered with and arsenic put into them. The box was packed by Fuller's on September 2nd. It may be that you would like to make a statement as to your own actions on October 26th, why Mr Martin was invited to tea, as to what became of the arsenic purchased by you and as to any other facts which may throw light on the matter. Also as to your movements during the period from the 2nd to the 20th September. You were away from Hay. Where and with whom did you stay; how were you occupied during that period, and whether you bought any chocolates? And I must tell you that anything you say will be taken down in writing and might be used in evidence hereafter.

Armstrong was surprised to hear this long, prepared statement and replied: 'Certainly, this is a very serious matter and I will help you all I can. I was not aware that arsenic was found in Martin's urine, and I appreciate that the circumstances call for some explanation from me. I will make a statement and tell you all I know.'

He had no idea at all that the purpose of the officer's visit was to arrest him, whether he said anything or not, and if there was ever an occasion for a man to keep silent for fear of self-incrimination by omission this was one of them, because the statement that he made featured heavily in the evidence against him and without doubt was used by the Crown to help secure his conviction. When the officers entered his room he was not told that he would be arrested, or that the charge of attempted murder had already been prepared against him. He was led to believe that the police were in the normal way processing enquiries into the circumstances of Martin's illness and the receipt of the poisoned box of chocolates.

Armstrong made a statement, which was written down by

Dr Bernard Spilsbury giving evidence at the assizes

Sir Henry Curtis Bennett and Sir Ernest Pollock

Left to right: Doctor Toogood, Doctor William Ainslie and Doctor Steed (in the background: Mr James (under-sheriff) and Doctor Buisson) at the assizes

Sir A. Bodkin (DPP)

Doctor Townsend and Mrs
Townsend at the assizes

Mr A.E. Chevalier at the
assizes

Mr Justice Darling

Left to right: Nurse Lloyd, Miss Una Baker, Nurse Kinsey, Miss Pearce and Miss Inez Rosser at the assizes

Mrs H. Price

Mrs Lily Evans

Mr William Jay, the
gardener

Madam X (Marion Gale)

Nurse Allen (*left*) and
friend at the assizes

Major Armstrong's bureau being taken to court

Major Armstrong in witness box being cross examined

Major Armstrong leaving the assizes under sentence of death

Sergeant Sharp in the presence of Weaver and Crutchett.
Armstrong read it over and corrected minor verbal
inaccuracies. Crutchett then suggested that he should add
that the statement had been made quite voluntarily without
him being questioned. Armstrong then signed it. It is clear
from the statement that he had been answering detailed
questions that were put to him. Crutchett's suggestion that
Armstrong had not been questioned was economical with the
truth.

I, HERBERT ROWSE ARMSTRONG after having been
cautioned by Chief Inspector Crutchett that anything I may
say may be used in evidence hereafter, wish to make the
following statement:
Mr. Martin is a brother Solicitor in Hay. He had been
married in June last but owing to my wife's death in February
last I had been unable to do any entertaining. I asked Mr.
Martin to have a cup of tea on Wednesday the 26th October
1921. At that time I had two men working in my garden,
which had been allowed to get into a very bad state. Their
names are Mc George, who was working in the garden and
Stokes who was erecting a fowlhouse. They both live in Bear
St. Hay.
I had no special reason for inviting Mr. Martin to tea other
than I had not entertained him since his marriage, and at that
time I was not entertaining on a very large scale.
On the day in question Mr. Martin arrived at my house
about 5 p.m. I had previously gone home to see that
everything was in order. I took him round the garden and
showed him various improvements that I proposed to make.
We then entered the drawing room where tea had been laid
out by my housekeeper Miss Pearce. As far as I remember the
food was placed in three plates on a wicker stand (I remember
the wicker stand as I have a more ornate one in brass and my
housekeeper had asked which I preferred) The food consisted
of buttered scone, buttered currant loaf in slices, and bread
and butter. I handed Mr. Martin some scone, on a plate. He
took some and I also took some which I ate and I afterwards
placed the dish of currant bread by his side on the table and
asked him to help himself. I shall be able to ascertain by going
to my house where the scone and currant loaf were bought. I
remember Mr. Martin saying that buttered loaf was a
favourite dish of his, and I know that he ate heartily and
cleared the dish. Afterwards I asked him to smoke, and I

remember that he said he was off colour and instead of having a pipe he would smoke a cigarette. At the time both Mr. Martin and I were working at high pressure on some sales of a Capt. Hope and this was probably the reason of his being below par. Mr. Martin and I discussed general office organisation, and I remember telling him that I was under-staffed. I also was feeling the effects of hard work. It was light when we began tea, but it soon became necessary for me to light the gas, and as I did so the globe came off and fell which caused it to break. Mr. Martin left about 6 p.m. and drove home in his own car. All the food which Martin consumed was prepared by Miss Pearce and was waiting for us when we entered the drawing room; and either she or the maid brought the tea and hot water in when we had taken our seats. Miss Pearce had previously asked if the food (which was subsequently placed on the table) would be satisfactory, and I had said 'Yes'.

The following morning I went to Mr. Martin's office to get various documents relating to Capt. Hope's sale which was to be completed on the 2nd November. It was a big property sale in which he was acting for several purchasers. I was told by one of his clerks (I cannot remember which) that he had been taken ill. I think now that it was Preene as I have a recollection of him saying that Dr. Hincks had been called and had said that he thought Mr. Martin was suffering from jaundice.

Mr. Martin's illness was causing great inconvenience as the completions were fixed for the following Wednesday and there was a great deal to be done. I sent a message to Mr. Martin by one of his clerks (I do not remember which) and said that if I could assist in any possible way and he would authorise his clerks that I would carry the matter through if he were not well enough. The next thing that I remember was that as he was not down at his office on Saturday I called at his house on the Sunday morning after Church. I saw Mrs. Martin and she told me that he had been very sick but was better and would be down at his office on Monday. It was not necessary for Mr. Martin to accept my offer of assistance as he was able to attend his office and carry through the completions by the stated date. After Mr. Martin's illness he told me that he had been very sick and that he had had a thorough clean out. Prior to his illness I had chaffed him about his practice of motoring to and from his office saying that if he did not take walking exercise he would be ill. I always walk to my office, not possessing a car.

I am continually meeting Mr. Martin professionally and he and his wife have a dinner invitation to my house when a date can be fixed.

The first time I purchased arsenic was in 1914. At this time I came across a recipe for weed killer consisting of caustic soda and arsenic which was very much cheaper than the liquid weed killer which my gardener had previously been in the habit of purchasing I therefore purchased arsenic and caustic soda from Mr. Davies Chemist of Hay and signed the book. I remember him telling me that the arsenic had to be mixed with charcoal and he mixed it accordingly. I made the weed killer at my house by boiling the caustic soda and arsenic in an old petrol tin. I think I put in all I purchased. It might have been in the proportion of equal parts of each but I don't remember. I think Miss Pearce will remember the preparation. It was all used in the garden as a weed killer. I have always had considerable trouble with weeds on the path of my vegetable garden.

The purchase of ½ lb of arsenic in June 1919, was for the same purpose and was used in exactly the same way.

The liquid and powder weed killer were purchased to my order by Jay of Castle Gardens, Hay who attended to my garden at that time. I don't even know how much was purchased and I never saw it. I believe it was kept in the stable.

In January 1921 I made a further purchase of ¼ lb of arsenic at Mr. Davies shop. A small amount of this was used as a weed killer after being boiled with caustic soda by myself. It was not a success which explains why I have some left at my house. When I purchased this arsenic it was mixed with charcoal. I am keeping this to make a further trial later on. I remember talking to Mr Taylor the Bank Manager of Hay respecting my recipe for weed killer. I remember being pleased at being able to make my own weed killer at a much cheaper rate than the prepared article which after the war was very dear and I could not afford it. This last preparation I carried out myself as before by boiling the arsenic with caustic soda in a petrol can. Although I have no motor car I use petrol for a petrol gas installation.

From the 2nd Sept to the 20th Sept 1921 as far as I can trace I did not leave Hay, but on the 21st Sept. 1921, I went motoring with Mr Lee, Surveyor of Taxes of Derby, who took myself and my son to Bath where my son was returning to school. We returned on the Sunday following.

I don't take chocolates myself and have not purchased any

of them since I bought a small box for my late wife in August 1920. These I bought in Hay but I can't remember the shop. They were certainly not Fullers, which I was of the impression were not procurable in Hay.

During the period between the 2nd and 20th Sept. 1921, I was in Hay transacting business at my office and residing at my house, I did not leave the town. I may have called on friends socially but I do not remember.

I am unable to throw any light upon the finding of arsenic in Mr. Martin's urine or as to the cause of his illness after having tea with me on the 26th October 1921. I did not touch the food he ate in any way and partook myself of what was on the same dish. If arsenic got into the food, I cannot account for it being there.

The cupboard where I keep the arsenic at my house contains boot cleaning materials and is unlocked. Nobody in the house so far as I know is aware of the presence of arsenic in the house. This arsenic I speak of is the only poison in my possession anywhere excepting of course any contained in medicine. I have a medicine chest in a bedroom.

I make this statement quite voluntarily and without being questioned.

As soon as Armstrong had read his statement and signed it, Weaver spoke to him: 'I am now charging you with administering arsenic to Mr. Martin on October 26th 1921, and you are under arrest. Empty your pockets on your desk.'

Armstrong was stunned. Before he could move Sergeant Sharp approached him and felt in his pockets for the contents, which he placed on the blotter on the desk. Armstrong was dumbfounded as he lifted his arms to allow the officer's fingers to pry into his pockets, removing the letters that he had placed in them that morning. The small bundle of his intimate personal belongings was arrayed before him, set upon a piece of brown paper that covered them but was not tied. He was then asked to sit in a chair in the middle of the room while the officers searched the drawers of his desk and began to examine closely the contents of the room. Sergeant Sharp was asked to go downstairs and carry out a search there.

Armstrong could not believe the position that he found himself in. There he was sitting on a chair in the middle of his room, with policemen rooting through his office, and he had been arrested on a charge of attempting to poison Martin. He looked out of the window and saw Martin walking along the street. Surely there had to be some mistake!

After some minutes had passed he asked Crutchett if he could have his handkerchief, his pipe and tobacco, which were given to him. He then asked if he could sit at his desk and go through some business letters that were there. Crutchett granted his request and stationed a constable to sit on the other side of the desk to keep an eye on him. Armstrong then noticed in absolute horror that caught in the flap of one of the envelopes was a packet of white arsenic which remained from his gardening experiments. At that moment Crutchett heard the rustle of paper and turned round. He saw that Armstrong was looking through the contents of the brown wrapper. He stopped him and moved him away from the desk and, tying up the brown paper parcel, handed it to Weaver.

After the most thorough search of his office Armstrong was taken to Hay Police Station. They locked up his office and then went to Mayfield to interview the astonished Miss Pearce and to conduct a search of Mayfield, politely but firmly refusing Armstrong's invitation to show them where he kept the arsenic and his gardening file, which contained the recipe for weedkiller.

Armstrong had been kept in his office that day for over six hours without food or refreshment of any kind. It was late in the afternoon when he was taken to a cell, which contained the hard mattress that had been slept upon by many vagrants, thieves and petty criminals who had passed through his court. When the cell door was shut and locked, it is difficult to imagine the horror and injury he must have felt. Here he was, an officer and a gentleman, solicitor, leading Freemason, rector's warden and clerk to the justices – in short, a pillar of the community – banged up in his own police cell, on a charge of attempted murder.

Armstrong could not sleep that night. He was desperate to see his solicitor and arranged for his clerk Arthur Phillips to contact Tom Matthews of Hereford to see him the following day. The news of his arrest hit the town like a bombshell. There was no other topic of conversation in any house or pub for miles around, and the news travelled like a bush fire. Major Armstrong has been arrested; it cannot be true!

THE TRIAL OF
HERBERT ROWSE ARMSTRONG

13

Tom Matthews of Hereford arrived to see Armstrong the next day and was dumbfounded to find his fellow solicitor in the cell of Hay Police Station. Armstrong gave him details of his arrest, and mentioned that there was some white arsenic at Mayfield that he had not reported to the police.

Matthews then went to Mayfield and saw Miss Pearce, who was in a state of shock and confusion. He entered Armstrong's study and asked her to open all the drawers in the bureau where Armstrong had told him the arsenic was kept. The drawers were opened one by one, but no arsenic was found. In the evening of that day Matthews had a conference with Ronald Bosanquet, junior counsel, who directed him that he had an absolute duty to believe his client and defend him accordingly.

The following morning Armstrong was escorted into the little courtroom at Hay which he knew so well, but on this occasion instead of taking his normal comfortable seat at the feet of the eight presiding magistrates, he was led to the dock. The deputy chief constable of Hereford gave evidence of his arrest and announced that in reply to the charge Armstrong had said: 'I am quite innocent.' No further evidence was given and Armstrong was remanded in custody to Worcester Gaol for one week.

A large crowd waited outside for a glimpse of him and when he stepped from the court to the waiting taxi to be conveyed to Worcester he was loudly cheered. A woman in the crowd cried out, 'Three cheers for Mr Armstrong', and the people took it up lustily. The applause was in stark contrast to the hatred expressed by the inhabitants of Kidwelly against Harold Greenwood.

Later that day the grave of Mrs Armstrong was opened. Standing by the open grave and an old yew tree were a police constable and grave digger, and at the gate by the roadside another policeman awaited the arrival of the pathologist, Dr Bernard Spilsbury. Shortly before 7 p.m. the lights of a motor car could be seen ascending the winding hill. Led by police officers carrying hurricane lamps, Dr Spilsbury and Detective Inspector Crutchett made their way to the graveside. Standing around the open grave, the party watched the coffin being brought slowly to the surface. A procession was then formed, led by a police officer with a lantern, and the coffin, borne on a bier by two policemen, was carried to the gateway, and then across the road to a small white-washed cottage whose windows had been covered in sacking. It was an eerie scene.

Spilsbury returned the following morning to begin his macabre work and in the presence of Dr Hincks, Deputy Chief Constable Weaver, Chief Inspector Crutchett and Dr Ainslie for the defence, the coffin was opened. Katharine's partially decomposed body was dissected and her vital organs removed. Spilsbury then left for London armed with sections of the liver, kidneys, spleen and several other tissues contained in sixteen glass bottles.

The inquest into Katharine's death was opened in the afternoon in Cusop school. After the jury were sworn in and a foreman appointed they were ordered to view the body. They filed out of the old school, past the lychgate, and entered the cottage with its bare unpapered walls. On a small table in the centre of the room, lay Katharine's coffin. Each man, with head reverently bowed advanced, and after a quick glance at the almost unrecognizable features of the occupant passed out again into the darkness and the snow. It was a scene not likely to be forgotten by the participants for the remainder of their days.

The court was then reconstituted in the schoolroom and the coroner, Mr Southall, charged the jurors with their duty of ascertaining the cause of death. He told them to put personalities out of their minds. He explained that in the normal course of events inquests were held immediately after a death, if one was deemed necessary. In this case, however, he had made an order for the exhumation of Katharine's body, but it did not follow that he accepted responsibility for the truth of the representations made to him before he made the order. He explained that it was a matter for the jury to listen to the evidence, without prejudice, and that he would be the judge of any legal questions that should arise. Their duty, he went on, was to decide questions of fact.

He called on one witness to prove the identity of the remains and stated that he would formally adjourn the proceedings until 24 January, when the inquest would be resumed.

14

Sir Archibald Bodkin, the director of public prosecutions, had at his disposal a unique medical team that consisted of the pathologist to dissect, the chemist to analyse and the physician to interpret the results. Dr Bernard Spilsbury, Mr John Webster and Sir William Willcox were a close band of men who always appeared for the Crown and never for the defence. 'They travelled together, stayed at the same hotels, compared their notes and discussed the evidence that they would have to give.'[4] The way they presented their evidence always gave the impression that their opinion was unanimous.

Three days after the exhumation Webster had completed his analysis of the packet of white powder found among Armstrong's letters. Bodkin made immediate contact with Willcox:

> ... when you recollect the almost importune repetitions of invitations by Armstrong to Mr Martin to come and take tea at his office, and the furnishing recently of tea cups and saucers at Armstrong's instance at his office and directions given that if anybody came to tea scones were to be provided, the significance of the composition of this little packet is obvious. I thought you would probably be interested in at once learning of these initial facts.

Willcox's evidence for the Crown was crucial in securing Armstrong's conviction. An expert may only give an opinion on issues in a case when the evidence, and the inferences to be drawn from the evidence, are directly relevant to his or her specialized knowledge and experience. The director of public prosecutions drew his own conclusions about the packet of arsenic found on Armstrong, by linking that packet with Armstrong's invitations to tea, inferring that Armstrong intended to poison a scone and hand it to Martin. Willcox will have read this letter and made up his mind that Armstrong was a poisoner and that the evidence required of him was to help secure a conviction. His reports substantiate that this was the case. The director of public prosecutions had in fact influenced his expert witness to give an opinion commensurate with the view of the prosecution. Bodkin was later criticized for being too active in the investigative or police role in proceedings; in fact he always took a vigorous role in his cases and was 'not content to instruct Counsel formally. He went to the scene of the crime and told his staff the line they must follow'.[5]

The prosecution team of eminent experts was not impartial. Its function was to help the prosecution win its case and they became personally involved in its preparation. Bodkin suggested that Willcox should have a word with Dr Hincks, who was even more emotionally involved in the case than his London superiors. Hincks was, of course, in a vulnerable position. He had certified Katharine's death as resulting from natural causes and he had been proved wrong, for there was now no doubt whatever that Katharine had died from arsenical poisoning. He stood to be criticized, however unjustly, for erring in his diagnosis of her final illness. But if he had to admit a mistake he should never have lost his impartiality and sided with the prosecution.

On 7 January Webster indicated to Bodkin that two grains of arsenic had been found in Katharine's liver and kidneys. Despite having this information, Bodkin allowed the case on the attempted murder of Martin to continue. His tactics in this respect were damaging to the defence. They had no idea that the more serious charge of murder would be laid against Armstrong, who was now languishing in Worcester prison with his practice in tatters and his family in turmoil.

Bodkin had only limited evidence to justify Armstrong's arrest on the attempted poisoning charge. This consisted of Martin's urine sample which contained arsenic, backed up by Martin's account of his sickness. He also had the box of chocolates containing arsenic and he fervently hoped that the police investigation would uncover proof that his suspect had bought and sent them. Crutchett of the Yard was asked to scrutinize Armstrong's call book in an attempt to discover which of the days between 2 and 20 September Armstrong had been away from his office. He found that only two of these days could not be accounted for: the 17th and the 19th. Armstrong's clerk, Arthur Phillips, produced a letter which Armstrong had signed on the 19th, demonstrating that although Armstrong had had no appointments on that day he had been in the office. The 17th was a Saturday and Crutchett discovered that Armstrong had been at Mayfield. Crutchett reckoned it was possible that the chocolates might have been sent to Armstrong through the post. He made enquiries of the postman, who stated that he had no recollection of delivering any parcel between those dates. The station master searched his inland parcel delivery sheets and could not trace the arrival of a parcel, and he confirmed that although Armstrong frequently travelled by train, there were no bookings until 21 September. Further enquiries from Mr Madigan, from whom Armstrong hired his car, revealed that no journey had been made between the key dates. The housemaid, Mrs Price, recalled that on 20 September there had been a dinner party at Mayfield. The next day, Armstrong had left Hay with Mr Lee, the inspector of taxes, to travel to Bath to return Sonny to his school; Armstrong was then away from Hay for three days. In short, Crutchett had drawn a blank.

Bodkin did not know quite what to make of the singular lack of evidence to connect Armstrong with the chocolates, but his concern had been suspended when he was told that the packet of white powder found in Armstrong's pockets was white arsenic. He knew that it was illegal to sell white arsenic in England and Wales and suspected an illicit purchase had been made when Armstrong was abroad.

Tom Matthews had very little time to complete his enquiries before the hearing resumed. He called again at Mayfield on 2 January and informed Miss Pearce of the outcome of the formal remand. He told her that the magistrates would begin to hear evidence at the court house on 9 January.

Miss Pearce was an elderly lady, with a rather poor memory, and she was generally nervous and excitable. When the police called to see her after arresting Armstrong, the effect on her can better be imagined than described. When the police left Mayfield on that day, her mind was thoroughly confused. Almost as soon as the arrest was announced, Mayfield was bombarded by pressmen, who were ready at any time to take advantage of its unfortunate occupants. Matthews agreed to arrange for Miss Pearce's removal, along with the three children, to a secret address in Hereford. However, before this could be arranged, three police officers again visited Mayfield and subjected her to a further examination. It was not until 6 January that the occupants were safely away from the house, which was then locked up.

Back at his office Matthews was inundated with calls and letters from all over the country. It seemed that everyone who wrote was as anxious as possible to help the defence, and asked him to convey support to his client in his darkest hour. The news was scarcely believable. Every true friend of Armstrong – and he had many – felt that he could hardly imagine, let alone execute, such a crime.

Matthews answered all the letters and began a correspondence with those that he felt could help Armstrong's case. He also arranged to deliver letters from the children to their father, which even after this long period of time make pitiful reading. Eleanor was by now fourteen years of age, and was fully aware of the charge brought against him. She wrote with words of support to 'My own dear loving Father' and Margaret sent him little pictures, scrawled on the back of envelopes.

Of vital importance was Arthur Chevalier, who initially pledged his wholehearted support for his great friend Armstrong, and to whom Matthews looked for help. Equally supportive were the ministers in the town: the Revd de Winton, vicar of Hay; Revd Buchanan, from Cusop; and the previous rector of Cusop, Revd Stredder. These three men were quite convinced that Armstrong was innocent and would soon be released. No one at that time believed that the charge of attempted murder (of Martin) would be sustained. No one, that is, except Sir Archibald Bodkin, Sir William Willcox, and the instigators of the arrest, Fred Davies, Laura Davies and Dr Tom Hincks.

15

The case that Mr St John Micklethwait, counsel for the Crown, opened at Hay Magistrates Court on 9 January 1922, was neither fully nor properly prepared. As a result he asked for lengthy adjournments throughout the proceedings, which were not concluded until 17 February 1922. Upon that date Armstrong was committed for trial.

The committal proceedings were not only extraordinary in the way they were drawn out, but also in the way that the murder charge was presented on the back of the attempted murder charge. The Crown should have delayed the committal proceedings until all the evidence had been obtained from the prosecution witnesses. As it happened, the evidence was presented piecemeal as it was collected, which was extremely prejudicial to Armstrong. All the evidence was reported verbatim in both the local and the national newspapers. The case itself achieved such notoriety that it is unlikely that any adult in Herefordshire would not have read every single detail of the extraordinary happenings in the little town of Hay.

On 9 January, when Armstrong was brought from Worcester Prison, he had no idea that the capital charge of murdering his wife was actively being considered. Neither did the eager crowd who tried to force its way into the little courtroom which was already filled to capacity. For the first three days of the hearing evidence relating to the attempted murder charge was given to the astonished magistrates, and at the end of each day Armstrong was allowed to sleep in the cell in Hay, hoping beyond hope that he would soon be released and allowed to rejoin his practice and family. At the end of the third day, the evidence against him was looking distinctly feeble and Matthews hinted that he might make a bail application. Evidence had just been given of the receipt of the box of chocolates and Dorothy Martin's illness at the dinner party. At this point Micklethwait addressed the court and told the magistrates that upon Armstrong's arrest a packet of white arsenic had been found in his pocket. His timing was superb, as he managed to associate the arsenic found in Armstrong's pockets with that lodged in the chocolates. In the process he effectively scuppered any chance of Armstrong's release. At the end of the fourth day Matthews made an impassioned plea for the case against his client to continue without delay and asked, in the event of a further remand, that Armstrong might remain at Hay. But his plea was rejected and the case was adjourned for a further week. Armstrong was returned to Worcester Prison.

On Monday 19 January the court reconvened. As if the whole proceedings were not bizarre enough the chief constable of Hereford was given a seat behind the Bench and there he sat in full uniform. Micklethwait was now beginning to enjoy himself and he proceeded to announce that Armstrong had now been charged with the murder of his wife. Without waiting for him to finish his address, there was a stampede from the room by reporters anxious to get the news to the four quarters of the kingdom. The *Hereford Times* issued a special edition on the day, which was snapped up in its thousands.

Micklethwait spoke for an hour, outlining the additional evidence he proposed to call in connection with the murder charge. He considered in detail the events leading up to Katharine's death and laid great emphasis on the fact that her symptoms were similar to those suffered by Mr Martin. He described the contents of Armstrong's diary which related to his holiday on the Continent, with its attendant dances, concerts and women. He told the Court that within twenty-four hours of his return from the Continent Armstrong had discussed marriage with another woman.

Micklethwait mentioned that one of the witnesses to Katharine's second will, made in July 1920, would testify that she had not signed her name in Katharine's presence. He went on,

If that evidence is true, the witnessing clause is a lie, and no one knew it better than Mr Armstrong. If that is so, that Will is not worth the paper it is written on. By that Will Mr Armstrong was not only defrauding his wife but robbing his own children as well.

He then stated that Armstrong had venereal disease. He would demonstrate that it had been contracted when his wife was at the asylum. 'Therefore it seems doubly strange that at a time of this sort he should seem anxious to have his wife back. One would think that that would be the last thing a man would do.'

He concluded his opening statement thus:

I have sketched the events of Mrs Armstrong's death, but one cannot leave it there, one must see what happened afterwards. We find that in the Summer of 1921 Armstrong comes back again. In cases of this character, unfortunately, you find that a man having once succeeded in carrying out one, would be emboldened to make a second attempt. But whatever the influence, whether he was influenced by hatred or financial ruin, or any other reason, I suggest that on the evidence before you there were two attempts made on Martin to take his life. Is it a mere coincidence that during these ten months in a little place like Cusop you have three clear cases of arsenical poisoning? You find, first of all, Mrs Armstrong suffering from arsenical poisoning. Is it a coincidence that in her body are found three grains of arsenic, and that one person – the only person who is going to gain any benefit from Mrs Armstrong's death – is the prisoner? The next thing is the box of chocolates. That box of chocolates was clearly doped with poison for the purpose of injuring or killing Martin. There can be no question with regard to the intention; and is it a mere coincidence that the powder that was found in the chocolates was white arsenic – pure white arsenic, which chemists by law are bound to tint or colour when they sell it? And is it a coincidence that the packet which was found in Armstrong's coat on arrest was white arsenic? Is it a mere coincidence that this deadly poison contained in these chocolates sent to Martin was precisely the same poison as that which was contained in the packet which Armstrong was carrying on his arrest? Is it a coincidence that Martin was nearly poisoned to death after taking tea with Armstrong – that a 1/33rd part of a grain of arsenic was found in his urine?

These are the links in the chain of evidence on which I am going to ask your Worships to commit the prisoner for trial on both charges – the charge of murdering Mrs Armstrong, and on the charge of attempting to murder Mr Martin.

Before he called his first witness Micklethwait mentioned that in his view all the evidence relating to the attempted murder charge was material to the murder charge and vice versa. He asked that evidence (linked to the first charge) already taken from the witnesses be read over to them. The reason was that the prosecution might want to have those depositions read over to the trial judge at the Assizes, and that they could only be read if they were at this stage formally made to apply to both charges. Finally, he concluded that from now on the evidence tendered would apply to both charges.

In this way the Crown inextricably linked two completely different events. It had associated the death of Katharine Armstrong in February 1921 with the sickness of Mr Martin in October of that year. The connection had been cemented by the find of white arsenic in Armstrong's pocket combined with that of the white arsenic found in the chocolates.

It was clear that Matthews had not anticipated this argument, and when his turn came to address the court he meekly pointed out that it was important for him to be presented with a list of what had been taken from the prisoner and from Mayfield. Matthews wanted to know whether or not the police had found the white arsenic at Mayfield. If they had, they were deliberately concealing it from the defence and if they had not, what had become of it? The absence of this arsenic perplexed him and went to the root of the defendant's credibility, for Armstrong had insisted that the arsenic purchased from Fred Davies's chemist's shop was white and not coloured; yet the evidence that Davies and his assistant had given was that it had been coloured in compliance with the Poisons Act. Micklethwait replied that Matthews would be granted his request.

16

Before the murder charge was announced there had been frantic activity by the police in the town and a host of new witnesses entered the frame. Of crucial importance were the three nurses who had looked after Katharine during her final illness. Equally important were witnesses who could give evidence of motive, which on the face of it appeared to be so lacking, for everyone who had any personal knowledge of the couple declared them to be both close and affectionate.

There are two time-honoured motives in the murder of a wife by her husband – money and another woman – and these were the motives that were fully explored by the Crown in their searching enquiries into the life of Armstrong. Unfortunately evidence for those motives was not readily available, and the Crown had to dig very deep. Despite the fact that Armstrong's affairs were in a muddle and that his costings book had not been written up for months, the police could find no evidence that he was insolvent. On the contrary his various accounts at the local banks were in credit and his client base was increasing, as evidenced by the Clifford sales, which had been successfully completed before his arrest. If a desire for his wife's money was a motive, there was no evidence that he needed it or that he had used it, despite the fiasco over the Velinewydd sales, and the undoubted fact that Williams Vaughan owed him a great deal of money, later calculated to exceed £7,000.

Notwithstanding his solvency the prosecution noted that Katharine's last will, made in July 1920, was in Armstrong's own handwriting and that it left him all her money and appointed him sole executor. They had taken a photograph of that will and had requested signatures of Katharine to see if her signature had been forged. Bodkin decided that this enquiry was not worth pursuing. They had arranged to interview the maid, Lily Candy, who was one of the witnesses to it, and she told them that she could not remember signing the will, even though there was no disputing that she had. However, she remembered signing a document in Armstrong's study and at his request, but not in the presence of Mrs Armstrong. She gave evidence to this effect. Thus, despite the fact that Armstrong had not transferred any of his wife's securities into his name and had maintained her account in Teignmouth, the prosecution decided to attack the validity of the will itself.

Bessie Friend was called to give evidence to establish that Katharine had not intended that her 1920 will should stand. Micklethwait spent nearly half a day arguing that the letters written to her by Katharine from the asylum should be admitted in evidence to demonstrate this intention, but the Bench overruled him on the grounds that they were hearsay. However, Micklethwait was not to be outdone and arranged for Bessie to be shown the 1920 will in the corridor outside the little courtroom. She was then recalled and told the court that she did not believe the signature of her late sister was genuine. The same tactic was employed in connection with Miss Hutchins, who had been a nurse companion to Katharine during the war and who had not seen her for two years before her death. As such it was recorded on the depositions that the signature was a forgery.

In this respect Micklethwait had exceeded his brief and acted entirely on his own initiative, as his instructions were to adduce evidence that the will had not been properly witnessed by one of the two attesting witnesses, namely Lily Candy, thereby making it valueless and an indictment against the prisoner. Lily Candy's evidence was later fully tested at the trial.

Upon his arrest several letters from Marion Gale were found in Armstrong's pockets. The letters indicated that marriage had been discussed but not agreed upon. Mrs Gale had been rigorously interviewed by the police and was distraught at having to give evidence for the prosecution; but when she did, she demonstrated that she was a woman of eminent respectability and virtue, far removed from the scarlet woman which the prosecution hoped that they would reveal. She arrived in the courtroom heavily veiled, and both prosecution and defence spared her the ignominy of having to state her name. She was reported only as 'Madam X'. There could be no doubt that whatever fuelled the relationship between Armstrong and Marion, it was not one of unbridled passion.

The two motives of coveting Katharine's money and wanting to marry Marion Gale were later described by the defence at the trial as 'ludicrous' and 'fantastic', but they were the only motives that the prosecution could find.

To augment these weak motives the prosecution embarked on a character assassination of the prisoner. After the housemaid, Harriet Price, had given her evidence on the attempted murder charge she was reinterviewed by the police and questioned about compensation money which she had been awarded as a result of the premature death of her farm labourer husband. After his death she had consulted Matthews, who advised her to apply to the court to apportion the award, which had to be shared between her and her late husband's mother. She then consulted Armstrong who acted for her and eventually the money was apportioned in the ratio of £225 to her and £75 to her mother-in-law. A cheque for the amount was paid to Armstrong on her behalf. She then started to work for Armstrong at Mayfield and asked him for £20. He gave her £17 saying that certain costs were due to him and that the balance had been invested on her behalf. The whole matter was greatly exaggerated by the prosecution in an attempt to prejudice Armstrong.

When Micklethwait opened the case on the attempted murder charge he mentioned that Armstrong was suffering from a disease, which everyone in court concluded was venereal. He confirmed this when he opened the case on the murder charge. He then addressed the court and explained that although this information had emanated from Dr Hincks, he wanted to make it quite clear that Hincks had only disclosed it after making a strong protest, and that Hincks might try to rely on professional privilege when he was later called to give evidence. Apart from this statement being untrue, for Hincks had readily disclosed to the police the reason why he was treating Armstrong, the only grounds for declaring it at all were to stigmatize the prisoner. Once again Micklethwait had cleverly exceeded his brief.

Dr Hincks was regarded by the prosecution as the most crucial witness – a belief, exhibited by his self-important demeanour, that he shared. Hincks professed outward friendship for Armstrong, and indeed he had partaken of his hospitality on many occasions. Despite this, he appeared anxious to do as much harm as he possibly could, introducing into his evidence unsolicited and extraneous statements that would clearly injure Armstrong as much as possible. He was not content merely to give evidence, but chose to air his opinions on the actions of his former friend.

He took particular care to express his views about arsenical poisoning, but he never detected anything resembling poison throughout any examination of Mrs Armstrong. It was quite obvious from his wording that he had seen the reports of the prosecution medical team, and as a result ventilated his views about arsenical poisoning as regards both Mrs Armstrong and Martin. The echo is particularly strong when he expressed the view that Martin's illness was caused by (not consistent with), his taking a possible fatal dose.

Hincks was not called by the Crown for a very considerable time, despite the fact that he lived within 200 yards of the police court. Throughout the long-drawn-out proceedings Matthews tried his very best to point out that important witnesses were available on the spot, but the prosecution maintained that despite 'superhuman' efforts it was not possible to obtain vital witnesses, and used this excuse to obtain long remands.

Hincks was not called until 25 January, even though the two reports of Willcox and Spilsbury were available before that date and Hincks had been in close touch with the prosecution from the early part of December. In fact Bodkin surprised everyone when he turned up in court on 12 January and met Hincks. Bodkin even went as far as writing to Willcox on 13 January, stating, '… I daresay you would think it right to have an opportunity of discussing the matter with Dr Hincks before any scientific evidence is given and this I will also bear in mind.' Further comment on this point is needless.

Hincks was anxious to impress everyone with his skill as a

doctor, despite the fact that his evidence contradicted that of Dr Townsend; but what was equally clear is that he kept no record in writing of any symptoms of which he spoke with such particularity. Bearing in mind that this man was extremely busy, it is difficult to believe that he could remember such details as the condition of the pulse, when he could not remember whether or not he had taken the patient's blood pressure. The evidence of Dr Hincks was deeply suspect. The fact is that when the prosecution team of London doctors gave evidence, Hincks spent the day in court sitting on the bench next to them.

On 9 February, before the court opened at Hay, Matthews again visited Mayfield, along with his managing clerk, Chivers. They both went into the study and immediately found the recipe for the weedkiller in the file marked 'Garden', in exactly the place that Armstrong said it would be located. They then looked at the bureau. Matthews pulled open the drawer that Armstrong stated contained the arsenic. It appeared to be empty, just as it had been when he had first looked at it on 1 January. He then put his hand inside the open drawer and felt some paper at the top of it. He managed to dislodge it and was astounded to see that it consisted of a blue paper wrapping tied with string. He took it out, opened it and found within it a wrapping of white paper. He turned the paper over and saw the label bearing the words, 'Arsenic, Poison, J.L. Davies & Son, Pharmacists, 7 High Town Hay.' He did the only thing possible at the time. He replaced the packet in the same drawer, exactly as he had found it, locked the study and went back to Hay, where he was due to appear in court in half an hour.

For Matthews the find of the packet of white arsenic was momentous, because it was now clear that Armstrong had been telling him the truth after all about his purchase from Davies. He was greatly relieved, as Armstrong's story fell into place and he could now accept that the packet of white arsenic found in his pocket had come from the same source. From that moment onwards he had no doubt that Armstrong was an innocent man.

When Matthews left the court he made immediate arrangements to speak to Bosanquet (Armstrong's junior counsel) to tell him about his discovery, which, the more he thought about it, seemed to vindicate Armstrong completely. He arranged a consultation the following day at Hereford. The following Monday he travelled to London to speak with his leading counsel Sir Henry Curtis Bennett. Both counsel advised him to call at Mayfield with Dr Ainslie and have him remove the packet, analyse it and say nothing to the police. Matthews did as requested.

On Friday 17 February the magistrates convened for the last time. Armstrong arrived as usual from Worcester and bowed to the familiar faces of his bench of magistrates, who again sat alongside the chief constable of Hereford. He looked round at the little courtroom that he knew so well, apparently unperturbed, but aware of the presence of the unfamiliar faces of Spilsbury, Willcox, and Webster, who had been summoned to give evidence against him and who sat in the well of the court alongside his foremost accuser and former friend, Dr Hincks.

Micklethwait rose and addressed the magistrates, saying that he hoped he would not detain them long. He then called Spilsbury to give evidence. Spilsbury, wearing a black morning coat, explained to the hushed court that he had conducted the post-mortem of Katharine's body and had removed certain parts of it for analysis. He commented that the liver, kidneys, stomach, intestines and uterus were unusually well preserved taking into account the time which had elapsed since death. The cause of death he gave as acute arsenical poisoning. He read his report, which had been handed to Matthews on the previous day. After concluding his evidence, he replied to a question posed by the chairman of the bench to the effect that the arsenic tonic given to the deceased at Barnwood would not have left any trace except, possibly, in her hair and nails.

John Webster then gave the results of his analysis of Martin's sample and confirmed that it contained 1/33 of a grain of arsenic in 17½ ounces of urine. Asked about the chocolates, he produced two of them mounted in plasticine, exciting much attention. He explained that a cylindrical hole, nearly half an inch long, had been bored into the two chocolates and that the holes had been filled with just over two grains of white arsenic. He confirmed that the remaining thirty chocolates from the box had not been tampered with.

He was then asked about the sixteen glass jars that he had received from Spilsbury and confirmed that over three grains of arsenic in total were present in the organs, and that wood shavings from the coffin as well as samples of turf and soil in the grave also contained arsenic. He produced the envelope found on Armstrong's person and confirmed it contained 3¾ grains of white arsenic. He stated that the tin found in Armstrong's study contained nearly two ounces of coloured arsenic and that a bottle marked poison contained a strong alkali solution of arsenic. He said he had tested the contents of a large number of bottles which contained or had contained homeopathic medicines and confirmed that only two of them contained small quantities of arsenic. The chairman, mindful that the chocolates contained white arsenic, as did the packet found on Armstrong, asked whether it was possible to dissolve the charcoal from coloured arsenic. Webster replied that although it was not an easy matter it could be done.

Out of the three experts Sir William Willcox was the one whom Armstrong had to fear the most and it was fitting that his evidence culminated the ten days of evidence which, at Micklethwait's request, had spanned six weeks. Willcox was Spilsbury's senior by only five years but his wizened little face made him look much older than Spilsbury's forty-five years. He took the stand and told the court that he had very wide experience of poisoning cases and particularly cases of arsenical poisoning. He confirmed that he had considered the evidence of Dr Townsend and Dr Hincks and that in his opinion Mrs Armstrong was suffering from acute arsenical poisoning before she went to Barnwood. He said he had weighed up the reports of Dr Spilsbury and Mr Webster and that in his opinion the cause of Mrs Armstrong's death was acute arsenical poisoning. He had no doubt that a fatal dose must have been taken within twenty-four hours of her death. He was careful not to criticize Hincks's death certificate, saying that it was correct from the point of view of the symptoms, but that they were not due to natural causes. Hincks, who was sitting a few feet away, must have been gratified to hear those remarks. When asked about the illness of Dorothy Martin, after eating a chocolate at a meal, he said that her symptoms were entirely consistent with acute arsenical poisoning. When asked about Mr Webster's urine analysis he said that the proportion of arsenic in the urine was larger than would be consistent with a medicinal dose and indicated that a poisonous quantity was taken on the 'Wednesday previous'. He confirmed that the cause of Martin's illness was acute arsenical poisoning.

When Willcox stepped down from the witness stand, Micklethwait addressed the bench and told them that his case was concluded and he invited them to commit the prisoner for trial to the Hereford Assizes on the charge of murder of his wife and on the charge of attempted murder of Oswald Martin. The Bench retired for five minutes and when they returned, they asked Armstrong if he wished to call any evidence in his own defence. The solicitor, who had sat silently throughout the whole proceedings, stood up very erect and in a clear, calm voice replied, 'I am not guilty of either charge, sir. I reserve my defence.' The chairman then said that he thought the evidence sufficient to warrant a committal to the assizes 'or other special place' where the trial would take place, and as the court rose Micklethwait thanked the Bench for their courtesy during the long-drawn-out hearing.

Armstrong rose and was escorted from the dock of his little courtroom – the courtroom which he would never see again.

17

Tom Matthews now had to prepare his brief for the defence and collate his team of experts. Sir Henry Curtis Bennett, who had been chosen as leading counsel, was at the height of his fame and had already appeared in forty-eight murder trials both for the prosecution and for the defence. Later he would defend Ronald True and Edith Thompson.[6] He was a brilliant advocate and his opening speech, which lasted over three hours, was delivered without a note in front of him. He was overweight, well connected and recently knighted for his services to the Bar.

However, in many respects he was an unfortunate choice for Armstrong. He accepted that Katharine had died of arsenical poisoning and knew that if his client had not poisoned her, she must have taken the fatal dose herself. If that was the case, she could have taken it accidentally, believing it to be something other than arsenic, or she could have taken it on purpose, intending to commit suicide. Curtis Bennett realized that no direct evidence existed and that out of all the circumstantial evidence so painstakingly assembled by the prosecution, the Martin evidence was the most damaging. He meticulously researched the obscure principles whereby similar fact evidence could be admitted and realized that attention centred upon the purpose for which the evidence was tendered. He noted that the possible purposes of admitting the evidence were put into categories: to prove intent, system or identification or to rebut defences of accident or innocent association; and that a tendency existed to admit the evidence if it fitted into one of these categories. He believed that on the facts there was no possibility that the alleged murder attempt on Martin's life could prove an intent to murder Katharine or provide evidence of a system of events and considered that the only possible ground for admitting the evidence at all would be to refute a possible defence of accident. He was convinced that if he stated to the court at the earliest opportunity that it would never be part of the defence case that Katharine had poisoned herself accidentally, the Martin evidence was inadmissible and that if it was admitted and Armstrong was convicted, an appeal on a point of law would succeed. Having made the vital decision to rule out the possibility that Katharine may have poisoned herself accidentally he presented the defence on the basis that she might have committed suicide, but at the same time distanced himself from that possibility, declaring that it was not up to him to prove that this was the case. He simply challenged the prosecution to prove beyond reasonable doubt that the prisoner had administered the arsenic to her.

The problem with Curtis Bennett was that although he was without doubt one of the most able advocates of the day he must have realized the inadequacies of his defence and known that his opposition would prosecute sternly and relentlessly. His decision not to attack the Martin evidence was a crucial mistake, because if he had made an issue of the chocolates and brought to the notice of the jury the inadequacies of the evidence, which failed to connect Armstrong with them, the whole hearing would have been transformed. As it happened he refused to attack the Martin evidence in any form. In addition, he failed to call any character witnesses for Armstrong; failed to call Eleanor to give evidence; failed to show that other gardeners had poisoned individual weeds in the same way that Armstrong had done; failed to call for an analysis of the weeds that Armstrong said he had poisoned individually; failed to analyse the bismuth mixture which had been given to Martin by Hincks; and failed to acknowledge the effect that the combined evidence of Willcox and Spilbury would have on the jury. The defence of his client, who was standing trial for his life, can only be described as reckless. He made a series of crucial blunders, not only in refraining to attack the Martin evidence but also in his misuse of the packet of white arsenic that Matthews had found in Armstrong's desk.

The way he employed this packet was instrumental in

allowing Armstrong's conviction – almost as much as the Martin evidence. Yet Armstrong, powerless in his own defence, had no part whatsoever in the tactics employed by Curtis Bennett.

Matthews had continually pressed Micklethwait for a list of items that the police had taken from Mayfield, but he was consistently fobbed off. The prosecution had built its case on the assumption that Armstrong had a secret source of pure white arsenic, which would explain the packet found in his pocket upon his arrest. They knew that Armstrong had openly purchased arsenic from the local chemist, but believed that all these purchases had been of the coloured sort. Matthews's discovery of the balance of the shop-bought white arsenic was going to be Curtis Bennett's trump card in disproving this allegation. However, the way it was used by him blew up in his face, as the judge maintained that Armstrong had deliberately concealed it from the police. With hindsight, Bennett should have advised Matthews to inform the police immediately of his find, and not chance his luck or the destiny of his client.

Curtis Bennett proved a liability for Armstrong, who would have been better served by Marshall Hall, or even by Mr Hogg, who had been suggested by Arthur Chevalier; but Armstrong was initially pleased with the choice of Bennett, who, like him, was a Cambridge man. There is some evidence that, as the trial progressed, Armstrong was becoming increasingly unhappy at the way his lawyer was putting over his defence. If this is true, it is easy to see why. In the words of Bodkin's biographer, 'For Armstrong, Sir Henry Curtis Bennett, a theatrical Counsel and no great lawyer, rose to the occasion and fought hard to prevent the evidence being heard but was unsuccessful.'[7]

Matthews had chosen three doctors to help Curtis Bennett with the defence. They were led by Dr Toogood, whose practice in the Temple, London, was largely conducted on behalf of insurance companies. In addition, for twenty-five years he had been medical superintendent of Lewisham Hospital. During his long career he had carried out 7,000 autopsies. Apart from those he performed in the hospital, he conducted many for insurance companies. The autopsies that they insisted on were thorough and included tests for poisoning. Dr Toogood's opinion was therefore a good one.

Toogood had appeared just over a year before in the

Greenwood case. His opinion strongly contradicted that of Willcox for the prosecution and Greenwood was acquitted. It was because of this successful defence that Matthews enlisted his help as the most eminent poisoning expert of the day, apart, that is, from those experts who only appeared for the Crown.

Dr Toogood was assisted by Dr Ainslie of Hereford, who had been present at the autopsy. Not only did Dr Ainslie have a better degree than Dr Spilbury's MB (Oxon), he was also a surgeon and innovator. He ran the first X-ray unit in Hereford and was widely respected, but he had no experience of arsenical poisoning. Dr Steed had a superior surgical degree to any of the Crown witnesses. Both Ainslie and Steed were Edinburgh men who had built up successful practices and were in demand as consultants.

All three were forced to defer to the collective wider experience of the London experts by the prosecutor, who browbeat them mercilessly.

It was customary for the Crown to brief the attorney general in major poisoning cases and if Curtis Bennett can be criticized for conducting a passive defence, the attorney general can be taken to task for conducting an unrelenting prosecution that bordered on the unethical. Sir Ernest Pollock was later to become Lord Hanworth, and master of the rolls, which latter position he held for thirteen years. This caused considerable criticism in both the press and the Bar on the grounds that he was neither legally nor intellectually able enough, and he never attained prominence as an advocate, despite his many qualities. Many believed that he was only nominated as a law officer because there was then a shortage of eminent advocates among politicians of the Conservative Party. He was often outclassed in difficult and complicated cases by the counsel who opposed him, and he relied heavily on intuition as opposed to close reasoning in his arguments. His conduct in the Armstrong case was much criticized.

He was aided by his juniors, C.H. Vachell KC and St John Micklethwait, but Sir Ernest must take the responsibility for the way the trial was conducted, and although it is to be expected that he would prosecute severely, he should have prosecuted fairly and honestly. However, it is clear that he was anxious 'to win his case' come what may, which is a deplorable ambition for a criminal prosecutor. The lengths to which he went is shown by his anxiety to pin a motive for the crime on the prisoner. Mrs Armstrong had expressed a desire to make a second will, leaving all her property to the prisoner, and this was done. Poor Pollock cross-examined the prisoner, suggesting that (although he had spent not a penny of the inherited money) he had omitted, on his wife's death, to execute a *fresh* will of his own leaving £12 a year to Miss Pearce. To that extent the latter had been a beneficiary under Mrs Armstrong's first will, but had not been mentioned in the second.

The presiding judge, Mr Justice Darling was not a great judge and

> often allowed himself to behave with a levity quite unsuited to the trial of a criminal case, thinking erroneously that he could thereby induce a jury to bring in the right verdict by an eventual careful and accurate summing-up. In fact he had frequently lost the respect of the jury to such an extent that they ignored or paid little attention to the judge. The Pemberton Billing case (1918) was a shocking example and went far to lower the status of the bench.[8]

In his long career he presided over some famous cases, including the notorious Steinie Morrison case (1911), and in the court of criminal appeal he presided over the Dr Harvey Crippen (1910) and Roger Casement (1916) cases. In the preface to Filson Young's *The Trial of H.R. Armstrong* in the 'Notable British Trials' series, Darling is recorded as being 'undoubtedly the greatest criminal judge, as well as one of the most distinguished men, of his day'. This is claptrap and if nothing else demonstrates Filson Young's weakness as an editor, for Lord Justice Avory was by far the greatest criminal judge of the period, if not long before it. Darling was never as great as Coleridge or Humphreys and in reality was comparable (alone of all criminal judges) to Ridley who was a true hanging judge.

Darling had been a sickly child, which isolated him from his peers and prevented him from going to school. He was called to the Bar without taking an examination and never gained any prominence on the circuit. In 1885 he took silk and in that year failed to gain the Conservative seat for South Hackney and again failed to be elected a year later. In 1888 he successfully fought a by-election and finally entered Parliament as a member for Deptford. In 1897 it was rumoured that the lord chancellor intended to appoint him to the High Court Bench and there was an outcry in the Temple. A leading article in *The Times* stated that he had shown 'no sign of legal eminence ... if he is raised to the Bench, it will be on political grounds'. However, the appointment was made and he resigned his parliamentary seat, no doubt to the great relief of the government, for which he had made little impression.

Darling was avid to try Armstrong and made some derogatory remarks about the coroner, whom he said had unduly delayed the committal. Southall rightly resented his remarks, for the truth was that the committal had been delayed by the prosecution in its anxiety to collect as much incriminating evidence as possible against the prisoner.

This was to be Darling's last murder trial and he was determined to demonstrate how such a trial should be conducted. He believed that Mr Justice Shearman had allowed Greenwood to escape the gallows, and he was determined that no such repeat performance would happen in his Court.

18

The trial opened at the Hereford assizes on Monday, 3 April 1922. The weather was particularly foul and a large crowd, including a small army of pressmen, besieged Hereford railway station, hoping to catch sight of Armstrong himself through the blizzard. However, they were outwitted by the police, who brought him to the Shire Hall courtroom in a closed car, and shepherded him in through the side door, practically unnoticed by anyone. The courtroom was filled to capacity and only fifty seats were available for the public, many of whom were women who had clamoured for admission. At eleven o'clock sharp, Mr Justice Darling arrived and a few minutes later entered the court wearing a full bottomed wig.

In those days there was another nominal check on the judicial process, ostensibly for the benefit of the prisoner, but in reality of dubious value. This was the grand jury, which had to be satisfied that there was a case worthy of investigation by the judge and the petty jury. As Mr Justice Darling addressed them in calm and measured tones, the whole court listened spellbound. He explained that they would have to consider two charges against Herbert Rowse Armstrong – one of attempting to murder Mr Oswald Martin and the other of murdering his wife, Katharine. He stated that he proposed to deal with the attempted murder charge last, but that both cases were inextricably linked in their details. He gave a résumé of Martin's illness and Katharine's death and went on:

There is a second count, that is that a little more than six months ago – on September 20th – the defendant attempted

162

to poison Mr Martin, it being alleged that he sent to Mr Martin, or to his house a box of chocolates. I have carefully read the evidence and formed an opinion but, of course, you are not bound by it – it is only an opinion. The impression I have come to is that there is not sufficient evidence to connect the defendant with the sending of these chocolates. It is very slight indeed, and I only commend this to your consideration. Whatever view you may take in this court depends entirely how you can connect the defendant with the preparation and the sending of these chocolates; further, that they should be consumed by Mr Martin.

The grand jury returned to the court half an hour after the judge had concluded his address and announced that they found a true bill (a case worthy of investigation) against the prisoner for the murder of his wife, but needed to retire to consider the other charges. Sir Archibald Bodkin entered the court and took his seat at the counsel's table. He was immediately followed by Armstrong, who entered the dock, wearing a neat brown suit. He stood to attention in true officer manner as the indictment of wilful murder was read out to him, and replied with perfect calmness, 'Not guilty, sir.'

The judge explained to the panel of jurors that the case would be very painful and would last a week, or more. He offered to excuse the two women on the panel and they instantly accepted. The jury of ten farmers and two gentlemen were sworn and Sir Ernest Pollock rose to open for the Crown, outlining the case he intended to prove, which he said would be borne out by the witnesses he would call. Before concluding his opening statement, the judge agreed that as a legal argument relating to the admissability of certain evidence would take place after lunch, it was neither necessary nor desirable for the jury to be present until that point had been settled.

When the proceedings resumed, the jury box was empty. Pollock told the judge that the defence wanted to protest against the admittance of certain evidence after the death of Mrs Armstrong – evidence which he thought was material to show that Mrs Armstrong had died not from arsenic taken by herself, but from that administered by the prisoner. He then outlined the Martin evidence and stated that he wanted to introduce it to rebut any suggestion that Mrs Armstrong's death could have been caused by her taking arsenic by misadventure and to demonstrate that the prisoner had arsenic in his possession on another occasion and definitely attempted to poison Martin. He then cited many precedents in support of his argument.

Bennett knew that the prosecution would attempt to call evidence in connection with the alleged attempt on Martin's life and submitted in a lengthy argument that the evidence was inadmissable on the murder charge that was before the court. He maintained that the precedents to which the attorney general had referred were cases where the defence was either that the person had not died of the particular poison in question, or that the death was a result of an accident. He suggested that accident had a double meaning in cases such as these: it might mean that the deceased had himself accidentally taken poison, or that the person charged with the murder had accidentally administered the poison. He indicated that his client would say that he had nothing to do with the taking of arsenic by Mrs Armstrong and that accident would not be part of his defence. He also suggested that Mrs Armstrong might have committed suicide by taking the arsenic herself. Mr Justice Darling responded:

> If the suggestion is to be or may be that she committed suicide, would it not be relevant to show that another person who displayed all the symptoms of arsenical poisoning although he did not die of it, displayed them because he had taken a meal administered to him by the defendant, and that the defendant was in a position to have given the same poison to his wife?

Bennett replied:

> When the defence is 'I didn't do the thing. I didn't administer the poison. I agree that my wife died from arsenical poisoning, but I never had anything to do with the administration of it,' surely it is going a very long way to say that he murdered his wife because nine months or nine years later some other person showed symptoms of poisoning after having had a meal with Armstrong?

The legal arguments lasted over two hours and the court began to grow weary. After Sir Ernest Pollock had replied to Bennett's submission, the judge said that he was of the opinion that the evidence intended to be given by the prosecution was admissible: 'It is not necessary for me to give any reason for my opinion, but if I am wrong the Court of Criminal Appeal will put me right.' The jury was then recalled and Pollock outlined the further evidence that he would call, avoiding any reference to the chocolates.

At the conclusion of the case certain commentators stated that it was a very plucky decision of the judge to admit the Martin evidence, which was so prejudicial to Armstrong on the murder charge; for one of the distinctive[9] features of the English law of evidence is how jealously it protects an accused person from being harassed and prejudiced by questions regarding other offences committed or alleged to have been committed by him. The common law rejects such evidence not because it is irrelevant (for logically it is relevant), but because it might be accorded an undue weight and is therefore potentially misleading. Give a dog a bad name and hang him. Place a man's bad record before the jury, and it is almost impossible for them to take an impartial view of the case in hand. Slight evidence becomes magnified. Every defence is liable to become suspicious. Instead of approaching the case with a presumption of innocence, the jury starts with a presumption of guilt, which the accused man has to displace; and he is lucky if his efforts to do so are not regarded as more or less ingenious attempts to wriggle out of a manifestly well-founded charge.

As soon as the judge had ruled that the Martin evidence was admissable, Armstrong was in trouble, as the jurors were bound to be prejudiced against him, because if they accepted that he had in fact tried to poison Martin, they had to be predisposed to believe that he had administered arsenic to his wife. In effect, this meant that Armstrong had to prove his innocence, not that the prosecution had to prove his guilt, and the basic law of evidence had been turned on its head. For in all criminal trials it is the cardinal rule that the prosecution must prove the 'persuasive burden' and the defendant has to prove nothing.

Even though the attorney general's case had been greatly

strengthened by the admission of the Martin evidence, the jury still had to be satisfied that Armstrong had actually poisoned his wife eight months before the tea party at Mayfield. The only available evidence consisted of the testimonies of those who had known and looked after her before her death, plus the opinion of the forensic teams.

The attorney general, in his opening speech to the jury, stated that 3½ grains of arsenic had been found in the samples submitted to Webster for analysis. Out of this total, over two grains had been found in the liver, rather more than half a grain in the bowels and a similar quantity in the large intestine. Sir William Willcox was certain that there must have been a course of poisoning during the last week of her life and a fatal dose within twenty-four hours of her death. However, even if he managed to convince the jurors to accept the expert opinion of Willcox, he still had to satisfy them that it was Armstrong who had given her the poison. This was necessary to rebut the defence suggestion that she could have taken it herself. It was crucial, therefore, to have her helpless in bed, unable to move her limbs and unable to move her hands to feed herself at the time when the experts said she had ingested the arsenic. Equally importantly someone needed to testify that she had had diarrhoea during her last day alive, as the absence of this symptom would have been very unusual in a case of acute arsenical poisoning.

The attorney general also had to eliminate any other contender who had the opportunity to poison Katharine, either unwittingly or on purpose. He was again helped by Willcox, who maintained that Katharine had been poisoned on the day of her admission to Barnwood in August 1920 at a time when Miss Pearce was on holiday and before the housemaid, Inez Rosser, had started her employment at Mayfield. By this circuitous logic Pollock declared that Armstrong was the only person who had the opportunity to poison Katharine on both occasions.

Although Pollock went to extraordinary lengths to satisfy the jury of the two 'motives', neither were considered important by the judge, who scarcely mentioned them in his summing-up. In fact the judge introduced a third motive, which the defence never had a chance to refute, and which flew in the face of the actual evidence. He said that

Armstrong may have wanted to be rid of a wife he considered a 'tiresome invalid'.

19

An even greater crowd of morbid sightseers had congregated outside the court on the second day of the trial, cheered no doubt by the bright spring sunshine that was in such stark contrast to the blizzard of the previous day. In the courtroom the public gallery was packed, and vacuum flasks and oranges were being passed around the wooden benches by those lucky enough to gain admission. A few minutes after Major Armstrong had been escorted into the dock the judge parted the curtain behind his presiding seat and entered the court. Micklethwait then rose to his feet and in a firm voice said, 'Miss Ida Bessie Friend'. The trial had begun.

She was called by the Crown to substantiate that Katharine's first will made in 1917 had remained in her possession throughout, and that a copy of it had been retained by her deceased sister at Mayfield. The letters that Katharine had sent her from Barnwood were admitted in evidence, despite the defence's objection that they were hearsay. The judge overruled the objection, declaring that they were admissable because of questions asked in cross-examination. Even at this early stage the judge was indicating his bias in favour of the prosecution case, because the letters were hearsay and no questions were asked of the witness that could possibly have rendered them admissable. Despite the text of these letters, Bessie admitted that her sister had indicated to her that she intended altering her 1917 will and that Armstrong had told her in August 1920 that a new will had been made. More importantly she told the jury that her sister had rheumatism 'under the knees' during the war years and neuritis in her hands in 1919, and that she realized that something would have to be done when she was called to

Mayfield in August 1920, which was the last time she saw her alive. The symptoms of her pains before August were important, but they were considered irrelevant by Willcox, who was anxious to support the prosecution line that she was first poisoned by Armstrong on the day of her admission to Barnwood and that before that date there was nothing really the matter with her.

After the judge ruled that the Barnwood letters were admissable the defence knew that he was biased against the prisoner. This knowledge was confirmed by his question to the attorney general at the close of the next witness's evidence. Miss Hutchins, who had witnessed the first will, and who described the Armstrongs as a most affectionate couple, was about to leave the witness box. The judge turned to Pollock and said, 'If you have the depositions before you, Mr Attorney, there is a matter just after the re-examination.' To which Pollock replied, 'No, I am content to leave that.' He was referring to Miss Hutchins's replies to Micklethwait's suggestion in the magistrates court that Katharine's signature on the 1920 will was a forgery. It may seem incredible that the judge should attempt to interpose in this way to help the prosecution, and remind the chief law officer not to forget to ask questions which would help his case, but the fact remains that he did.

The young housemaid, Inez Rosser, then told the jury that when Katharine returned from Barnwood she had delusions and imagined that she (the housemaid) was wandering about the house when she was in bed. The judge noted this remark and when Miss Pearce gave evidence and said the same thing, he carefully framed the question, 'Was Mr Armstrong at home then?', implying to the jury that Katharine was not deluded that Armstrong had been pursuing the housemaid. As the trial continued, the judge's technique of putting a question loaded with innuendo was used with stunning effect.

There was a thrill of anticipation when the old friend of Mrs Armstrong was called to give evidence, but Miss Pearce was treated shabbily by both Pollock and the judge, in the same appalling way that she had been treated at the magistrates court. Micklethwait had then actually lost his temper with her and desired it to be recorded on the depositions that he refused to ask her any further questions. She was a very important witness and should have been regarded as such by the judge, whose duty of impartiality should have extended to her. However, her evidence did not help the prosecution case, particularly when she said that as soon as her mistress had returned from Barnwood she had asked her if she would break her back if she threw herself out of the attic window. She went on to say that she remembered the circumstances of the signing of the 1920 will: Mrs Armstrong had put her hand on the document and told her where to sign and then stated, 'There is Lily; she will sign it.' The attorney general was worried. He asked the judge permission to refer to the statements that she had given to Crutchett. Curtis Bennett quite rightly objected, declaring that what the attorney general wanted to do was cross-examine his own witness and that he could only do this if she was hostile. He remarked further that not one single question had been asked of Miss Pearce at the magistrates court in connection with the will. The judge asked her a few questions, to which she replied dispassionately and without preference. He declared that she was a hostile witness and allowed the attorney general to proceed. The very fact that she had been pronounced a hostile witness meant that her evidence to the jury was belittled. Moreover, her testimony went to the heart of the case, particularly when she mentioned that Mrs Armstrong returned from Barnwood worse than before her admission. She was definite that Mrs Armstrong sat out in the porch on 14 February and that it was not until 16 February or the next day that her final illness began.

Despite Miss Pearce's statement that she had actually signed the 1920 will in Mrs Armstrong's presence and remembered Mrs Armstrong saying 'There is Lily; she will sign it,' Lily Evans (née Candy) was certain that she signed only one document during the whole time she was at Mayfield and that she did so at Mr Armstrong's request and in his study. If her evidence was true, the will was invalid, as a will must be witnessed by two attesting persons, who must sign in the presence of each other and in the presence of the testator. But was her evidence true? When Curtis Bennett cross-examined her, he asked her if she was quite certain that she had signed one document only during the whole time she was at Mayfield and she emphatically replied that she was quite certain of this fact. Curtis Bennett paused for a moment to allow her answer to achieve the maximum effect. He then handed her a different certificate that bore her signature and she had to admit that she had signed it in Armstrong's study. So where had she signed the will, which she accepted bore her signature? The position was equivocal.

Harriet Price was the next witness called to give evidence. She spoke of the tea party at Mayfield and was adamant that Miss Pearce had made the currant scones, which were whole and not buttered. If she was telling the truth, and there is no reason to disbelieve her, Martin must have been lying when he told the magistrates that the scone he had eaten had been buttered, because there was no butter on the table. It was kept in the diary and Miss Pearce stated that Armstrong never entered the kitchen, which led to the dairy. Crutchett had already carefully checked if Armstrong had bought scones or butter in the town and found that he had not.

Nurse Kinsey was the last witness of the day. She had been telephoned by Armstrong on 23 January and asked to assist Mrs Armstrong in dressing and undressing. The attorney general knew perfectly well why Nurse Kinsey had remained at Mayfield for only four days. Because she feared Katharine might commit suicide she had urgently seen both Dr Hincks and Armstrong to inform them that Katharine required a full-time psychiatric nurse. However, he deliberately evaded asking her the questions which would have revealed those answers. There can be no excuse for this omission. Kinsey was a witness to fact and that part of her evidence, even though it did not suit the prosecution case, was material. Instead Pollock concentrated on her account of when she called at Mayfield on 10 February and noticed a great change in Katharine's condition, explaining that she looked like a jaundice case, with a deep discoloration of the skin and very wasted. She said that when she arrived that day Armstrong was with Katharine, who was lying down on the sofa in the drawing room complaining of severe pains in her abdomen, having been vomiting badly. Nurse Kinsey was a truthful witness. She had no axe to grind for any party. She must have articulated what she had seen, but her date must have been wrong, for the evidence from the other witnesses, including Dr Hincks, was that there was nothing acutely wrong with Katharine before 15 February at the earliest. If Nurse Kinsey had mixed up the dates of her visit it is likely that she was a week out and that she had visited Mayfield on 17 February; otherwise her testimony cannot be explained. Curtis Bennett readily obtained from her that Katharine had asked 'if she thought it would be sufficient to kill anyone if they threw themselves out of the attic window'. In very quiet tones, Curtis Bennett asked her, 'Did you really fear that Mrs Armstrong might commit suicide?' to which Nurse Kinsey replied, 'After the remark I thought she was not safe to be left.'

Nurse Kinsey's evidence concluded the second day of the trial.

The evidence of the next witness was probably the most important of all. Nurse Allen had relieved Nurse Kinsey on 27 January and had been with Katharine, apart from one night only, until 22 February, the day Katharine died. Matthews recorded in his brief to Curtis Bennett that he believed her to be a particularly truthful witness. However, what was so strange is that her evidence at the trial contradicted her evidence at the magistrates court. It is difficult to fathom the reasons why she changed her story, but when her evidence is tested against the other witnesses not only does it fail, but more interestingly it actually supports the prosecution argument that Katharine could not have taken the poison herself. As mentioned, the prosecution case depended on her being consigned to bed as early as possible, demonstrating that she was unable to get up to take anything, and had to rely on what was given to her. If she had not been able to take arsenic herself, she must have been given it and in the words of the attorney general in his opening speech to the jury, 'Who else could have given it, who else had possession of it, who had the motive to give it to her? We will show that all the facts point to no other person apart from the prisoner.'

Perhaps this was the real reason why she insisted that Katharine had taken to her bed on Sunday 13 February. In the magistrates court she had given the date as Sunday 20 February. The judge was aware of the importance of her evidence and posed several questions to her:

'During the last four days did she get out of bed at all?'

'No, not to my knowledge, she did not.'

'Do you believe she could have done it?'

'I do not think she could have.'

' ... As I understand it it is suggested that she could after the 13th have got out of bed and have got a bottle out of the cupboard above the fireplace. What do you say to that ...?'

'I do not think it was possible.'

'You have said you did not think it possible that she could have done it after the 13th, that is the Sunday; but what do you say to any time during the last four days?'

'I do not think it was possible then because she was so much weaker.'

There is no escaping the conclusion that Nurse Allen must have been 'got at' by the prosecution. The only other explanation is that she had become completely confused, apparently failing to see the glaring inconsistencies in her evidence. Yet the parts of her evidence that supported the prosecution case were used by the judge in his summing-up as evidence to be believed and accepted.

This is what Nurse Allen said in the police court in answer to Micklethwait's questions:

'With regard to her appetite, what do you say as to that?'

'It was very good.'

'And did she have her meals with the rest of you?'

'Yes, in the dining room.'

'How long did that state of affairs last?'

'I can't remember very well. I think it was about a fortnight. She was all right in health and taking her food.'

'What happened then?'

'She complained of feeling sick at certain times. She complained of nausea and could not vomit at times.'

'Did you stay until she died?'

'Yes.'

'Tell us in your own language when was it?'

'After lunch.'

'Did she vomit much?'

'Not a great deal at that time, but it was a good amount.'

'She died on Tuesday, February 22nd?'

'Yes.'

'When she started this vomiting, what did you do?'

'I undressed her and put her to bed and applied hot water bottles.'

'Did you give her anything to take?'

'No, except she had some hot water in a glass with bicarbonate of soda to stop the vomiting.'

'Did it have the effect of stopping it at all?'

'It is such a long time ago that I really cannot remember, I have taken other cases since then.'

'If you do not remember much about it of course, say so. I only want what you remember. Did you send for the doctor.'

'No, she requested me not to do so.'

'What happened after that?'

'On the Monday or Tuesday it ceased.'

'Do you mean it went on on Monday and ceased on Tuesday?'

'That I can't remember.'

'You say the vomiting had ceased on Tuesday. Had it ceased on the Monday?'

'I do not remember, but it was not so incessant as on the Sunday.'

'Do you remember at all what her condition was on the Wednesday, Thursday and Friday following?'

'On the Wednesday there was no vomiting. On the Thursday it started again.'

Matthews then posed her some questions:

'And right from the commencement she was suffering from delusions?'

'Yes. At times she would get up and walk round the house, thinking there was something about during the night, and I got up to bring her back. Mrs Armstrong never went out of the room without my knowledge, because I was a very light sleeper, and I used to follow her about and watch her, because she was a patient who required observation.'

'Did that, at all events, continue until two or three days before the end?'

'Up to the Sunday before her death.'

'From that time she was not up at all so far as you know?'

'Well, I was always there, and I do not think she was.'

'She did not get out of bed from the Sunday before she died?'

'That is so – before that day I remember Mrs Armstrong

going round the garden, following which I had a conversation with Mr Armstrong as to his wife having caught a chill, but I cannot remember the date.'

There is nothing really wrong with this account as far as the facts go, at least as narrated by Nurse Allen in the magistrates court, except that it allows Armstrong a loophole. His wife could have poisoned herself either by intention or accident if she was up and about forty-eight hours before her death. The prosecution would have a better case if Katharine were completely powerless in bed for as long a time as possible, to avoid the suggestion to the jury that she might have taken the poison herself. Indeed Pollock did not want the jury to consider the possibility that Katharine could have taken arsenic from the medicine cupboard, which was crammed full of potions and lotions, pills and powders with cryptic names on the labels and mysterious contents.

No one, not even Nurse Allen, suggested that Mr and Mrs Armstrong were anything but a devoted and affectionate couple. And as a loving husband he would read to his wife in the evenings after he returned from work. The prosecution knew this and could thereby show the prisoner alone in the same room with the poisoned woman.

Yet Dr Hincks was not called by Nurse Allen on 13 February, because Katharine did not want him to come. She had taken a hearty dislike to Dr Hincks, anyway, having never forgiven him for sending her to an asylum. She cannot have been that sick and there is no evidence to suggest otherwise, apart from the evidence of Nurse Kinsey, who must have confused her dates. Katharine was put to bed with a hot-water bottle and the nurse sprinkled some powder in a cup or glass of hot water to settle her stomach. The powder was bi-carbonate of soda, which in appearance is similar to a number of white powders, including white arsenic. If her nurse was giving her a white powder in the form of bi-carbonate of soda to soothe her stomach, and it worked, Katharine must have considered this treatment to be a good one. What should be noted is the fact that she was sick so soon after the meal on Sunday 13 February consisting of preserved gooseberries. Nurse Allen suspected her after-dinner pills and removed them from a vessel in the sideboard in the dining room. However, the nurse did not remove her homeopathic medicines which were contained in the medicine cupboard in her bedroom. The little chest and the fact that the contents were not properly examined at the time is something of a mystery.

A discussion had taken place between Dr Hincks and Katharine when the subject of her homeopathic medicines was raised. She persuaded him to allow her to continue taking them, although he was averse to the idea. Hincks was not a homeopath and did not know what the bottles contained. But as far as Katharine was concerned she had been given permission to continue taking these medicines, and she did so right up to the end.

Nurse Allen confirmed this in reply to Matthews's question in the magistrates court:

'She was a woman who knew perfectly well what she was doing except for these delusions? She knew what you were giving her?'

'Yes, I think so.'

'She was, at any rate, taking homeopathic medicine up to the end?'

'I asked the doctor if he was agreeable to her taking them. He was not agreeable at the beginning, but he afterwards gave his consent.'

'I think she took them on the Sunday previous to the day she became sick? She took them up to the last day?'

'Yes.'

'Had she a medicine chest in her own room?'

'She had.'

'Containing, I suppose, homeopathic medicines?'

'I suppose so. I never took much interest in it.'

'You slept in the same room as her.'

'I did.'

The evidence is clear that Katharine was allowed to take her homeopathic medicines herself, without proper scrutiny, along with the medicine prescribed by her doctor, up to the day she died. The caveat to this is that for the last few days of her life she was without doubt bedridden and could not have reached her medicine cupboard, but she still could have taken her medicine if she had some by her side, or secreted about her person. What must be remembered is that Katharine had always taken her digestive pills after a meal to ward off dispepsia. It was these pills which had been removed by Nurse Allen, who had given her bicarbonate – pills replaced by white powder. The pills that Nurse Allen removed were completely innocuous and harmless but they were used by Katharine to ward off feelings of discomfort, and were in fact comforters, because she dreaded indigestion and had become neurotic about it.

There can be no doubt, despite what Nurse Allen said at the trial, that she was not desperately ill on Monday the 14th. It was an important date for the defence and much hinged upon it, because the prosecution contended that Armstrong had started his slow poisoning of his wife the day before, and that her sickness on that date was the result of arsenic being given to her then. What was difficult to reconcile, however, was Nurse Allen's insistence that Katharine had not sat in the porch on the Monday, and although she recalled the event, she maintained that the true date was the Thursday or Friday before, that is, the 10th or the 11th. Luckily for the defence there was a completely independent and impartial witness who confirmed that she had seen Katharine on the 14th, although no weight was given to this evidence by the trial judge in his summing-up. The witness was Inez Margaret Price, the wife of Owen Price, the manager of Barclays Bank at Hay, who stated that she visited Mayfield sometime between three and five o'clock that afternoon and had sat and talked for about three-quarters of an hour with Katharine, who was sitting out under the veranda by the front porch. She stated that she thought Katharine looked very frail. She was certain that it was the 14th because she had been wearing a new costume bought that day. On returning home, she sent a cheque to her tailor for the balance due to him for it. She produced the actual cheque dated the 14th, made payable to Messrs. Hartley and Co. alongside the receipt for it dated the 15th, marked 'by cash in settlement of account'. She also remembered that she had seen Miss Pearce on that day and that she may also have seen the maid. Even Armstrong recalled that when he returned home from work that evening Katharine told him that she had sat out in the garden and Mrs Price had visited her. This was confirmed by Miss Pearce.

There is no evidence of anything untoward happening on the following day, Tuesday the 15th. However, the exact dates and times are in conflict at this crucial time. Nurse Allen said in the magistrates court that there was no sickness on the Wednesday and that on the Thursday it started again. Dr Hincks said in the magistrates court that he had an urgent message to go to Mayfield on Tuesday the 15th and found Mrs Armstrong in bed. She had been very sick in the night and complained of abdominal pains. Armstrong said he had telephoned for the doctor either on the afternoon or the early evening of the 16th, and that Hincks arrived that evening. Emily Pearce was not sure whether it was the 16th or the 17th that Mrs Armstrong finally became very ill. But whatever the exact day she did become ill and took to her bed.

All the evidence states that she was now desperately ill, and it was agreed by both the prosecution and defence doctors that she had ingested a poisonous dose of arsenic. The question for the jury was a simple one: had Armstrong given it to her?

Much now depended on the expert evidence. The distribution of the arsenic in various organs was known – the interpretation of this distribution was the subject of controversy. The prosecution case was simplicity itself. All it had to prove was that a fatal dose had been administered within twenty-four hours of death. If the Crown experts could deduce this from the evidence of the body, it would be a simple step to inculpate Armstrong. After all, the victim was on her death-bed, practically paralysed by this time, taking only liquid food given to her by other hands. During this 24-hour period she could not even hold a glass to slake her own thirst, and was entirely reliant on others to feed her and give her a drink. Who else could have given arsenic to her but Armstrong? However, the matter was not quite that easy, because the poor lady had taken to her bed desperately sick five days before her death. To account for that sickness, it was necessary to say that arsenic had been given then; but what about the sickness on the 13th February? Perhaps arsenic had been given then also. But what about the solitary vomit on the evening of 26 January? Why not allege a series of small doses of poison, to account for each and every bout of vomiting? But why stop there? Why not allege an earlier dose given on 22 August, to account for her sickness before her admission to Barnwood?

To wrap the whole thing up, the prosecution had the benefit of the Martin evidence: his sickness after taking tea with Armstrong; the trace of arsenic in his urine; the packet of white arsenic found in Armstrong's pockets. Could anybody doubt that Armstrong was a poisoner, if the facts were presented in this way?

The third nurse was Miss Lloyd, who had relieved Nurse Allen, on the night of Sunday, 20 February and had stayed with Katharine throughout the night. She recalled that her charge had vomited twice in the night. The judge wanted to know if Katharine had vomited after taking her milk food. Nurse Lloyd replied that she had vomited after her first feed, but not after her second feed and that she had then slept fitfully throughout the rest of the night. She recalled that Katharine had one motion, but could not recall whether or not it was diarrhoea.

When she left the sick-room on the morning of 21 February, Katharine had only twenty-four hours to live. The prosecution case was that Katharine must have been given arsenic within those twenty-four hours. There was a jug of milk food in the room, which Nurse Lloyd had used to feed Katharine in the night and Katharine had not been sick after her second feed from it. It was unlikely that the jug had been salted with arsenic, which would in any event have curdled the milk. The prosecution argued that Armstrong must have entered her sick-room and given her arsenic. But how and in what? Where is the evidence or the proof? So far there is none.

Before the attorney general embarked on the selected part of the Martin testimony which Bodkin had instructed him to call, Marion Gale and Arthur Chevalier gave evidence. In fact Arthur Chevalier had already taken his place in the witness box but had been quickly replaced by Marion. The attorney general stated she had little evidence to give and it could be fitted in before lunch.

Appearing without a veil, Marion Gale was reported as a woman past middle age, of average height and wearing a brown costume. Her name was written down and given to the jury, and the judge, in deference to her feelings, requested the press not to report her name even if they discovered it. Marion, unlike Miss Pearce, was treated civilly by both prosecutor and judge alike. She made it clear that Armstrong had never disguised from her that he was married with three children and she recounted that she first met him when he was stationed in Essex in 1915. She dined with him in 1920 while staying in London and she remembered that both she and her mother had expressed sympathy when they learned of the death of his wife. She recounted his visit to see her on his return from the Continent. On the subsequent visit, at Whitsuntide, he asked her to consider the idea of marriage. When asked by the judge whether or not she had ever promised to marry him, she replied that she was considering it but at no time had she promised it. She recounted her visit to Mayfield in October 1921, when she had been staying with friends at Cheltenham. When asked whether she knew that some of her letters had been found upon him when he was arrested, she replied that she did not. She confirmed that from 1915 until May 1921 she was merely a friend of the family and that from May 1921, although there was a suggestion of marriage, she was never formally engaged. It was no wonder that Curtis Bennett later described this friendship as a 'ludicrous' motive for Armstrong to kill his wife.

Arthur Chevalier took the stand after lunch. He was Armstrong's greatest friend and they had known each other for over thirty years. Chevalier had visited the family every year, except during the war, and knew both Mr and Mrs Armstrong intimately. Initially, he had pledged his support for Armstrong and with gratitude Matthews had turned to him for help in the preparation of his client's defence. Bodkin knew of this relationship and had arranged for Chevalier to be interviewed by Crutchett. He then informed him that as he would be required to give evidence for the prosecution, it would be preferable if he would not communicate with Matthews until he had given his evidence. Matthews was furious with Chevalier and expressed his feelings very strongly to him. Chevalier had been placed in a very difficult position, and was torn between his friendship with Armstrong and his duty to the Crown, borne out of his sense of obligation to his legal profession. Furthermore, he had been appointed an executor of Katharine's first will and had been told in no uncertain terms by Crutchett that the prosecution believed it to be invalid. He took advice from his own counsel and was advised not to communicate further with the defence until he had given his statement to Bodkin. More importantly, he was told to place a stop on Katharine's assets, none of which had in any case been transferred into Armstrong's name. There was no legal aid in those days and Armstrong had to finance his own defence. Matthews had instructed brokers to sell some of Katharine's war loans to defray the rapidly mounting defence costs, and found to his alarm that Chevalier refused to allow the sale to proceed. The effect of Chevalier's actions was incalculable, as not only had he withdrawn his support from his oldest friend but he had actively undermined the preparation of his defence. A cynic would suggest that he wanted Katharine's estate intact, because if Armstrong had used her money to pay for the costs of his defence and had still been executed, there would have been nothing left for the children. Chevalier might then have had to support them out of his own funds. Cynical or not, that possibility was a real one and the thought had not escaped Chevalier.

Matthews reported his consternation to Curtis Bennett in his brief, but recorded that whatever the reasons for Chevalier turning his back on Armstrong, his evidence at the magistrates court had been overwhelmingly in favour of the defence. When Chevalier was called to give evidence at the trial, he reiterated his earlier statements and there was no doubt that Matthew's comments were justified: Chevalier's testimony did not advance the prosecution case. For example, he told the jury that when he visited Mayfield in September 1919, he found Katharine to be in a nervous and excited condition; and when he had been summoned in August 1920, by Armstrong himself, he thought it likely that Katharine might commit suicide and that there was no alternative to her being committed to a mental hospital. It was, of course, the prosecution case that Katharine had been poisoned on the day she went to Barnwood. According to Chevalier, however, he had been summoned by Armstrong, who immediately agreed to a joint consultation with Dr Hincks, during which they all agreed that she had to be sent away. It was

Armstrong who insisted that her sister had to be party to this decision; when Bessie saw Katharine's state, she agreed at once that Katharine had to be committed for her own good. However the evidence is treated, it is hard to believe that Armstrong would arrange for the best friend of the family and his wife's sister to be present just at the time when he was trying to poison his wife. He knew full well that she would have to be examined by two doctors before certification and that she would then be examined by doctors in the asylum. That was the prosecution case, however, absurd as it may appear.

After Chevalier had finished giving his evidence, the prosecution turned to the witnesses who would help sustain its case that Armstrong had tried to murder Martin. Micklethwait examined the gardener, McGeorge, and elicited from him that Armstrong never mentioned either weedkiller or arsenic to him, even though he had seen a tin containing weedkiller in the stable. When McGeorge was cross-examined by Curtis Bennett he stated that on the morning of the tea party he had asked Armstrong to return in the early part of the afternoon to tell him where to move some fruit trees. He said that Armstrong arrived just after four o'clock, immediately went up to him and after speaking to him, went into the house.

'Did he come out again immediately?'

'He came straight out to me.'

'He was only in just for a moment?'

'Only just time to take his cap and coat off.'

'And was out again immediately into the garden?'

'Yes.'

'Coming out again into the garden, was he with you right up to the time when Martin arrived?'

'He was.'

'Did you actually see Mr Martin come?'

'I did.'

The attorney general in his opening speech had stated that January was an extraordinary time for putting down weed killer. When William Jay was asked to comment, he said that as a gardener he preferred to put down weedkiller in January. Another plank in the prosecution case should have been demolished.

It was reported in the *Hereford Times* of the day, 'There was a craning of heads when Mr. Oswald Norman Martin, the Hay solicitor, whom Armstrong is charged with attempting to murder, went into the box.' By way of comment, if the press, who had avidly sat through all the proceedings, thought that Armstrong was being tried for the attempted murder of Martin, what did the jury think? Even the attorney general had been at a loss to know how to present all the evidence to do with the alleged attempts on Martin's life – particularly in relation to the delivery of the poisoned box of chocolates, the count of attempted murder rejected by the grand jury. In this respect the letter of instruction which the attorney general had received from Bodkin three days before the trial began makes illuminating reading:

You were good enough to say you would like me to consider the question of whether in the forthcoming trial evidence as to the chocolates should be introduced. I have done so and am writing upon that.

We have had enquiries made at all agencies of Fullers within about 100 miles of Hereford. We know from enquiries approximately the date on which the particular box of chocolates was packed, but we have been absolutely unable to directly connect Armstrong with its purchase or transmission by post. Its wrapper was destroyed; the writing of the address was in printed characters, there was nothing in Armstrong's house to indicate that he had manipulated the chocolates; and in short, there is no direct evidence indicating that he caused them to be sent. On the other hand they are filled with white arsenic; they were sent to Martin at his new address; it is believed that the letters 'ford' appeared on the postmark; and Armstrong was in possession on his arrest of arsenic of a similar appearance to that in the chocolates, and he stated that he had given chocolates to his wife in August 1920; and Fullers chocolates were not procurable in Hay. I believe this is substantially all the evidence. It would be said that if he did not send the chocolates someone else acquainted with and having animosity against the Martins in the same neighbour-hood was in possession of arsenic and sent the chocolates, whereas there is no one whom the Martins can suggest would have been so wicked as to attempt to poison them thereby. Further, it would be said that the sending of the chocolates in

September was followed by the tea party in October and the circumstantial evidence that the man who was in possession of quantities of arsenic then administering it to Martin is clear and strong ... but if the evidence as to the chocolates is insufficient to connect the prisoner with the incident, then the case for the prosecution would not seem to be advanced or bettered by giving it. To introduce it would give the defence a great deal of material, and in view of the thinness of the evidence, the defence would undoubtedly place the question about the chocolates most prominently forward and might get the Jury to look at it as being the real important issue in the case and to take a thoroughly wrong perspective of it. Following this line of thought I have come to the conclusion that it is better to omit reference to chocolates as Armstrong would say 'I know nothing whatever about them'.

As the unfortunate Martin entered the witness box he knew that the Crown would not question him about his receipt of the box of chocolates, even though they had been the vital factor in impelling Dr Hincks to request a urine sample. In addition, two of them containing arsenic had been mounted in plasticine and had been handed round the magistrates court.

The vital question begs to be answered. If Armstrong had not poisoned the chocolates, who else could have been so wicked to do so? There can only be one reply.

Micklethwait examined the witness and took him through his marriage and the Velinewydd contracts. Martin carefully omitted to say that his clients wanted to get out of their contracts. He said that on 20 October he wrote to Armstrong confirming that the contracts were rescinded. Armstrong had insisted on speaking to his clients, who refused to reconsider their position. On the next day Armstrong invited him to tea, which was arranged for the Monday, but Martin cancelled and they rearranged a date for Wednesday 26 October. On that day he arrived by car at ten past five and, having met Armstrong in the garden, finally entered the house at about twenty to half past five:

'It was getting dark when we sat down for tea. Mr Armstrong poured out the tea and handed it to me. He handed me a scone in his fingers, saying "excuse my fingers" – or something like that.'

Micklethwait: 'What sort of scone was it?'

'It was a buttered scone.'

The judge: 'Did he ask you what you wanted?'

'He may have. The scone was cut horizontally in two halves.'

Micklethwait: 'Plain or currant?'

'That I can't tell.'

'Did you have anything else?'

'Yes: I had some currant cake and butter.'

Martin said that Armstrong did not mention the Velinewydd sale or indicate the object of asking him to tea.

The attorney general then told the judge that they were about to enter a new phase of Mr Martin's evidence and the trial was adjourned to the following day.

20

When the fourth day of the trial opened Martin resumed his evidence. He said he returned home at about twenty to seven and remembered feeling slightly unwell when he started to dictate to his clerk Alan Preen. He ate a dinner of jugged hare and coffee cream between 7.30 and 8.15 and then did some more work.

I kept on feeling more unwell until about twenty minutes to nine. I thought I was going to be sick, and went up into the bathroom. I felt very sick, but was not actually sick. I went downstairs again, and found Preen, my clerk, had gone. I was actually sick for the first time about ten past nine. I was sick again about three times after that before I went to bed. I eventually went to bed, and was sick at intervals throughout the night. The vomit was exceedingly violent, and the vomit was very dark and offensive. The vomit eventually became lighter. I had pain in the abdomen as well. I first noticed it when I went to bed about 10 o'clock. In addition to the pain, my heart was beating very fast all the night and the next day. I had two or three attacks of diarrhoea during the night. When it began to get light, my eyes were very sensitive to the light, and I could not bear it. Dr Hincks came and saw me on the Thursday morning at about 9 o'clock. He came again in the evening, and again on the Saturday, Sunday and Monday. I had never had any attack similar to that before. In consequence of what Dr Hincks told me I gave him a sample of the urine in the bottle.

It was about November 14th that I received another invitation to tea at Mayfield and he persistently asked me to go to tea either at Mayfield or at his office until December the 12th, which was the last time he asked me. I refused all the invitations to go. He used to ring me up in the morning and talk about business first and then ask me to come to tea. Altogether I think I had quite twenty invitations to tea from Armstrong. At first he invited me to Mayfield, and subsequently I took tea at my own office in order to have some ready excuse for not accepting his invitation. Armstrong then started to have tea in his own office and invited me to have tea with him there.

When questioned by Curtis Bennett, Martin showed clear animosity towards Armstrong, which did not impress the jury, particularly when he replied to the many questions that Curtis Bennett posed to him about Armstrong's acts of kindness towards him. Martin had to admit that a letter by itself could not rescind a contract and agreed that it was Armstrong who had issued the writs against his clients to force them to complete the Velinewydd contracts. Throughout his cross-examination Martin was very evasive. He could not remember what he had for lunch on the 26 October, nor what the evening meal consisted of, yet he was very precise about other details.

When the medical experts later gave evidence they all agreed that there was nothing particularly characteristic about Martin's sickness which could exclusively point to arsenical poisoning. The diagnosis of arsenical poisoning suggested by both Hincks and Willcox depended entirely on the finding of arsenic in his urine.

It is very hard to determine the exact role that Martin played throughout. Stredder believed him to be rather delicate – something of a war crock – and he had more knowledge than most, because they were next door neighbours. His mother-in-law Laura had warned Martin to be suspicious of the invitation to tea and told him that her premonition that Armstrong would harm him had come true. He may have needed little persuasion to make up the story that he had been passed a buttered scone in Armstrong's hand, for the fact remains that Martin replied to the judge that Armstrong may have asked him what he wanted to eat and in response was handed a scone: not that Armstrong picked up a scone and placed it on his plate without asking him what he wanted to eat, which Martin inferred was the case.

From all accounts his sickness was severe, but the effects of gastric influenza are severe. Neither vomiting nor attacks of diarrhoea are pleasant for anyone, but even according to his wife, his illness cleared up relatively quickly; and at any rate within twenty-four hours. This in itself indicates that he had not been subjected to a near lethal dose of arsenic. Afternoon tea is a light meal and it is very unlikely that he would have been able to eat a further meal of jugged hare within two hours of being poisoned by arsenic. He was shivering in the night and extra blankets and a hot-water bottle were supplied. This denotes a rise in temperature, which is consistent more with gastric influenza than arsenical poisoning. Armstrong related that Martin had told him he was feeling off colour and preferred to smoke a cigarette rather than his usual pipe. All the evidence of his illness, apart from the discovery of the trace of arsenic in his urine five days after the tea party, points to either food poisoning or gastric flu.

Dr Hincks, the country doctor, was well used to similar bouts of sickness and believed at the time that Martin's illness was not out of the ordinary. It was only when Martin was visited by Laura Davies that the former was persuaded that he may have been poisoned. If he was as weak a character as Stredder suggested, it would not have been difficult to influence him in this way, particularly as he was sorely vexed about the Velinewydd business. The fact remains that he knew he had played a dirty trick on Armstrong, who could have completed the two sales if he had been given a further week to do so. Equally he knew that Armstrong, whose strength as a solicitor was in litigation, would sue his clients for specific performance. Armstrong was a powerful adversary. Martin had advised his clients not to complete their purchases and a court case was bound to ensue. If Martin's clients had lost the case, Martin would have lost a great deal of prestige.

Whatever the truth about the actual tea party, it may seem difficult to fathom why Armstrong was so insistent to have tea with him again, for even though Martin may have exaggerated the number of invitations he received, his account of many invitations was undoubtedly true. But there was a valid reason all the same, which was not connected with their office business. Both men were Freemasons and although Armstrong later said in evidence that they had discussed licensing arrangements at the tea party in Mayfield, neither man informed the court that together they were proposing someone to be balloted for membership of the Hay Lodge.

The summons was dated 30 December 1921. It would have arrived at every Lodge member's house on 31 December, the day of Armstrong's arrest. The summons stated:

> To Ballot for Mr Albert Howard, age 31, The Prospect, Hay, Clerk to Guardians. Proposed by Wor. Bro. H.R. Armstrong, Chaplain P.G.J.D.; seconded by Bro. O.N. Martin.

The Lodge meeting had been fixed for 9 January 1922, but the hapless Howard was not elected, because on that day Armstrong was in the cell of his own court and Martin was giving evidence against him.

By Martin's own admission the invitations to take tea with Armstrong began on 14 November; the day of the Lodge meeting to which Armstrong had brought a bottle of brandy and a bottle of port and where he had sat next to Dr Hincks. The last invitation by Armstrong to Martin was on 12 December, the day before the next Lodge meeting: a meeting which Martin did not attend.

There are two conclusions to be drawn from this sorry affair. Martin must have been an exceptionally weak character to agree to second Armstrong's nomination of Howard at the very time that he was trying to avoid all contact with him. More importantly, Armstrong cannot have remotely considered poisoning the very person whom he had chosen to support his candidate for the Lodge, which he adored.

Oswald Martin was replaced in the witness box by his wife, Constance, and as she gave her evidence, Armstrong folded his arms, stretched back and gazed at the ceiling. Her statements did not progress the prosecution case far, apart from confirming Martin's sickness. Neither did the evidence of Una Baker, one of Armstrong's clerks, who told the court that tea was taken in the office towards the end of November on about half a dozen occasions, and that it had only been suggested because she had started to boil a kettle on a new oil stove that made the air rather dry. She confirmed that she heard Armstrong invite Mr Martin to take tea on three occasions and stated that Mrs Armstrong's will of 1920 had been proved quite openly in the office.

Dr Hincks, the last witness to be called that day, had much to lose if Armstrong was acquitted. Prior to the trial he was employing a locum, called Dr Lamb, who was helping to run his practice. A legal agreement had been prepared for the sale of Hincks's practice to Lamb, which would have been executed in the event of Armstrong's release. Before the verdict was announced the Hinckses and the Lambs were sitting in the doctor's surgery and the sale agreement was open on the table in front of them. They were awaiting a telephone call from Hereford. When the telephone rang and the caller announced that Armstrong would hang, the agreement was ripped up. If the verdict had been 'not guilty', the agreement would have been signed and Dr Hincks would have left Hay, where he had practised for twenty-eight years. Dr Hincks reconstructed Katharine's illness and death in the way which suited the prosecution case. In many respects his evidence was dishonest. Dr Hincks was not an impartial witness.

Although Armstrong had always consulted Hincks, Mrs Armstrong had not. She had returned to Mayfield in December 1918 and was joined there by her husband in March 1919. She complained of pains in her arm and Armstrong begged her to see Dr Hincks. Her first appointment with him was on 13 May 1919, and having listened to her describe symptoms of numbness and tingling of the fingers, he diagnosed brachial neuritis, that is damage to the nerves in the shoulder. She returned to his surgery on 19 May for the same condition and again went back on 24 June, complaining of pain in the wrist joint. Hincks still believed that his diagnosis of neuritis was correct, but now considered the cause to be rheumatism. Katharine consulted him again on several occasions during the summer. In September 1919 Chevalier paid a visit and Katharine played the piano for the first time in months, if not years. This suggests that Katharine may indeed have had something wrong with her joints in her arms and fingers throughout 1919. It bears out the evidence of both Bessie Friend and

Miss Pearce to the effect that Katharine suffered from pains in her arm and knee joints during the war years, which, according to Bessie, the doctors believed to have been caused by worrying.

There could never be any suggestion that Armstrong had poisoned her during the war years or during 1919 for that matter; the question must therefore be posed: what was the cause of Katharine's digestive disturbances and pains in her joints between 1915 and 1919, if not arsenical poisoning?

Hincks was not consulted again until August 1920. On 1 August he was asked to call at Mayfield to take out a speck from Eleanor's eye. He recalled that he spoke to Katharine, who appeared to be quite rational. On 15 August, Armstrong called to see the doctor and asked for sleeping draughts for Katharine. He was then consulted jointly by Armstrong and Chevalier on 18 August and asked to visit her as a matter of urgency. On arriving at Mayfield, he immediately realized that Katharine was mentally deluded and advised that she should be sent to Barnwood asylum. He said that he had examined her heart and found she had a mitral systolic murmur. The judge asked what it meant and Hincks replied that it was a type of heart disease. He immediately corrected himself: 'I won't say it means heart disease; it means that there is something wrong with one of the valves of the heart.' He said that on examining her urine, he had discovered albumen, which indicated that 'there was some disturbance of the kidney'.

He called again on the morning of the 22nd, examined her with Dr Jayne and as a result they both certified her as insane. Before Hincks examined her in the morning, he had been told that she had been vomiting, but apparently thought nothing of it. He returned in the afternoon with the car and said that he noticed 'that her general condition had changed for the worse. The first thing I noticed was that she was cyanose; she was blue about the lips; she had a sallow complexion; sallow and pallid in appearance. I examined her and found her with a rapid pulse – a pulse of 120.' He said that he saw her retch in his presence and was concerned whether or not it was safe to allow her to travel. He asked her what was wrong and Katharine told him that she was suffering from one of her bilious attacks.

At Barnwood Dr Hincks examined her with Dr Townsend. A sample of her urine was taken by catheter and was found to contain albumen. 'Her pulse was rapid. She was in an exhausted condition ... there was a systolic murmur [in the heart].' The judge asked him what caused the murmur and Hincks replied, 'I did not know then, but in the light of what I now know from the autopsy I think that that was the cause of the murmur.'

Hincks did not go to Barnwood again. He helped arrange for Nurse Kinsey to tend Katharine after her release and visited on 25 January, when he found 'really nothing wrong with her'. He was then asked by Armstrong to visit her occasionally and keep her under observation, and called again on 6 February, when again he found nothing wrong with her. He called again on 11 February when he found her complaining of the return of the 'curious feelings in her feet', which he later described to be high-steppage gait, and helped her upstairs where he examined her. At the time he cannot have thought there was much wrong with her, because he did not prescribe and did not arrange a time when he would call again. If his dates were correct, Nurse Kinsey could not have called on 10 February.

Hincks called again on 16 February as a result of a telephone call and noticed that she was acutely ill. 'Her pulse was 120; she looked very seriously ill; she had an acute expression on her face, her lips were cyanosed, blue; and it was about now that I began to notice, I can recollect, the discoloration of the skin, but it got more marked in the latter days.' When asked which part of the body was discoloured, he stated, 'The face more particularly, and the abdomen.' He said that he remembered discoloration in August. 'In February again I would describe it, that her discolouration when I saw her on the 16th (February) was about equal to what it was when she went into the asylum, but towards the latter end of her illness it assumed a much deeper bronze or copper colour.' When he was asked about the lips and tongue, he said, 'Brown and dry.' When questioned about her final days he was emphatic that 'it was impossible for her to leave her bed certainly from the 18th onwards.' On being pressed by the Crown, he said, 'She could not convey a cup to her lips.' The judge interposed 'When would that be?' Hincks replied, 'That would be about the 16th or 17th I should think, the beginning of her acute illness. She had to be fed.' He then gave his opinion, 'My opinion now is that her illness when she went into the asylum was caused by arsenical poisoning; she had a remission of heart symptoms while she was in the asylum and her last and final illness was again due to arsenical poisoning.' Mr Justice Darling: 'A fresh dose?', to which he replied 'A fresh dose.'

Hincks was particularly careful to say that he never saw any delusions at all or any sign of the return of her mental trouble.

> During that time after she came back from the asylum her great anxiety all the time was to get better; that was her great wish, she desired to get better ... I was never worried with regard to any question of suicidal tendencies during the time I was in attendance on her ... I do not recollect anything said about her having spoken of throwing herself out of the window ... I had not the slightest misgivings, otherwise I should never have consented to a nurse just visiting her night and morning.

Of course, this was entirely untrue, as Nurse Kinsey had made a special visit to him and told him that she feared suicide. Indeed it was Hincks who arranged for a psychiatric nurse to stay with Katharine at all times, day and night.

There is no doubt that Hincks believed that Armstrong was a poisoner, and as he had nailed his colours to the mast, he had to justify his beliefs. He was the vital medical witness, since he was Katharine's doctor and had treated her both before her admission to Barnwood and after her return. However, he was biased. Willcox had based his opinions on what Hincks had said had happened, and then fed his bias with more information, which enabled Hincks to feed his recollections with hindsight. Hincks told the jury that when Katharine returned from Barnwood there was nothing wrong with her. This statement did not conform to Townsend's evidence, which was that although she was improved physically she was very little better mentally. Hincks said she had 'high steppage gait', but no one else had noticed it, not even the nurses or Miss Pearce. He said that she had suffered from peripheral arsenical neuritis when she was in

Barnwood, but he had not seen her while she was there and his opinion again contradicted the medical evidence of the asylum doctors. Hincks's new opinions were the ones he was told to have.

21

An even larger crowd had collected outside the Shirehall, on Friday, the fifth day of the trial. Despite the fact that the day's session had begun, a line of several hundred people pressed themselves against the railings in the hope that a few of them would be admitted when the court adjourned for lunch. To break the monotony a harpist kept them entertained.

Hincks was recalled to the witness box and stuck steadfastly to his opinions, even though he had to admit he had no experience of arsenical poisoning since his student days. Armstrong scarcely moved, except to make a note or whisper to Matthews, and displayed an attitude of confidence and indifference throughout.

Hincks spoke of Martin's illness and had to admit that there were a number of medicines that contained arsenic and that 1/33 of a grain would not affect a person at all. When asked whether or not arsenic was one of the impurities of bismuth, he replied that as he was not a chemist, he would not know, but had to agree that, in the case of Martin, the 'whole thing' depended on finding that 1/33 of a grain. Hincks could not say anything else, because that too was the opinion of Willcox and every other expert, whether called for the prosecution or for the defence.

After being in the witness box for over five hours, at one o'clock Hincks was replaced by Dr Townsend of Barnwood asylum, who was a fair witness and a credit to his profession. Townsend did not jump to conclusions about arsenical poisoning. He had no reason to do so, for unlike Hincks he was not emotionally involved in the Crown case. He described Katharine's admission and stated that he attributed her failure to pass urine for the first twenty-four hours to the vomiting and loss of body fluids. He had made an examination of it and confirmed that it contained albumen, which cleared away in three to four days. He did not know if her urine had been examined later during her stay. He stated that he kept her in bed until November, and that in September he had noticed some wasting of her muscles and that she had lost 'her power in her hands and feet'. He related to the court that she had taken a tonic containing arsenic for a month beginning in October and that he held the view that her loss of power was functional, in other words that it was a real inability, but caused by a disassociation of the mind and not from an organic cause. Armstrong had followed his suggestion and visited at about three-weekly intervals. The solicitor readily agreed that a specialist should be called, and Townsend declared that even if she had been released on leave of absence, he would have accepted the death certificate without making any further enquiries. Of extreme importance was his statement that upon her release she had recovered to a degree physically but not mentally, which was an inconvenient detail overlooked by both Hincks and later by the judge in his summing-up.

Mr Fred Davies then took the stand and described the sales of weedkiller recorded in his ledger and the sales of arsenic recorded in his poison book:

27 July 1912	one gallon of weedkiller
23 June 1913	three gallons of weedkiller
2 May 1914	one pound caustic soda and ½ lb arsenic
7 June 1919	½ lb of arsenic
4 May 1920	four gallons of liquid weedkiller
4 August 1920	two tins of powdered weedkiller
11 January 1921	¼ lb of arsenic

He told the court that on 30 October 1921 he selected a clean bottle, washed it half a dozen times, took it down to Dr Hincks, who later brought it back to his shop.

Davies always denied that he had any real involvement in the inquiry. In cross examination before the magistrates he said that he did not give instructions for anything to be done and suggested that Hincks had acted entirely on his own initiative. This statement is entirely untrue, as he certainly knew and approved of what was being done. Matthews had asked Revd de Winton for local knowledge, and received the following response:

1. In the first week in January to a fellow tradesman 'he certainly did it. There is no doubt of that' that was referring to poisoning Martin.
2. In the middle of January over the counter in his shop to a farmer 'we should all have been poisoned if it had been allowed to go on'.

The second statement demonstrates his positive involvement.

He stated that none of the sales of the weedkiller had been entered in his sale of poison book, because the gardener, Jay, had made those purchases. He admitted that the amount of weedkiller purchased during the last two years was not excessive considering the amount of ground it had to cover. He agreed that Armstrong had told him that he had his own recipe for making weedkiller. Curtis Bennett then produced a small cigarette tin, inside which, wrapped in paper, were two ounces of white powder. The wrapping was handed gingerly to the jury, and eventually to the judge, who looked curiously at it, and when he had finished with it, he dusted his fingers daintily and dropped his handkerchief away from him. Curtis Bennett produced it, like a conjuror produces a rabbit out of his hat, but his theatrical trick outraged the judge. Davies was equally startled when he was handed the wrapper to examine. He had to admit that the inner wrapping bore his label and conceded that the packet might contain the arsenic that Armstrong had purchased on 11 January 1921. He said he had not made the sale himself and accepted that it was possible that it had been sold uncoloured.

Curtis Bennett must have known that the production of white arsenic in the middle of a murder trial was reckless in the extreme and that the police would rigorously deny that they had been inefficient in their most thorough of searches. It is hard to know what he anticipated, but no doubt he had been looking forward to disclosing his little tin to Fred Davies all morning. Yet he should not have concentrated on his disclosure but should have cross-examined the chemist mercilessly and brought to light the chocolates episode and the lack of evidence associating Armstrong with them. Juries do not like important matters to be hidden from them, as they are suspicious about the reasons for the concealment, which may go against the accused. The undoubted fact remains that most, if not all, the jurymen, along with practically everyone else in the court from the judge down, knew about the arsenic in the chocolates, for it featured prominently in the magistrates court and had been widely reported in all the newspapers.

The only slight inroad Curtis Bennett made was to establish that Davies prepared liquor arsenicalis (Fowler's solution) and liquor arsenici hydrochloric from the powdered arsenic which he kept in tins. The same cupboard contained all the empty bottles, and from this supply Davies had given Martin a bottle that had previously contained hydrogen peroxide. Davies had stated this to be empty in the magistrates court and clean at the trial. Curtis Bennett asked no questions at all about Davies's involvement prior to the sample being taken, even though Davies had said in evidence that he had taken the bottle to Hincks and later said he had taken it to Martin. Bennett also failed to elicit that Davies knew a great deal about arsenic, its preparation in a number of forms and its use in a wide variety of agricultural and domestic contexts. In fact Davies had the apparatus in his chemist's shop to test for arsenic and could have analysed the white powder in the chocolates and the urine sample; but equally Davies did not want to take this step, as he was the only other person who had the means and the opportunity to tamper with the chocolates. It would have been very suspicious indeed if it had been his analysis that had discovered the arsenic in the chocolates and in the urine.

The judge had been taken aback by Bennett's little trick and finally intervened when poor Hird, who had actually sold the white arsenic to Armstrong, protested that he had coloured it before selling it. Mr Justice Darling noted that Matthews had not raised the issue in the police court and he wanted to know why.

The next witness that should have been called was Laura Davies, the wife of Fred, but both defence and prosecution lawyers indicated that her evidence was not required.

As the day was drawing to a close, Officers Weaver and Crutchett gave their evidence. Weaver spoke of Armstrong's arrest and Matthews's find of the packet of white arsenic was left for Crutchett to explain. Crutchett protested very strongly indeed when it was suggested to him that he had failed to find the packet of white arsenic in the bureau of Armstrong's study. In fact he was as stunned as Armstrong had been when he was arrested to be confronted with such an accusation. At this stage, the trial began to take a sinister turn, which was very unfavourable to the prisoner, who sat back and listened to the dialogue. Crutchett was now on the defensive, protecting his position as a senior policeman. Not surprisingly he stated that he had examined the drawer of the bureau and did not discover any white arsenic. Curtis Bennett then overplayed his hand and commented that traces of white powder could be seen in the drawer itself, and suggested that Crutchett did not make a thorough search, because he was looking for coloured arsenic and not white arsenic. Crutchett replied, 'Oh yes; there were other things that caused me to look for white arsenic.' Crutchett also stated that he had not found the recipe for the weedkiller in the file marked 'Garden', or the advertisement by the Boundary Chemical Company indicating the method for killing individual weeds. He made a point of remarking that although he had given permission for Armstrong to look at his business letters, he had not authorized him to look at the letters that had been removed from his pockets. When he heard a rustle of paper and noticed that Armstrong was looking at the contents of the brown wrapping, he stopped him and placed him on a seat in the middle of the room. The judge noted this remark with interest.

The sixth day of the trial was held on the Saturday. The production of Bennett's little tin had deeply upset the police officers in the case and Deputy Chief Constable Weaver was recalled to the witness stand. He insisted that the drawer in question contained only keys and had been pulled right out. He denied that the recipe containing weedkiller had been in the study. The judge asked, 'Do you believe it possible that the little packet, two ounces of arsenic, could have been in that drawer, or in the cavity behind it, at the time you searched?' to which he replied, 'Well, I say it is absolutely impossible, my Lord. I do not think we left an inch of the bureau untouched.'

Harriet Price was recalled and said that she went into the

study on the Sunday, the day after the police search and saw two silver salt spoons on the floor. She opened the bureau and found the key to the silver chest: there was no packet of arsenic in the drawer. By this time the whole affair had been blown out of all proportion and everyone in court had become thoroughly confused. Bennett's attempts to discredit the police for the inefficiency of their search had backfired. The judge later used the episode to cast more doubt on the honesty of the prisoner, who was unjustly accused of deliberately concealing the white arsenic from the police until the trial.

The remainder of the day was taken up with the forensic witnesses called by the Crown. Their evidence made a deep impression on the jurors, because they heard at first hand from the pathologist who had conducted the post-mortem, the chemist who had analysed the organs of the dead body and the physician who interpreted the results. The latter's inferences were based not only on their deductions but on the evidence of Dr Hincks who had treated Mrs Armstrong during her lifetime.

Spilsbury was the first to be called, and with the help of a coloured diagram, explained the workings of the digestive system. He explained that the progress of food through the alimentary canal depends on many variables, but that in the normal course of events, it passes from the mouth and out through the rectum within twenty-four hours. As there was arsenic in the stomach and the small intestines, it follows that the poison must have been ingested within that period of time. The liver and kidneys had also been damaged by quantities of arsenic. He explained that the poison must have been taken before the final dose to account for these features, and the damage to the heart wall could be similarly explained. He concluded that 'the poison must have been given in a number of large doses over a period, certainly of some days, probably not less than a week ... [and] ... a fatal dose must have been taken certainly within twenty-four hours of death'.

In cross-examination he readily admitted that a person could take a fatal dose many days before death and agreed that there were cases on record where a person had survived for seven or more days. It would be expected that in such a case, quantities of arsenic would be found not only in the liver but also in the large intestine and that the vital organs would be affected by the poison. He even admitted the possibility that arsenic could become 'encapsulated' in the stomach and be slowly released, causing symptoms, followed by periods of remission and relief. He concluded, 'I should not like to exclude it entirely.' But when he was re-examined, he denied that this scenario was possible in the case before him and reiterated his view that Katharine had died from a fatal dose of arsenic administered within twenty-four hours of her death.

When asked his opinion on Katharine's illness in August 1920 he declared that vomiting, the presence of albumen in her urine followed by the development of peripheral neuritis pointed clearly to arsenical poisoning. In cross-examination he admitted that the albumen could have been caused by kidney disease, but that it should be discounted because the albumen completely disappeared soon after her admission to Barnwood. Bennett pointed out that there was no evidence that any further examinations were ever made. The attorney general then shot to his feet and declared that Dr Townsend had told the court on more than one occasion that an examination of Katharine's urine had been made in November and found to be albumen-free. This was, of course, completely untrue, as no examination had been made after 29 August; albumen could have been present throughout her stay, and Pollock's intervention reflected badly on his own honesty. Despite Spilsbury's assertion that the symptoms on her admission and her subsequent paralysis pointed to arsenical poisoning, he had to admit that the arsenic tonic given to her would have tended to retard her recovery if she had been suffering from arsenical neuritis. This point should have weighed heavily in favour of the defence.

When he was questioned about Martin's illness he readily admitted to Curtis Bennett that the urine sample was not taken scientifically and the bottle selected could have been contaminated by its previous contents. Arsenic was also known to be an impurity in glucose and bismuth, both of which had been given to Martin – the glucose in the form of port wine jelly and the bismuth in the form of Hincks's 'white mixture', which had been tablespooned into Martin four times a day. Yet when he was re-examined on these important statements, he changed his opinions.

He knew full well that the whole case revolved around the time that Katharine had ingested the arsenic. If it could be proved that it had been taken within twenty-four hours of her death, the prosecution case would be immeasurably strengthened. Yet he dismissed the phenomenon reported by an American doctor, called Witthaus, whose research into the effects of arsenic injected into cadavers indicated that the arsenic 'migrated' from tissue to tissue, and that meaningful deductions about the distribution of arsenic could not be made with certainty from findings in the body after death. When Spilsbury was queried by the attorney general the following dialogue took place:

'And lastly Dr Spilsbury, paying every tribute of respect to Dr Witthaus' writing in 1911, have you during the course of the last ten or eleven years since that book was published had the opportunity of making examinations of dead bodies; may I say by the score since that time?'

'I think I may say almost by the thousand.'

'And without undue modesty might you say have your researches during that period contributed to advancing knowledge in that ten years?'

'I hope so.'

'Has there been anybody who has had a larger opportunity from his experience and examinations of forming an opinion on this subject?'

'There have been many, but I do not know that so many go into toxicological cases.'

'What might toxicology be?'

'Poisons.'

'Then when a new edition comes out, Dr Spilsbury, perhaps some tribute may be paid to you for your researches?'

'I will leave that.'

Needless to say Dr Spilsbury's researches never modified Dr Witthaus's conclusions, or any other writer on forensic medicine who reported on the effects of arsenical poisoning, for that matter. What was equally interesting in this exchange was Spilsbury's comments that he had examined thousands of dead bodies during a ten-year period. When John Webster gave evidence he stated that he examined about thirty to forty bodies per year, totalling three to four hundred during the ten-year period. Cases of arsenical poisoning were rare and accounted for a tiny percentage of all poisoning cases that were submitted to him for analysis. Webster had given evidence in both the Seddon and Greenwood case. Spilsbury had appeared for the Crown in the former but not the latter. In reality, whatever Spilsbury intended to convey, his experience of arsenical poisoning was limited to one case only.

Armstrong was obviously distressed when the ghastly details of his wife's exhumation were recounted. Although not a muscle of his face moved, his eyes were downcast as though he was consciously detaching himself from the proceedings, but when the cross-examination began he followed every word that fell from Curtis Bennett's lips. He knew that whatever had taken place in the first five days of the trial was nothing compared to the damning rhetoric of Dr Spilsbury, whose evidence went to the root of the issue more surely than arsenic had ever penetrated a dandelion root.

John Webster's evidence dealt mainly with his analysis of the various bottles that had been handed to him, which included Martin's urine sample, but not the chocolates. He told the court that he had never found a larger quantity of arsenic in the organs of any body and was almost as theatrical as Curtis Bennett when he produced a little tube containing 3½ grains of arsenic and held it up for the jury to see. The judge rammed the point home: 'That represents the amount actually found. That means a very, very much larger amount taken in the body.'

Willcox was the last of the prosecution witnesses for the Crown and effectively summed up the medical evidence. He differentiated the neuritis which Katharine had undoubtedly suffered during the war years and in 1919 from the peripheral neuritis that she suffered in Barnwood. He also declared that her heart trouble in August 1920 could not have been caused by either neuritis or rheumatism. When asked about her sickness on the afternoon of 22 August (the admission to Barnwood) he said that she must have ingested an irritant poison. The suppression of urine could have indicated a toxic poison, although it might have been due to other causes. He laid great store on the disappearance of the albumen in her urine and the onset of peripheral neuritis which developed in the course of a fortnight, explaining that it indicated arsenical poisoning. When asked whether or not it was easy to diagnose arsenical poisoning during life, he made an important admission: 'It is difficult; the symptoms of arsenical poisoning may be imitated by disease.' He was then asked about Katharine's symptoms when she had returned home and pointed out that the high steppage gait, of which Hincks spoke, was a common disorder or sensation in peripheral neuritis. Her high pulse and sickness on 16 February were due to an irritant poison, and the return of the peripheral neuritis symptoms before the 16th indicated that poison had been taken before the 11th. The symptoms on the 16th were symptoms of latent poisoning, indicating that arsenic had been taken a few hours before the onset of these symptoms. From the distribution of the arsenic in the alimentary canal, 'I have no doubt that a possibly fatal dose was taken within twenty-four hours of death.'

Finally, shortly before twenty past seven that evening, the judge interposed and asked Willcox three telling questions:

'You thoroughly understood the hypothesis put to you by Sir Henry Curtis Bennett as to the last two days of the life of Mrs Armstrong and what might have happened during those two days?'

'Yes.'

'Taking that hypothesis as he put it and remembering all the evidence that you have heard as to everything, is that hypothesis in your opinion a possible one to account for Mrs Armstrong's death?'

'Quite impossible.'

'You understand it to be a suggestion that it was suicide committed according to the system of that hypothesis?'

'Yes.'

As the court adjourned for the day, Sir Henry Curtis Bennett turned at the door and nodded with a bright smile to Armstrong, who returned the salute. Bennett was going home to prepare his opening speech and Armstrong was going back to his solitary cell. The prosecution case had finished. On the Monday Armstrong would enter the witness box and for the first time in the whole proceedings give an account of himself. Everyone in court wondered how he would react and what his voice would be like, for up to now he had been silent and passive, sitting between two warders in the dock of the court.

22

When the trial resumed on the Monday, there was an expectant air in the court, for not only was Armstrong going to enter the witness box, but Curtis Bennett would set out the case for the defence.

Curtis rose to the occasion and with effortless oratory captivated the jury and public alike. He submitted that the case for the Crown was based on a falsehood and had been developed backwards from the finding of the arsenic in Katharine's body. Not only was there an insufficient motive for murder, but the prosecution had not been able to make any suggestion as to how Armstrong was supposed to have administered the poison. He emphasized that the prosecution had to prove their case and it was not enough to put a man in the dock and say, 'Look, this is suspicious', 'that is suspicious' and 'the other is suspicious'. It was not for Armstrong to prove that his wife took the poison herself or that someone else gave it to her. It was for the prosecution to prove what they had set out to prove. 'If you take the ordinary possibility or the ordinary chances, the case that Mrs Armstrong took the poison herself is infinitely stronger than the case made out against Major Armstrong.' This remark caused the judge to intervene for the first time. 'You mean,' he quietly remarked, 'that she took it knowing it to be poison?', to which Curtis Bennett replied, 'Certainly. I have answered you, my Lord, with what is in my mind; but it is not for me to prove that.' He continued:

On August the 15th this man, alleged to be poisoning his wife, sends for the doctor! That is a good start in a poisoning case. Why! You are going to be left to the end of all time wondering. There is no evidence, as Sir William Willcox admitted, of any vomiting up to the 22nd August, and then this alleged poisoner sends for the best friend of the family, Arthur Chevalier. An amazing poisoner this! He then sends for the sister of the person he is alleged to be poisoning! There is not one scrap of evidence of arsenical poisoning or the administration of any poison by anyone in August 1920, and it is suggested – for there is no sort of evidence that Armstrong administered arsenic – that he did this on August 22nd. You have got to swallow something if you swallow this assumption on evidence of that sort and on the evidence of that sort hangs this man's life.

He turned to Katharine's death and again pointed out that all the evidence indicated suicide, but that he could no more prove suicide than the prosecution could prove that Armstrong poisoned her. He referred to Nurse Allen's evidence, which he said he could prove was wrong: Katharine was not in bed from 13 February onwards. 'You are dealing with a man's life and you are dealing with it through opinions based on reports and symptoms which I have shown cannot be relied upon.' He dealt with Martin's evidence and pointed out to the jury that he refused to say a good word about Armstrong and that Martin had a stronger motive for getting rid of his rival than the other way round.

You see, Mr. Martin was a newcomer in Hay, a man who had only just started in the county. If Major Armstrong did try to poison Martin because of the motive suggested, then there is only one proper verdict, and that verdict was that he was insane. Can you imagine that any sane man would try to poison Martin because of this trouble over the Velinewydd estate? Armstrong is not being tried for trying to poison Martin. You won't be asked for your verdict on that. The prosecution have got to prove murder. It doesn't matter twopence about Martin.

Armstrong entered the witness box after lunch, standing erect with both hands resting on the ledge. He was examined by Bosanquet and answered in a firm voice, free from hesitation and embarrassment and his voice carried to the far reaches of the court. All eyes were on him as he recounted his early career and family life. He explained his wife's health

problems and her delusions, which became so acute in
August 1920 that a decision was made to send her to
Barnwood. He said that he did not see his wife until noon of
the day of departure and emphatically denied that he gave her
arsenic on that or any other day. He narrated his visits to
Barnwood and said that when she returned she could not use
her hands and feet, but denied that she suffered from high
steppage gait and that she never complained of anything of
the kind.

On the evening of 15 February Katharine took to her bed,
but she had been up and about on that day. He said that he
continued to go to work and used to sit with her, and always
looked into her room after he had lunch, but denied that he
had anything to do with her food. When asked about an
entry in his diary, 'Ask M.G.', he explained that as Miss
Pearce would be away on holiday he wanted someone to keep
house and made the entry to remind him to mention it to
Marion Gale, who may have known someone who could
help. 'She was the only friend I could discuss this matter with.
I have no relatives.'

When asked about his relationship with Martin he said
that it was always 'absolutely friendly' and that it was
'perfectly incorrect' that he handed him a scone, saying
'excuse fingers'. He told the court about his purchases of
arsenic and said that when he returned from Italy he noticed
that the 1921 purchase that he had placed in his cupboard in
his study had apparently been opened and that the string had
been removed. He had then placed the open packet in his
bureau. He was clearly impressing the jury and the judge was
forced to intervene: 'Where is the bureau?' Curtis Bennett
replied that it was in the possession of the under-sheriff. The
judge then ordered that the bureau be brought to the court so
that Armstrong could place the packet within it. The
conveyance of the bureau through the streets of Hereford was
watched with great interest by the crowds that had gathered
outside the court. Armstrong left the witness box and placed
the packet in the desk, which had been positioned in the
grand jury room. The drawer fitted and there was no cavity
behind it. He then resumed his evidence, giving details of his
use of the other two ounces of the white arsenic: killing
individual dandelions in his garden and conducting

experiments in the nursery relating to its solubility with caustic soda. This took place while he was staying with his friend, Tunnard Moore.

When asked if he had deliberately interfered with the letters taken from his pockets he said that he had interpreted the consent to look at his business letters to mean that he could look at those letters taken from his pockets. It was then that he noticed for the first time that the little packet of white arsenic was among them. Finally he was asked if he had proposed marriage to Marion Gale and he replied that he had, on 'either May 14th, or May 15th, just after my birthday.'

At 6 p.m. the attorney general rose to begin his cross-examination. At 6.35 p.m. the Court adjourned part heard. Armstrong was again in the witness box on Tuesday morning, the seventh day of the trial.

23

Armstrong had weathered the storm on the previous day and had responded to the attorney general's brief cross-examination with confidence, despite the signs of a brewing storm. One method favoured by the attorney general was to distort quite neutral evidence by interpreting it unreasonably. At the time of his wife's admission to Barnwood Armstrong had answered a questionnaire on her health and had replied that her health had been 'generally good but of livery tendency', and that he had not disclosed her suicidal tendencies which had been indicated to him by Chevalier. 'Did you not think it fair to the asylum authorities not to make any disclosure as to your anxiety as to her suicidal tendencies?' asked the devious Pollock; and later: 'Out of mercy to your wife, sir, did you not attempt to conceal from her that she was going to an asylum?' If Armstrong thought that these questions were loaded he had no inkling of the savage onslaught that would be inflicted upon him by both prosecutor and judge when he re-entered the witness stand. The most potent weapon of all is the destruction of the prisoner's credibility in the eyes of the jury.

Pollock attacked the making of the second will and tried to prove that Armstrong had destroyed the rough draft of it found by Bessie after Katharine's death. He tried to adduce evidence by way of letters from New Zealand, but Curtis Bennett's objections were sustained. However, Armstrong had to admit that after the second will was made he did not arrange for the first will to be destroyed, and the judge again intervened with telling effect.

Armstrong readily admitted that he was often at the sick bed when the nurse was out of the room, but repeated that he had never given her food or drink. 'It was never necessary. The nurse was always present when it was required.' His card to Bessie, which indicated his belief that Katharine was getting better, was used against him, Pollock suggesting that he had written it after Hincks had told him that his wife would not recover. Armstrong was taken through the Martin evidence, which he countered firmly but effectively. He stated that he only remembered the white arsenic in his bureau when he noticed the little packet caught up in the letters which had been removed from his pockets. He stated that he had not told the police about it, because he had been arrested and was waiting to see his solicitor. The judge again intervened: 'And you wanted to wait,' he queried, 'until you had seen your solicitor to see whether you should tell the police the truth?' The questions about Armstrong's omission to tell the police about the white arsenic continued with unremitting persistence. All Armstrong could say was that he was very shocked to be arrested and that when he saw the little packet after the arrest he was so stunned he thought it better to say no more. For a period of an hour in his cross-examination he was attempting to balance a copy of the New Testament on the ledge before him, allowing it to sway one way or the other before quickly catching it before it fell. His actions were mechanical, but showed signs of his nervous tension during the long ordeal.

His story was convincing and made sense and the judge knew that it had impressed the jury. His evidence finished at 2.30 p.m., almost exactly twenty-four hours after he had entered the witness box on the previous day, and as he was about to step down fatigued more than he knew, the judge indicated that he should remain where he was and began a remorseless interrogation.

'With regard to the white arsenic: you have told us how you made up the four ounces you bought in January into two parts of two ounces each?'

'Yes, my Lord.'

'And the experiment you made with one packet of two ounces and caustic soda which you afterwards poured down the sink or the lavatory. And the rest you made up in a packet?'

'Yes.'

'And the two ounces left you put in a cupboard?'

'Yes.'

'Had you then forgotten all about that four ounce packet of arsenic?'

'Yes, my Lord.'

'Had you ever had white arsenic before?'

'No, never.'

'Always coloured with charcoal?'

'Yes.'

'It was rather remarkable, was it not, that you should then have had four ounces of white arsenic which you had never had before?'

'No, my Lord.'

'How was that – how was it when you made your statement to the police you were so particular as to tell them you had mentioned all the arsenic you had except any that might be in medicine of which you would not know; how was it when you told them so carefully of all you had got you put in that statement that there might be other in medicine. How can you account for having forgotten all that arsenic – the only white arsenic you have ever had?'

'I cannot account for it.'

'You had tried an interesting experiment by mixing it with caustic, not in a tin but in a glass. Is that so?'

'Yes, quite correct, my Lord.'

'And that accounted for one ounce of it, and as to the rest you had made it up into twenty little packets?'

'Yes, my Lord.'

'And with regard to nineteen of them you gave separate doses to nineteen dandelions?'

'Yes.'

'You made a hole at the root of the dandelions and administered nineteen doses of arsenic to nineteen dandelions. Did you notice what became of them; did they die?'

'Afterwards they died.'

'That was very interesting, was it not?'

'It was at the time, but it had passed from my mind.'

'A very interesting experiment if you wanted to get rid of weeds, was it not?'

'It was.'

'Do you tell the jury that you absolutely forgot about that

white arsenic?'

'I do, my Lord.'

'And the dandelions?'

'The whole incident had passed from my mind for the time when I was making that statement.'

'Did it not strike you that it was very remarkable, after, to forget. You are a solicitor?'

'I follow that.'

'Does not it occur to you it would have been a very very bad case for you if you had to tell the police that you had not only weed-killing arsenic but white arsenic in your possession?'

'But I did not remember it.'

'That is not what I asked you. Does not it appear to you if you had got white arsenic in your possession it would have been a very bad thing?'

'It would have to be explained.'

'You see that?'

'Yes quite, now.'

'When you saw the little packet and you realised that you had got white arsenic in your pocket, did you realise that it was just a fatal dose of arsenic, not for dandelions only but for human beings?'

'No, I did not realise that at all.'

'It appears now if every one of these little packets you made up were the same as the ones found in your pocket, every one contained just a fatal dose of arsenic for a human being. You realise that, do you not?'

'I do now, my Lord; I did not at the time.'

'The suggestion is that the moment you remembered that, you tried to get it back?'

'I could not, my Lord, because Worthing was the other side.'

'The police officer, Worthing?'

Sir Curtis Bennett: 'Crutchett, my Lord.'

Mr Justice Darling: 'Well, Crutchett.'

'You know now what you saw there was a fatal dose of arsenic?'

'I know now since the evidence in this case.'

'And you realise what you had given the dandelions was a fatal dose of arsenic for a human being?'

'I have realised it since, I did not know it at the time.'

'If you were simply dosing dandelions, why did you make up that one ounce of arsenic into twenty little packets such as that found in your pocket wrapped up in paper?'

'Because of the convenience of putting it in the ground.'

'But you did it all in one day?'

'I dosed them all at the same time, yes.'

'Why go to the trouble of making up twenty little packets, one for each dandelion, instead of taking out the ounce you had got and making a hole and giving the dandelions something from the one ounce?'

'I do not really know.'

'Why make up twenty little packets, each a fatal dose for a human being, and put it in your pocket?'

'At the time it seemed to me the most convenient way of doing it. I cannot give any other explanation.'

'And according to you you did not tell them anymore about it although you knew your statement did not tell the whole of the truth?'

'That is so.'

'Would it not have been better to make a clean breast of it and say – it is in the drawer of the bureau?'

'It did not occur to me, my Lord.'

'I understand you kept all this to yourself, and sent for Mr Matthews the next morning?'

'Yes. And after the consultation with him you did not even mention to the police that the arsenic was in the bureau?'

'I will not go as far as that. I told Mr Matthews on Sunday where it was.'

'You did?'

'Yes.'

The judge then deviated from the truth and allowed his rancour to overcome him:

'And as far as the police officers and the prosecution were concerned they knew nothing about it until Sir Henry Curtis Bennett opened those facts to the jury yesterday. Is that so?'

This brought an immediate response from Curtis Bennett who told the judge that he had produced it last week (as the judge well knew), but the judge continued: 'Was it, as far as you know, purposely concealed from the police until last Thursday?' 'And what you say is you thought when the police were going to search they would find it?' 'If you thought they were going to find it why did not you try to get credit for yourself by telling them where it was?' 'Yes, but according to you, you had done your best to keep it secret till last Thursday?'

This vehement attack left the jury in no doubt whatsoever that the judge believed that Armstrong had deliberately concealed the white arsenic from the police, that his story about poisoning individual weeds was nonsense and that he could have used the packet in his pocket to take a human life. Yet the packet at Mayfield had been caught up in the drawer; it was Curtis Bennett who had decided to conceal it from the police; the Boundary Chemical Company did retail a device for killing individual weeds; and there were five witnesses who would come forward to give evidence that they had poisoned individual weeds in much the same way as Armstrong said he had. As for the packet itself, the judge did not ask Armstrong whether there was other detritus in the pocket of his gardening coat, which he had been wearing when he was arrested. No, because such questions would have been fair ones, and that was not the object of the judge's intervention, which was to inform the jury in the strongest of terms that he did not believe a word of Armstrong's story.

For the greater part of the 7½ hours that Armstrong had stood in the witness box he had maintained his dignity but the last quarter of an hour had tired him more than he realized, and as he finally left the box to return to the dock he marched with a military step to his accustomed seat in the dock, sat down and stretched out his legs luxuriously.

Matthews was then called to give evidence in support of the find of the packet of white arsenic. His story was corroborated by his clerk, Chivers. There was never any doubt that Matthews had found both the arsenic in Armstrong's desk and the recipe for the home-made weedkiller in the garden file. Yet two senior policemen stated that all the drawers from the desk had been removed completely in their thorough search, and that they had not seen the garden file. If they were lying on oath, can their evidence be accepted that Armstrong was not given permission to look at the business letters that had been taken from his pockets? Matthews's discovery of the packet of white arsenic should have been dropped there and then, but the judge thought otherwise and reserved his astonishing attack on his honesty and integrity until later in the trial.

Messrs Toogood, Ainslie and Steed then gave their evidence for the defence and as each of them were cross-examined they were browbeaten mercilessly by the attorney general, who forced them to admit that the Crown experts were more experienced than they were. He was helped throughout by the judge who had allowed free rein to the prosecution experts, but on occasions restricted the defence experts to answering complex questions by a simple yes or no.

Toogood was examined by Bosanquet and established his opinion that from 1915 to 1920 Katharine suffered from auto-intoxication caused by chronic indigestion. He associated this with the presence of gallstones and the fact that she also suffered from neuritis and rheumatoid arthritis. These conditions in turn fully explained the albumen found at times in her urine and the dilated heart with a murmur. He believed that before her admission to Barnwood she was suffering from melancholia and that the loss of power in her limbs was functional weakness associated with the previous neuritis. He was quite clear that she could not have been suffering from arsenical neuritis, because she could change her postures; the arsenic tonic given to her also helped her to recover and, more importantly, there were no delayed contractions of her muscles and no fibrillary tremors. He agreed with the reports from the asylum that her condition was functional.

Pollock was by this time getting worried, because Toogood's clear thinking was impressive. When Bosanquet asked Toogood about her condition on 11 February when she was examined by Dr Hincks, Pollock whispered very loudly 'high steppage gait', to which Toogood replied that it was often found in functional diseases. Toogood then confidently stated that there was no evidence consistent with arsenical poisoning up to 16 February and that on this date she must have taken a considerable quantity of arsenic, possibly ten grains or more, although he could not possibly state for certainty the amount, due to the vomiting which occurred. He accounted for the symptoms which followed by stating that if a large dose had been taken, a portion of the arsenic may have become covered with mucus and become attached to the wall of the stomach. There it might have remained for some days before gradually dissolving and passing into the intestine. He explained that it was quite possible to survive for some days after taking a large dose and that he had known of a case where the person had survived for seven days. He said that it was impossible to interpret the results of the post-mortem, because the jejunum and ileum had been placed in the same bottle, together with the fluids found within them, and any inferences drawn would be absolutely valueless. He was definite that migration after death was a well-known phenomenon and that it was impossible to form any correct opinion of the distribution of arsenic from the findings of a post-mortem made several months after death.

Toogood was then questioned about the Martin case and stated that his illness was consistent either with an attack of acute indigestion or gastro-intestinal influenza, or any irritant poison, which could include arsenic. However, he did not believe that a person taking a fatal dose of arsenic at half past five would be likely to eat dinner two hours later. The judge was increasingly aware that he was making an impression on the jury and asked him,

'Is there anything in what Mr Martin describes from which you could say he had not taken arsenic at tea time?'

Toogood: 'At which period during the whole course of his illness?'

Judge: 'I will not ask you again.'

Bosanquet was forced to repeat the judge's question, but the judge insisted that the shorthand writer read it out and Toogood replied that he did not believe that any person who had taken a fatal dose of arsenic would have been able to return to work so soon, as the constitutional disturbance would be too great. Toogood then stated that samples of bismuth could contain very considerable quantities of arsenic and cited an example where a medicinal bismuth contained 0.44 per cent of the poison. He maintained that the sampling of the urine was not, in any event, taken scientifically at all, and that the water which had been used to wash out the bottle should have been sent for analysis to make certain that there was no arsenic in the bottle itself. Finally, before the court rose for the day he said that a fresh cork should have been taken from a fresh packet to ensure that it was arsenic-free.

24

When Toogood was called to resume his evidence on the Wednesday the trial was drawing to a close and Armstrong reappeared in the dock looking utterly worn out. The attorney general lost no time in taking Toogood to task.

'Would you place Sir William Willcox as one of the great authorities on arsenical poisoning?'

'I should, emphatically.'

'Would it be putting it too high to say that he is perhaps the highest authority?'

'He is the highest authority I know.'

'I suggest in the United Kingdom.'

'Undoubtedly.'

'Dr Spilsbury – is he a man of unrivalled experience in post-mortem examinations? Is there anyone in the United Kingdom you would suggest has had greater experience in post-mortem examination than Dr Spilsbury?'

'No.'

'And Mr Webster is a man who, as an analytical chemist, holds the highest reputation?'

'Very high.'

'As high as anybody?'

'I think so. [after a pause] I have no doubt of it.'

'In the cases that come before you in your various capacities would you rely upon the analysis of Mr Webster?'

'I can think of no one better qualified to whom I could send.'

Judge (sharply): 'Answer the question.'

Toogood (answering): 'I should.'

This browbeating of an expert witness was absolutely unethical and should never have been allowed, whereas the judge actually encouraged and welcomed it. Toogood maintained that Katharine had rheumatoid arthritis and relied on Hincks's description of the swelling in the wrist in July 1919. This answer brought the response from Pollock: 'Do you pit your opinion against the doctors?' – these being the eminent trio, whom Toogood had been forced to recognize as 'the greatest authorities'.

The most heated exchanges occurred when Pollock asked what Toogood meant when he said the urine sample had not been taken scientifically.

'What is the suggestion?' queried the attorney general. 'Is it that Martin put it in his urine when the doctor was not present?'

'No,' replied Dr Toogood, 'I say there ought to have been a scientific test.'

'That is not what you mean,' persisted Pollock irately.

Toogood answered, 'It is exactly what I mean.'

'Let us see,' continued the attorney general, with exceptional heat, 'what your charge is. Put it in plain words. Do you suggest that if Dr Hincks had been present the urine would have been of a different character?'

'Of course not,' was the emphatic reply.

The attorney general then asked: 'What do you mean in this case? You attach importance to the fact that the urine was not passed in the presence of a doctor?'

Toogood repeated, 'Because it was not a scientific test.'

At the end of Curtis Bennett's re-examination, the judge decided to clarify the reasons why Toogood believed Katharine was not suffering from arsenical neuritis when she was in Barnwood, and read out a part of Townsend's report. Curtis Bennett then intervened and made him read a further paragraph of the report and Dr Toogood retorted, 'I had that in mind, my Lord.'

'Then why did you not tell,' said the judge, with rather more than a trace of annoyance and rebuke.

'You put a question to me and I answered it categorically,' responded Toogood.

Lord Justice Darling fixed Dr Toogood with a steady glare and said, 'That will do.'

Dr Ainslie's evidence was essentially brief, but it confirmed the opinion of Dr Toogood. He believed that Katharine had not been suffering from poison when she was admitted to Barnwood and that if she had been, the arsenic tonic given to her would have made her condition worse. He was certain that she had taken a massive dose on either the night of 16 or the morning of 17 February and that the scenario was quite consistent with the findings during life and at post-mortem.

Despite the brevity of his evidence the cross-examination conducted by the attorney general was lengthy and vitriolic, but throughout Ainslie maintained that a large dose of arsenic had been taken on either 16 or17 February and he agreed with Toogood that it might have encysted in her stomach. Ainslie was then questioned about Martin's urine sample and was referred to the experiments of Willcox with salvarsan, which he maintained were not comparable, stating that the effects of salvarsan were quite different from the effects of arsenic on its own. Ainslie was standing up well to the attorney general's onslaught and was making real inroads into the prosecution case. Pollock then introduced a deliberate lie and forced Ainslie not only to accept Willcox's experiments but also defer to the experience of Willcox himself. He asked Ainslie,

'Do you know that he [Willcox] has tested with white arsenic?'

'No; if he says so I agree.'

'Do you know that these results are found in white arsenic as well. If he says he has done it with white arsenic would you accept it?'

'Yes, I always accept an expert.'

'And do you agree that Sir William Willcox is the greatest authority on arsenical poisons?'

'Yes; at least I do not know any better; I cannot think of anybody better known.'

However, the truth is that salvarsan is an organic preparation of arsenic used for the treatment of syphilis (a parasitic blood disease). Two to three grains of salvarsan may be given intravenously without toxic effects, whereas two grains of white arsenic can cause death. There can be no excuse for the chief law officer to deliberately mislead a witness, the judge and the jury in such a way.

When he was re-examined by Curtis Bennett, Ainslie was referred to a textbook and an extract was quoted to him: 'A single dose of arsenious acid may cause a prolonged fatal illness.' He agreed with the quotation and continued to maintain, via a lengthy explanation of Katharine's symptoms before her final illness commenced, that a single large dose of arsenic could have been responsible for her death. The judge again intervened:

'Are you answering the questions or are you acting as an advocate?'

This brought a furious response from Curtis Bennett: 'Surely he is answering the question, my Lord.'

Judge: 'No, he is giving a good deal more.'

Bennett: 'I was told to wait while the Crown witnesses were giving their explanation.'

Judge: 'He was not giving an explanation, but he was going into a different subject.'

Bennett: 'If any of my witnesses gives an explanation they are told to answer the question, but with my friend's witnesses I have to wait for their answer.'

The court was then adjourned and the judge had words with Curtis Bennett.

After lunch the attorney general acknowledged that Matthews's evidence was not disputed and it was mutually agreed that the bureau could be removed from the court. The last defence witness was called. Dr John Steed agreed with his two colleagues that the facts were quite consistent with a large fatal dose being taken on 16 February. When he was cross-examined by the attorney general he stated his qualifications, to which Pollock replied, sarcastically, 'You come with good qualifications, Scotch degrees, to which we always pay attention.' Bennett then said that his case was closed.

The judge fully realized that the combined evidence of Toogood, Ainslie and Steed had impressed the jury, particularly as the latter two men were well respected in Hereford. They had also supported Toogood's contentions, which on the face of it made sense. To combat this favourable impression he decided to launch a personal attack on the defence solicitor himself and immediately recalled Tom Matthews to the witness box.

'I want you to understand in what I am about to say I do

not make the very slightest suggestion against the propriety of anything you did. You begin by understanding that.'

To this the puzzled Matthews replied, 'I am much obliged.'

He then took him through the whole of his evidence again and launched a fierce attack on his honesty and integrity.

'You are acquainted, I suppose, with the law concerning being an accessory after the fact to a felony? ... You realised, I take it, that from that moment you might not destroy that arsenic?'

'Yes, I had not the slightest intention.'

'What I want to arrive at is that you appreciated that it would not do for you to make away with that arsenic?'

'I did.'

'Or to allow anyone else to?'

'Certainly.'

'And you appreciated, did not you, that anybody who did that would most certainly be interfering with the administration of justice. I suppose you have read Coke's Institutes?'

'In my earlier days.'

'You realise that it would be at least that?'

'I cannot say I appreciated it to that extent, but I realised that I could not destroy it.'

'And if you did destroy it that you would be making yourself an accessory after the fact to a felony and if you knew that felony had been committed.'

'I cannot say that I appreciated it in that light; I will be quite frank.'

'Did you before this case look at the case of the King against Levi in 1911.'

'No, I did not; I consulted Sir Henry and I was quite content.'

'Having consulted Sir Henry Curtis Bennett you did not mind what Lord Coke thought or what Mr Justice Hawkins thought?'

'If I may say so, I thought the responsibility was shifted from me.'

Mr Justice Darling knew perfectly well that Matthews had been acting on the advice of Sir Henry Curtis Bennett, but he dared not attack the Bar; he picked on the solicitor instead. In fact he accused Matthews of nothing, but his comments, which were pure humbug – that the defence should not attempt to pervert the course of justice – distracted the jury from the important evidence of the day. Lord Justice Darling had achieved his objective.

When this exercise of well-aimed selfish indulgence had finished, Curtis Bennett rose to make his final speech. The court rose early and the judge indicated that the trial would finish the next day.

25

It was unfortunate for Armstrong that the last day of the trial was reserved for the two speeches that both insinuated his guilt. The first was that of the attorney general, who summed up the case for the Crown; the second was the speech of the judge, who summed up the case to suit his own beliefs; for as somebody who was present in the court said, 'It was Mr Attorney [the attorney general] who summed up', and this was a fair description.

It would be hard to find a judge's summing-up in the annals of crime that was more perverse and damaging to any prisoner. Darling was a hanging judge and in the trial of Armstrong he excelled himself.

He opened by saying that the real dispute between the prosecution and defence was whether or not the prosecution had proved that the defendant gave Mrs Armstrong the arsenic. In this he was correct, but he then skewed the balance.

And in order to persuade the jury that the prosecution has not proved their case, the defence contend that Mrs. Armstrong took the poison intending to kill herself. If you come to the conclusion that she did commit suicide, then you cannot possibly convict the defendant – he is as innocent as you can be, but if you do not come to that conclusion you will deal with the rest of the case.

Put that way, he was giving the jury a choice – to believe either the prosecution's version or the defence's version. But that is not in line with legal principle, which states that it is up to the prosecution to prove their case. It is not up to the defence to prove their version of what happened. The defence has to prove nothing.

Having begun to sum up in this way Darling then began to demolish the suicide theory.

> Do you honestly believe it credible that that woman, in the condition she was, got up with the intention of committing suicide? What evidence is there as to what time she did ever intend to commit suicide? Where did she get it from? Where did she take it from? What evidence have you that she went to get a dose of arsenic? If the theory of Dr Spilsbury that she must have had a fatal dose within 24 hours of her death is correct, then the whole line of the defence is gone. The doctors for the defence are confident that the first and last dose of arsenic taken by the deceased was taken on February the 16th, but Dr Hincks and the nurse gave evidence of arsenical poisoning before that date. Again Dr Spilsbury said he was certain that from what he saw arsenic was taken within twenty-four hours of death. He is not theorising. He has told you of what he saw. Dr William Willcox, one of the greatest living authorities, says he is perfectly certain that the dose was taken within twenty-four hours of death. Thus the theory of suicide is demolished, it being certain that she died of arsenical poisoning. There is no evidence that she ever took any arsenic, knowing what it was. There is a great deal of evidence that she could not have taken it if she had wished.

Having obliterated any thoughts in the jury's mind that she had committed suicide, he continued:

> If you come to the conclusion that this woman did not destroy herself, then you will look round to find who did give her the stuff from which she undoubtedly died. There is no evidence in this case to show that anyone had arsenic except the defendant and he had arsenic for weed killing, and had mixed the weed killer for many years. Who had arsenic in that house? No one but the prisoner. Did anyone but the prisoner know there was arsenic in the house? He says 'No' in his statement. Why, when he made that statement to the police he never mentioned white arsenic. Why didn't he mention the white arsenic? After what I have read to you, do you believe that? If you think he has told you a falsehood about that, what do you think of his evidence? Do you believe he could have forgotten that? Do you believe that he had forgotten

what he did in the summer; that he had forgotten what he did with the rest of it; that he made up twenty little packets? He is charged with administering the arsenic to murder his wife. She died of arsenic. If you are satisfied beyond reasonable doubt that he gave it to her intending to kill her (and he had the opportunity to give it to her: You can see how easy it is to put some arsenic into an invalid's food), and that she died of that, you will find him guilty. You will never consider, of course, a motive sufficiently adequate for murder, but that does not mean that it is not sufficient for another person.

Darling's interpretation of the facts amounted to lynch law. Armstrong's wife had died of arsenical poisoning; Armstrong had arsenic; therefore he had administered it to her. The essence of lynching is that a man's guilt is self-evident, unless he can prove his innocence.

Lynch law is not the law of the land, which can be stated thus:

> While the prosecution must prove the guilt of the prisoner, there is no ... burden laid on the prisoner to prove his innocence and it is sufficient for him to raise a doubt as to his guilt. Throughout the web of the English Criminal Law one golden thread is always to be seen, that it is the duty of the prosecution to prove the prisoner's guilt ... If, at the end of and on the whole of the case, there is a reasonable doubt, created by the evidence given either by the prosecution or the prisoner, as to whether the prisoner killed the deceased with a malicious intention, the prosecution has not made out its case and the prisoner is entitled to an acquittal. No matter what the charge or where the trial, the principle that the prosecution must prove the guilt of the prisoner is part of the common law of England and no attempt to whittle it down can be entertained.[10]

Darling's interpretation of the facts followed the logic of the initial investigation. Fred Davies had accused Armstrong of attempting to poison Martin and Martin believed him. Mrs Armstrong had been exhumed and was full of arsenic. Armstrong must have attempted to poison Martin. It followed that Armstrong must have poisoned his wife. The prosecution was launched to demonstrate this proposition and placed it before the defence to disprove. It was not launched to examine the facts. The law had been turned on its head, and there was nothing that Armstrong could have done to prevent it, for whatever he said, or did, could and was used against him.

As the jurors filed out of the court to begin their deliberations, Armstrong was taken to the cell beneath the court. Curtis Bennett could not bear the tension and went for a walk. He stopped to buy a paper and in the shop the telephone rang. The caller announced the verdict. When Bennett returned, it was all over. The deputy-clerk of assize had said:

'Herbert Rowse Armstrong, you stand convicted of the wilful murder of Katharine Mary Armstrong. What have you to say why the Court should not now give you judgement to die according to law?'

Armstrong, drawn stiffly to attention, with his feelings almost overpowering him, with his lips giving an occasional tremor and twitch, and with a deathly pallor showing from beneath his usually ruddy countenance, made a great effort to appear composed, and to answer the question put to him. With a gulp and a shudder he ejaculated the one word, 'Nothing' – that was all. It was reported that he was crying when he was taken back to prison.

There was an outcry against the verdict. Curtis Bennett thought it was 'a poor show' and lodged an appeal, requesting leave to call five witnesses to give evidence that they had all dosed individual weeds with arsenic. But his application was refused.

The appeal began on 11 May and was heard by the Lord Chief Justice Hewart, sitting with Avory and Shearman. There were four main grounds of appeal, three of which related to the admissibility of the Martin evidence and the fourth specified misdirection on the whole case; this fourth ground gave details of seven examples. The fifth ground maintained that the trial judge misconstrued certain of the evidence and in consequence misdirected the jury.

The appeal lasted three days and was dismissed. This was not really surprising, because although the court of criminal appeal had been established for fourteen years only one appeal against a verdict of wilful murder had ever been successful. In those days the judges stuck together: theirs was a collegiate force.

The lord chief justice in delivering the unanimous judgement declared that there was evidence that a fatal dose had been administered within twenty-four hours of her death; that she suffered from the same kind of poisoning both in August 1920, before her removal to an asylum, and in February 1921, soon after her return home; that the defendant purchased arsenic shortly before each of those occasions; that he was the only person who, on both occasions, had the opportunity of administering arsenic to his wife; and that his possession of arsenic, made up in small packets of fatal doses, including the packet found upon him at the time of his arrest, was not consistent with any legitimate purpose; that there was a twofold motive for murder, namely, the desire to obtain the benefit to be derived under the new will, and the desire to contract another marriage; that the suggestion that his wife committed suicide was refuted, not only by the words she used on more than one occasion, but also by her physical condition, which, for a considerable time, made it impossible to leave her bed.

In dealing with the admission of the Martin evidence, his lordship pointed to a section in Darling's summing-up and declared that if it was likely to be understood to mean that the appellant was a man who was in the habit of committing, and might be expected to commit, this particular crime, then it would obviously be a misdirection.

> But it is difficult to imagine that the learned judge, with or without the authorities before him, intended to convey such a thing … but in any event it was the evidence, and not the reason for its admission, that must have influenced the jury, and we are clearly of the opinion that the jury in this case would certainly have returned the same verdict, even if the summing-up had not contained the passage to which reference has been made.

The director of public prosecutions lost no time, and without hearing the judgment which was delivered on 16 May, wrote direct to the attorney general.

As it seems possible that Armstrong's advisers may apply to

you ... authorising an appeal to the House of Lords, I venture to put some considerations to you ... an appeal to the House of Lords might tend to imply doubt in the principle involved by which the Martin evidence was admitted and I venture also to think that the House of Lords could throw no further light upon this question beyond that which the elaborate arguments in Armstrong's case have enabled the Lord Chief Justice to deal with. I doubt whether the Criminal Appeal Act was intended to be made the reason for elaborate technical discussions which perhaps may a little tend to obscure the righteousness of a Jury's verdict. I believe that it is far more in the public interest, if real substantial justice has been done to the accused at the trial, that the decision of the Court of trial should be relied upon and supported so long as our modern system of trying these important cases before single judges continues. The enforcement of criminal justice is far too serious a thing, I sometimes think, to be made the subject of technical discussions, unless the technicality is one which involves an injustice to the accused, and it is hardly possible I venture to think, in this case to say that there was injustice done to Armstrong in the course of his trial.

This stark expression of false logic set out by the director of public prosecutions to his own advocate epitomizes his attitude to the whole case: he believed his suspect to be a poisoner and did not want him to escape justice on a technicality. But was the admission of the Martin evidence a mere technicality? The answer is no, because it went to the root of the case and an appeal to the House of Lords should have been allowed on a point of law of public importance. Unfortunately for Armstrong only the attorney general could grant leave to appeal to the House of Lords and it was hardly likely that he would do so, particularly as he had prosecuted the case and defended the appeal; and it was not in his interests to risk a further hearing. The rule of law that justice must not only be done, but must appear to be done, did not feature in Sir Ernest Pollock's repertoire.

Without doubt the Martin evidence should not have been admitted in the murder trial, because its prejudicial effect outweighed its probative force, which is the current test laid down by the House of Lords in 1975.[11] If Sir Ernest had granted his fiat, Armstrong may well have been freed.

Nevertheless, for good measure, he did not make a decision

until 25 May, when he formally refused leave to appeal on the basis that there were no grounds to justify one. On 27 May the home secretary stated that he could find no grounds for advising His Majesty to interfere with the due course of law. With unseemly haste the date of the hanging had been fixed for 31 May and there was nothing else that could be done to save Armstrong's life.

On 29 May, Marion Gale wrote to Matthews:

A few hours ago, the Governor wired me, asking if I would go to Gloucester, but I honestly don't feel equal to the terrible ordeal and it does not seem to me it would be any good. I have replied to that effect. I wish to keep clear in my mind my last meeting with Major Armstrong in October 1921 and dwell only on his kind friendship and years of good pal-ship – in spite of all, I want to think of him only as he was as equals myself. I think you will understand what I mean. Please if you see him again or have anything else to tell me I shall appreciate your confidence – this last request that I am unequal to facing has considerably upset me.

The Revd Stredder wrote to Matthews on 30 May.

... so there is no question that about 9 tomorrow morning poor Armstrong swings. It is a most unexpected end, and one feels so intensely sorry for those three children, for this tragedy will affect them all through life. Some kind friend is sure to remind them of their father's fate. They ought to change their name. What is your candid opinion – of course one ought not to ask that, but those in intimate touch with him will have formed their own opinion.

Nothing will ever convince me of the infallibility of the Home Office experts. I always shall hold to the opinion that they were wrong in talking about chronic arsenical poisoning. I don't believe that Mrs Armstrong had any arsenic prior to February 15th. My wife's sister motored over from Tunbridge Wells a couple of days ago and she could remember Mrs Armstrong complaining of 'pains like pins and needles' in her right arm so long ago as nine years. Judge Darling would say she was telling lies – she couldn't possibly remember so long. But she dates the time from her coming over to Cusop for the boy's christening. He was born on the 20th February 1912 – christened about April. So the neuritis must have been troubling Mrs Armstrong so long ago as that. It seems to me that you have been up against an impossible task. Darling took every word that Spilsbury, Webster and Willcox said as Gospel truth. Anything to contradict their opinion would be regarded as untrue. It is a most unsatisfactory state of things. I was disgusted to read in the Express last week that Armstrong is now stated to have done for Mr & Mrs Cheese and Davies the estate agent. It is a pity they can't be sued for libel.

Of course people swallow all they see in the papers with the result that Armstrong is regarded as a perfect fiend. I felt the appeal would fail, and I believe it would have failed had it been allowed to go to the House of Lords. But there is no question as to the neuritis being of far longer standing than August 1920. Well anyhow guilty or not guilty poor old Armstrong pays the penalty and I should think that now he will be glad to get it over....

On the day before the execution Armstrong attempted to put his affairs in order. He made a list of gifts to all his friends and handed it to Matthews, to whom he wrote a final note:

My dear Matthews,

My heart was too full today to say all I wished. Thank you, my friend, for all you have done for me. No one could have done more. Please convey also to all your staff my gratitude for the ungrudging work they put in. No team could have worked more loyally or with more devotion to duty.

Ever your grateful friend,

H. Rowse Armstrong.

26

There can be many 'if onlys' in a case such as this. If only
Curtis Bennett had attacked the Martin evidence; if only
Bodkin had still been Treasury counsel and not director of
public prosecutions; if only Pollock had remained an
undistinguished MP and not been conducting his first murder
trial as attorney general; if only Hincks had not become
emotionally involved in the Crown case; if only Spilsbury and
Willcox had been fairer to their profession; if only the judge
had not been biased.

Martin wrote to Armstrong on 29 September stating that
unless the Velinewydd contracts were completed by 20
October, his clients would rescind and demand the return of
their deposits. The motive suggested by the prosecution was
that Armstrong then faced financial ruin and as a result tried
to kill Martin. However, in the short time that was allotted,
Armstrong arranged for the bank to seal the reconveyances to
enable the sales to be completed on time. On 20 October he
met with Martin and produced a telegram from the bank
confirming that the reconveyances had been sealed. Martin
refused to accept the position and insisted that as the
reconveyances had not been actually produced to him on that
day, he would rely on the terms of his letter of 29 September
and would refuse to complete. If the prosecution motive is to
be accepted, it had only arisen on that day.

However, the chocolates arrived at Martin's house on 20
September, nine days before Martin's letter. At that time it
was in Armstrong's interests to keep Martin at work. It was
only misfortune on Armstrong's part that the sealed
reconveyances had not been delivered to Hay by 20 October,
for if they had been, Martin's clients would have had no

excuse not to complete. The prosecution cannot have it both ways, either the motive existed, or it did not; and lame as the motive sounds it had not arisen on 20 September, so who sent the chocolates, which arrived on that day? Whatever the answer, it cannot have been Armstrong.

If Armstrong had not sent the chocolates it is unlikely that he had tried to poison Martin at all, and the unlikelihood is more or less a certainty when the evidence of the masonic installation is taken into account. Why should Armstrong attempt to murder the only person he had chosen to second his proposal for Howard to be balloted for membership of the Lodge? No doubt the prosecution would have said that this was a clever ruse on Armstrong's part to divert suspicion from him. But such a suggestion would have to take into account that the invitations by Armstrong to take tea recommenced on 14 November (the day of the Lodge meeting) and terminated on 12 December (the day before the next Lodge meeting). Armstrong was about to issue high court writs against Martin's clients and held counsel's opinion to the effect that the case would succeed. Yet, despite the difficulties that existed between their respective clients, Armstrong had asked Martin to second his proposal. Why should he do this if he was intent on killing him? The invitation to Martin to stand as a seconder for his candidate shows the opposite intention and confirms that Armstrong was disposed to Martin, not the other way round.

The evidence of the arsenic in Martin's urine looks convincing, but both Toogood and Ainslie were surely correct in saying that the sample was not taken scientifically. The bottle had been provided by Davies, who retailed arsenic and it could have been contaminated with arsenic, either accidentally or on purpose by him. However, it is not vital to suggest that Davies tampered with the urine – even if he must have doped the chocolates – for the fact remains that arsenic was a known impurity of bismuth and could have explained the presence of 1/33 of a grain in 17 1/2 ounces of urine. As the whole case is full of coincidences, Webster found traces of bismuth in Katharine's intestine, together with minute traces of arsenic. Who is to say that Hincks's 'white mixture' did not contain arsenic? In any event there were too many symptoms of arsenical poisoning lacking. There was no burning sensation in the throat; no acute diarrhoea; no straining of the stools; no intense thirst; no cramps in the calves; no furred tongue; no weak or irregular pulse. Martin's illness was not characteristic of arsenical poisoning.

Moreover, if Armstrong had conceived the idea of poisoning Martin on 26 October he stood the risk of Martin commencing to persistently vomit and suffer from insistent and painful diarrhoea during the tea party itself. Afternoon tea is a light meal and the onset of symptoms could have been immediate. No one in their right mind would attempt to murder another in such a way as the risk of discovery would have been too great.

If Armstrong had not tried to poison Martin, there were no 'three clear cases of arsenical poisoning in the little village of Cusop'. There was only one case of poisoning, which led to one death. But was arsenical poisoning the only cause of Katharine's death?

Katharine believed that the doctors did not know what was wrong with her, before, during, and after her stay in Barnwood. In the war years her doctor had told her that rheumatism was the cause of her pains in all her limbs, exacerbated, according to her sister, by her tendency to worry. Miss Pearce had said that she was a 'martyr to indigestion' and Bessie had confirmed this to be the case. The fact is that Katharine had suffered from what she thought was indigestion for years and she had told Hincks on the day of her admission to Barnwood that she was suffering from one of her bilious attacks. Armstrong had written to Chevalier in December 1919 'that she still gets troublesome indigestion'. It was, of course, the prosecution case that her vomiting was caused by arsenical poisoning, but the fact remains that Katharine had a considerable history of vomiting, at a time when she cannot have been poisoned. She also suffered from feelings which she described as 'pins and needles'. If all these symptoms are taken together – the biliousness, sickness, indigestion, pains in her joints, wasting of the muscles – and, importantly, the discoloration of her skin before death, it is possible to build a clinical picture which cannot solely be explained by neuritis or neuropathy. There must have been something else wrong with her.

There is a possible explanation which would account for

all these long-standing symptoms. Although Dr Ainslie had mentioned it to Matthews, who passed it on to Curtis Bennett, it was never raised at the trial.

There is a real possibility that Katharine was suffering from Addison's disease, which is a malfunction of the adrenal glands that produce the hormones necessary to metabolize carbohydrates, fats and proteins. The effect of hormone deficiency is a weakening of the body and the consequent electrolytic imbalance impairs the function of the heart, muscle and nerve tissue. The most dramatic sign is a progressive darkening of the skin caused by increased production of the skin pigment melanin. Other symptoms include aching joints, progressive weight loss, nausea, vomiting, abdominal pain, weakness and fatigue (caused by low blood pressure). Untreated, these signs and symptoms progress to a collapse of the circulatory system and death. Jane Austen died of Addison's in 1817. It can be easily treated by the administration of cortisone and President J.F. Kennedy, an Addison's sufferer, led a normal life. The disease was first diagnosed by Thomas Addison in 1855, who suspected the cause to be tuberculosis of the adrenal glands. However, tuberculosis is rare in Western Europe and the leading cause of Addison's disease is now described as an 'error' in the immune system: the normally protective antibodies attack and destroy adrenal gland tissue. Addison's can also be caused, however, by physical damage to the adrenals. Apart from feelings of faintness, especially when standing, caused by postural hypertension, a sufferer is liable to develop mental symptoms such as depression. Addison's disease is known to be strongly influenced by mental stress and is characterized by periods of relief followed by periods of ill-health. The disease may take tens of years to fully develop. The marked skin pigmentation is especially evident in the mouth and on the tongue.

The diagnosis of arsenical neuritis over other forms of polyneuritis depends on certain abnormalities being observed: these include skin eruptions, eczema, thickening of the skin on the palms of the hands and the soles of the feet (keratosis) and cutaneous pigmentation absent from the face or inside of the mouth and which consists of a fine mottling of the skin, with patches of light chocolate colour, the intervening area being white (leucodermia).

In the final stages of Katharine's illness, her face went a dark coppery colour and her tongue went brown. This form of pigmentation is not to be expected in a case of arsenical poisoning, whereas it is a typical sign of Addison's disease. During the final stages of her illness, she vomited whatever food she was given within twenty minutes of being given it, and this is another common symptom of Addison's. All the symptoms of Addison's were present and if her blood pressure had been taken by Dr Hincks, the diagnosis would have been confirmed.

Unfortunately, despite Dr Hincks's excellent memory of many important symptoms, he could not remember whether he took her blood pressure at any time in her illness. More importantly, perhaps, her adrenal glands were found to be so decomposed that no damage or disease, even if present, could be made out in them.

The prosecution never attempted to dispute that every symptom almost to the end could have been caused by ordinary natural disease. Even Willcox admitted in cross examination, 'that the symptoms were consistent with natural disease but he did not think so in this case'.

Armstrong's conviction was based on a correct interpretation of the arsenic found in her body ten months after death. Both Spilsbury and Willcox based their opinion that arsenic had been taken within twenty-four hours of her death on the findings of arsenic in her alimentary canal. Such statements of opinion should be treated with caution. According to Sir Sydney Smith[12]:

A certain amount has been written about the relative distribution along the alimentary canal affording an index of time since administration. Considerable care must be taken in regard to this, for there is a great tendency for arsenic to remain in the stomach while it is rapidly eliminated from the intestines. I have repeatedly found powdered arsenic in the stomach forty-eight hours after its administration, and at the same time no sign of it could be found in any portion of the intestines, although its presence in the walls of the intestines could be demonstrated.

Glaister[13] accepts this phenomenon: ' ... arsenic may be recovered from the stomach after relatively long periods, despite vomiting, due to its tenacious association with gastric mucosa.'

These statements of opinion are borne out by a modern case study[14] of a man who died eight days after ingesting arsenic. The report confirmed that in an acute case of arsenical poisoning, despite modern intensive care, stomach pumps and surgery the concentration of arsenic remaining in the digestive tract can stay high for many days after ingestion.

There was no evidence to support Spilsbury's contention that there was a gradual increase in the concentration of arsenic from the stomach downwards, as the stomach contained more than the jejunum, and the jejunum and ileum and contents had been placed in the same bottle, rendering a correct interpretation impossible. Spilsbury was incorrect in dismissing the phenomena reported by Witthaus, as according to Sir Sydney Smith (Ibid.): 'In exhumations the possibility of imbibition of arsenic from the stomach into the neighbouring viscera must be remembered in discussing its distribution ...'

Spilsbury's evidence as to the likely duration of a fatal illness conflicted with his evidence in the Seddon case when he said that a single dose would not be likely to prove fatal in less than three days, 'and it might be longer'. Willcox contradicted his evidence in the case of Edward Black who was hanged nine weeks before Armstrong for the poisoning of his wife by arsenic. In that case, Willcox said: 'Death may therefore be delayed for days or even weeks after a single dose which might be much less than the normal fatal single dose – usually considered to be two grains.'

Katharine could have taken the arsenic from the study cupboard on 16 February accidentally, believing it to be something other than arsenic. She could have removed some of it and continued to take it during her final illness. She could have taken it intending to take her own life. Equally, Armstrong could have given it to her.

However, there was no evidence that he did and his conviction rested on expert opinion and on prejudice alone. No man should be condemned in this way. There must be proof of guilt and there was no such proof.

After this long period of time only one of the motives suggested by the prosecution deserves scrutiny. Was

Katharine's 1920 will improperly witnessed as alleged by the prosecution or was her signature forged? The latter view was held by Odell in his book *Exhumation of a Murder* in which he presented evidence of the late Mr Henry T.F. Rhodes, a document examiner. However, that analysis is the subject of controversy and the question was never raised at the trial. In fact Mr Justice Darling did not refer to the disputed will in his summing up at all.

It was unfortunate that Armstrong was tried by Mr Justice Darling. Filson Young wrote, ' ... but the unconventional common sense of his utterances, and the piercing and clean-cut analysis to which he subjected the essential evidence could only have been employed by a judge equipped, like him, with immense experience, the most lucid mentality, and the clearest understanding of the ultimate character of justice'. This comment could be interpreted another way by saying that whenever he destroyed a valid point made in favour of the prisoner he did so with such skill that its unfairness could never be made a ground for appeal. For the undoubted fact remains that Armstrong did not receive a fair trial and, without the slightest shadow of a doubt, the present court of appeal would have ordered a retrial on the grounds of Darling's gross interference alone. Darling never once made a point in favour of the defence and every single one of his utterances favoured the prosecution. He was entrusted to try the case fairly and in the words of Lord Chief Justice Lane:[15]

> However distasteful the offence, however repulsive the defendant, however laughable his defence, he is entitled to have his case fairly presented to the jury by judge and counsel ... [and] where the cards seemed to be stacked most heavily against [him] the judge should be most scrupulous to ensure that nothing untoward took place which might exacerbate the defendant's difficulties.

There were two real villains in this case: Fred Davies, whose suspicions generated the inquiry, and Lord Justice Darling, whose belief in Armstrong's guilt at the outset interfered with the fairness of the inquiry itself.

What if every man were to lose his life who, in a battle against weeds, resorts to destroy them individually?

What if every man who retained a packet of weed killer in his gardening coat was to die because of it?

What if every man who did not tell the police he was in possession of more weed killer than he said he owned, was condemned to death?

What if every man was hanged for a friendship with another woman during his wife's lifetime?

If every man who lost his wife was unfortunate to live among men who were malicious enough to contrive evidence, how many more innocent men would have been hanged?

The chocolates were a plot. It matters little whether it was hatched out of envy or greed, or whether the originators, believing that Armstrong was a poisoner, felt they had a duty to expose him – it was a conspiracy all the same. Once the finger of suspicion had been pointed, every gesture and word takes on a sinister significance, a duplicity that does not, in fact exist.

Which of the men in this story displayed the most base behaviour? The man who openly bought arsenic and boiled his weedkiller in full view of his household, or the man who invented the evidence against him? Which man was the more deviant, the man who showed open hospitality, or the man who, whilst maintaining a friendly exterior, plotted and schemed with unparalleled viciousness to determine his death? Which of these men display the cunning and devious behaviour of a secret murderer? For a murder was committed and the victim was Armstrong himself.

His was an infamous death, one that must at last be accepted as a travesty of justice and another indelible stain, not only on our legal system, but on our collective conscience.

Epilogue

After the hardback edition of this book was published in 1995, Channel 4 commissioned Just TV ('Trial and Error' Series) to produce a documentary. The director Gerry Troyna filmed an interview with Professor Bernard Knight, the Home Office pathologist who appeared for the Crown in the Fred West case – and who kindly wrote a foreword for this paperback edition. Bernard Knight stated to me that 'with a decent defence with medical back-up Armstrong could never have been convicted today'. I was then flown to Florida State University to interview Dr Gerald Quatterhomme – a French pathologist with experience of arsenic cases. He agreed with Bernard Knight that after a ten-month interment in the grave, the distribution of the arsenic found in Katharine Armstrong's body could not reliably indicate the amount of arsenic actually present in those organs at the time of her death. He stated that it was impossible for any expert to say – given the evidence available at the time of the trial – whether Katharine had ingested the poison a few hours, twenty-four hours, or a few days before her death. Yet Armstrong was hanged on the expert evidence of Sir Bernard Spilsbury who stated categorically that she must have ingested arsenic within twenty-four hours of her death.

On this evidence alone the Criminal Justice Review Commission should review this case and submit the evidence to the new Home Secretary who should advise Her Majesty to grant a Royal Pardon. Wherever miscarriages of justice occur they should be rooted out and righted. Our faith in the judicial process depends on that.

References

1. Excerpts from the *Gloucester Chronicle*, 1922
2. The case of Harold Greenwood
3. Presence of serum albumin or serum globulin may be due to functional causes or to renal diseases
4. D.G. Browne & E.V. Tullet, *Bernard Spilsbury: His Life and Cases* (George G. Harrap & Co. Ltd, 1951)
5. Robert Jackson, *Case for the Prosecution: A Biography of Sir Archibald Bodkin* (Arthur Baker, 1962)
6. Ronald True was tried in 1921 and Edith Thompson a year later
7. Ibid.
8. *Dictionary of National Biography* (Oxford University Press, 1949)
9. 'Evidence of Similar Facts', *Law Quarterly Review*, No. 149, January 1922, page 63
10. Woolmington *v.* DPP (HL) (1935) AC 462
11. DPP *v.* Boardman (HL) 1975 AC 421
12. Sir Sydney Smith and Frederick Smith Fiddes, *Forensic Medicine*, 9th edn (J & A Churchill, 1949)
13. Glaister's *Medical Jurisprudence and Toxicology* edited by the late Edgar Rentoul and Hamilton Smith 13th edn (Churchill Livingstone, Edinburgh & London, 1973)
14. 'Acute Arsenic Intoxication: Forensic & Toxicological Aspects (An Observation)', *Journal of Forensic Sciences*, Vol. 37, No. 4, July 1992, pp. 1163-71
15. Marr (1989) 90 Ct. App. R. 154

Bibliography

Bailey, Guy, *The Fatal Chance* (Peter Davies, 1969)

Bosanquet, Sir Ronald, *The Oxford Circuit* (Thames Bank Publishing Co., 1936)

Browne, Douglas G., & Tullett, E.V., *Bernard Spilsbury: his life and cases* (Harrap, 1951)

Cecil, Lord David, *A Portrait of Jane Austen* (Book Club Associates, 1978)

Darling, Lord, *Musings on Murder* (J.A. Allen, 1925)

Duke, Winifred, *Trial of Harold Greenwood* (William Hodge, 1930)

Fairs, G.L., *A History of Hay* (Phillimore, 1972)

Glaister, John, *The Power of Poison* (Christopher Johnson, 1954)

Grice, Edward, *Great Cases of Sir Henry Curtis Bennett KC* (Hutchinson & Co. 1937)

Graham, Evelyn, *Lord Darling and his Famous Trials* (Hutchinson, 1929)

Jackson, Robert, *A Biography of Sir Archibald Bodkin* (Arthur Barker, 1962)

May, Richard, *Criminal Evidence*, 2nd edn (Sweet & Maxwell, 1990)

Odell, Robin, *Exhumation of a Murder* (Harrap, 1975)

Picton, Bernard, *Murder, Suicide or Accident* (Robert Hale, 1971)

Rentoul E. & Smith H., *Toxic Materials in Medical Jurisprudence and Toxicology*, 13th edn (Churchill Livingstone, 1973)

Simpson, Keith, *Forensic Medicine*, 4th edn (Edward Arnold, 1971)

Smith, Sir S. & Fiddes, F.S., *Forensic Medicine*, 9th edn (J. &

A. Churchill, 1949)

Sutherland, Halliday, *The Arches of the Years* (Bles, 1933)

Thompson, C.J.S., *Poisons and Poisoners* (Harold Shaylor, 1931)

Walter-Smith, Derek, *The Life of Lord Darling* (Cassell, 1938)

Willcox, Philip H.A., *The Detective Physician: The Life and Work of Sir William Willcox* (Heinemann, 1970)

White, Bryan, *Hangings in Gloucestershire* (Home Office 1985)

Wild, Roland, and Curtis Bennett, Derek, *'Curtis': the Life of Sir Henry Curtis Bennett* (Cassell, 1937)

Young, Filson (ed.), *The Trial of Herbert Rowse Armstrong* (William Hodge, 1927), *The Trial of the Seddons* (William Hodge, 1914)

Papers and Journals

DPP file of Rex *v.* Armstrong, PRO ref DPP1/63

The defence papers

Hereford Times

Lancet

John Bull

Brecon and Radnor Express

Gloucester Chronicle

Journal of Forensic Sciences

Postgraduate Medicine

Archives of Internal Medicine

Annals of Emergency Medicine

Law Quarterly Review

et al.

Index

Index